THE FUNCTION OF APOCALYPTIC AND
WISDOM TRADITIONS IN ROMANS 9-11

SOCIETY
OF BIBLICAL
LITERATURE

DISSERTATION SERIES
J. J. M. Roberts, Old Testament Editor
Charles Talbert, New Testament Editor

Number 109

THE FUNCTION OF APOCALYPTIC AND
WISDOM TRADITIONS IN ROMANS 9-11

by
E. Elizabeth Johnson

E. Elizabeth Johnson

THE FUNCTION OF APOCALYPTIC AND WISDOM TRADITIONS IN ROMANS 9-11

Scholars Press
Atlanta, Georgia

THE FUNCTION OF APOCALYPTIC AND WISDOM TRADITIONS IN ROMANS 9-11

E. Elizabeth Johnson

Ph.D., 1987
Princeton Theological Seminary

Advisor:
J. Christiaan Becker

Library of Congress Cataloging in Publication Data

Johnson, E. Elizabeth.
    The function of apocalyptic and wisdom traditions in Romans 9-11 /
E. Elizabeth Johnson.
    p.   cm. -- (Dissertation series / Society of Biblical
Literature ; no. 109)
    Originally presented as the author's thesis (Ph. D.) -- Princeton
Univ.
    Bibliography: p.
    Includes indexes.
    ISBN 1-55540-226-7 (alk. paper.) --ISBN 1-55540-227-5 (pbk.)
    1. Bible. N.T. Romans IX-XI--Criticism, interpretation, etc.
2. Apocalyptic literature--History and criticism. 3. Wisdom
literature--History and criticism. I. Title. II. Series:
Dissertation series (Society of Biblical Literature) ; no. 109.
BS2665.2.J64 1989
227'.106--dc20

89-35508
CIP

64,049

Printed in the United States of America
on acid-free paper

CONTENTS

Preface

Dissertations are at once solitary and communal endeavors.

One struggles alone to discover the reasonable limits to set to the project, the precise questions to ask, the appropriate methods of research to employ. The countless hours of combing the library, staring at the text, and sitting in front of blank paper are very private ones. I have been fortunate to work on a project that has intrigued me from the moment of its inception; even during the inevitable periods of frustration I have never been bored. And I have learned from the solitude.

The best theology is always done in community, though, and to the extent that any dissertation qualifies as good theology it is the product of many people's labor. Years of learning are also years of being taught, which means that one's teachers past and present leave their marks on every page. J. Christiaan Beker's passion for Paul's gospel, his uncompromising demand that Paul's letters speak for themselves, and his comprehensive understanding of Paul's thought have for fourteen years taught me how to ask the questions. Paul W. Meyer's meticulous attention to the text and keen theological sensitivity have taught me not to stop with the first questions I ask or to settle for easy answers. David R. Adams's critical acumen and methodological rigor have taught me how to begin answering the questions. Their shepherding of this dissertation has been wise, creative, and compassionate. I owe them— and all my teachers—a deep debt of gratitude.

Not all my teachers have been Princeton faculty members. My parents taught me to love the Bible and to love scholarship, and although they never dreamed I would do both at the same time, they have nurtured me every step of the way. My colleagues in graduate school, especially Jeffrey S. Siker, R. Neil Elliott, Gordon Zerbe, and O. Larry Yarbrough, have often been the best critics and have always been the most supportive questioners. Bart D. Ehrman, my constant conversation partner and friend, has read every word of this dissertation innumerable times, relentlessly forcing me to think and write more clearly, and consistently suggesting improvements.

The faculty and students of New Brunswick Theological Seminary suffered with me through the birth pangs of final production and rejoiced with me in a successful defense. Thomas Jordan meticulously—and cheerfully—compiled the indexes. Russell Gasero labored harder than anyone should have to, producing a camera-ready manuscript for publication. Many thanks to them all.

Introduction

Students of the Apostle Paul are increasingly convinced that Jewish apocalyptic language and thought play a substantial, if not constitutive role in his letters. Since Ernst Käsemann's declaration 25 years ago that "die Apokalyptik ist...die Mutter aller christlichen Theologie gewesen,"[1] it has become almost a scholarly commonplace to affirm this renaissance of Albert Schweitzer's turn-of-the-century insistence on the importance of apocalypticism in early Christianity.[2] Indeed in a recent major monograph on Paul, J. Christiaan Beker identifies the apocalyptic horizon of God's impending victory to be the very center of Paul's thought.[3]

Beyond this broad, growing consensus, however, there is profound disagreement concerning the nature of Paul's debt to apocalyptic traditions. No common definition exists of what exactly constitutes such an 'apocalyptic tradition,' no standard delineation of the elements of 'apocalyptic theology,'[4] and only recently has there emerged a generally accepted description of the literary genre 'apocalypse.'[5] This wild diversity of opinion forces scholars either to choose from among existing (and often

---

[1]"Die Anfänge christlicher Theologie,"*ZThK* 57 (1960) 180.

[2]See the review of scholarship below, Chapter One.

[3]"The coherent center of Paul's gospel is constituted by the apocalyptic interpretation of the Christ-event"(*Paul the Apostle: The Triumph of God in Life and Thought* [Philadelphia: Fortress, 1980] 135).

[4]Handbooks on the subject abound, each cataloguing the supposed characteristics of apocalyptic literature and thought; few of the lists, however, appear to describe the same range of phenomena. See further below, Chapter Two.

[5]The Apocalypse Group of the SBL Genres Project has published its initial results, edited by J. J. Collins, in *Semeia* 14 (1979). See further below, p. 66.

contradictory) definitions of the phenomenon,[6] or to come up with new ones of their own. Leander Keck has recently observed:

> ..."apocalyptic" may be the most misused word in the scholar's vocabulary because it resists definition. To begin with, "apocalyptic" is an adjective which should be used to characterize the thought and imagery of those texts regarded as apocalypses. However, it is commonly used as a surrogate for "apocalypticism."
> ...Furthermore, the theological content of "apocalyptic" (and of apocalypticism) remains hard to define because the content of apocalypses varies so greatly on the one hand and because ideas found in apocalypses are found in quite different texts as well.[7]

Regardless of the definition of the adjective "apocalyptic" chosen, however, there remain features of Paul's letters that stubbornly refuse to be classified under that rubric, and appear rather to derive from other religio-historical quarters. Still other elements of Paul's thought bear resemblence to Jewish apocalyptic literature but are so greatly modified that one suspects the influence of other religious traditions in these instances as well. It contributes little to the cause of precision to assert that Paul is an original thinker who employs all the richness of his Hellenistic-Jewish heritage to preach the gospel. It can be helpful, though, to ask in what ways he combines some specific aspects of that varied background in the service of a particular argument.

Chapters 9-11 of the letter to the Romans provide a useful test case for such an investigation. Paul's wrestling with the place of historic Israel in God's plan of salvation is clearly driven by a concern for the faithfulness of God, and ultimately (11:25) reaches a conclusion that can only be termed apocalyptic: in the end, God will save all Israel. There are nevertheless throughout the three chapters numerous other images and ideas familiar from the Jewish wisdom literature (e.g., the potter in 9:20-23 and the word that is near in 10:6-8), and the entire section concludes with a hymn in praise, not of God's faithfulness, but of God's wisdom (11:33-36). Surely in Romans

---

[6]For example, Beker, who prefers K. Koch's criteria (*Ratlos vor der Apokalyptik* [Gütersloh: Gütersloher, 1970]) to those of P. Vielhauer ("Introduction"to Apocalypses and Related Subjects in E. Hennecke, *New Testament Apocrypha*, ed. W. Schneemelcher, tr. R. McL. Wilson [Philadelphia: Westminster, 1965], vol. 2, 581-642) (*Paul*, 135-136). See further below, pp 18-21.

[7]"Paul and Apocalyptic Theology,"*Int* 38 (1984) 230.

9-11 apocalyptic categories alone do not exhaust Paul's theological resources. Yet interpreters of Romans 9-11 have commonly viewed its wisdom features atomistically, in isolation from the overarching apocalyptic thrust of the passage.

This study inquires into the function of these sapiential elements in the development of the largely apocalyptic argument of Romans 9-11. Chapter One reviews the research on Paul's use generally of apocalyptic and wisdom traditions, and reveals the long-standing dichotomy in scholarly minds between the two. Chapter Two explores the relationship between wisdom and apocalyptic thought in Jewish literature roughly contemporary to Paul, testing the hypothesis of Robin Scroggs that there exists a "Jewish and Christian apocalyptic-wisdom theology"[8] that informs Paul's thought. Chapter Three is a detailed exegesis of Romans 9-11 that asks how the different wisdom and apocalyptic elements function together in the argument, and what impact their confluence has on the passage as a whole. An Excursus to Chapter Three examines the role Romans 9-11 have played in the debate about Paul and Israel, and responds to current exegetical attempts to absolve him of charges of anti-semitism. Chapter Four gathers the results of the study and draws conclusions about the Apostle's conflation of apocalyptic and wisdom traditions in the formulation of his argument in Romans 9-11.

---

[8]"Paul: ΣΟΦΟΣ and ΠΝΕΥΜΑΤΙΚΟΣ," *NTS* 14 (1967) 35. See the discussion of Scroggs's thesis below, pp. 37-38.

1

The Problem of
Paul's Background

The twentieth-century quests for Paul's theological heritage have
travelled in numerous directions, operating from widely differing theological
presuppositions and employing diverse investigative tools.[1] The searches
have often been undertaken in very exclusive terms: the background of the
Apostle was either Jewish or Hellenistic,[2] his thought either theological or
religious,[3] his letters either systematic or spontaneous.[4] Even among

---

[1] See the reviews of scholarship in W. G. Kümmel, *Das Neue
Testament: Geschichte der Erforschung seiner Probleme* (Freiburg: Karl
Alber, 1970; ET *The New Testament: The History of the Investigation of
Its Problems*, tr. S. M. Gilmour and H. C. Kee [Nashville: Abingdon,
1972]) and S. Neill, *The Interpretation of the New Testament: 1861-1961*
(London: Oxford University, 1964). For histories of Pauline research, see
A. Schweitzer, *Geschichte der paulinische Forschung* (Tübingen: J. C. B.
Mohr, 1906; ET *Paul and His Interpreters*, tr. W. Montgomery [London:
SCM, 1912]); R. Bultmann, "Neueste Paulusforschung," *ThRu* 8 n.f.
(1936) 1-22; E. E. Ellis, *Paul and His Recent Interpreters* (Grand Rapids:
Eerdmans, 1961); J. Munck, "Pauline Research Since Schweitzer" in The
Bible in Modern Scholarship, ed. J. P. Hyatt (Nashville: Abingdon, 1965)
166-177; W. D. Davies, "Paul and Judaism" in ibid., 178-186; and H.
Koester, "Paul and Hellenism" in *ibid.*, 187-195.

[2] Compare A. Schweitzer's insistence on Paul's fundamental Jewishness
(*Paul and His Interpreters*) with W. Wrede's portrait of the Hellenistic
'second founder of Christianity' (*Paulus* [Tübingen: J. C. B. Mohr, 1904];
ET *Paul*, tr. E. Lummis [London: P. Green, 1907]).

[3] The classical nineteenth-century presentation of Paul as a systematic
theologian was strongly opposed by A. Deissmann (*Paul*, tr. W. E. Wilson
(London: Hodder and Stoughton, 1926 2 ; original 1911) who portrayed

scholars who agree in general terms about the broad outline of Paul's life and thought, dichotomies of definition continue to appear, particularly regarding the religious and cultural antecedents to his theology and the historical influences on his ministry.

This chapter explores two such separate quests for Paul's background-- in the Jewish apocalyptic and wisdom traditions--and suggests that the bifurcation of the two has ignored an important characteristic of Paul's thought. As Helmut Koester observes in his reflections on recent scholarship:

> The various attempts to relate certain aspects of Paul's thought to a particular feature of his religious background usually tend to overemphasize one single element of his theology at the expense of others.[5]

The claims made about Paul's debt to the apocalyptic and wisdom traditions are a case in point. This segment of Pauline research divides itself naturally into two distinct and parallel tracks: Albert Schweitzer and his successors, who emphasize Paul's apocalyptic background, and Hans Windisch and his, for whom Jewish wisdom thought is more important. Throughout the twentieth century, with only rare and recent exception, neither group of scholars has paid significant attention to the priorities of

---

Paul as "primarily 'a hero of the religious life' for whom 'theology is a secondary matter'" (Schweitzer, *Paul and His Interpreters*, 172). In light of W. Wrede's somewhat earlier *Paulus*, which had adroitly replaced the alternative with a both/and (Paul's religion is theological; his theology is his religion), Schweitzer called Deissmann's book "a kind of anachronism" (ibid., 173). See also Kümmel, *The New Testament*, 295-299.

[4]F. C. Baur sounded the first call for a contextual reading of Paul's letters in *Paulus: Der Apostel Jesu Christi* (Stuttgart: Becher and Müller, 1845; ET *Paul the Apostle of Jesus Christ: His Life and Works, His Epistles and Teachings*, tr. A. Menzies [Edinburgh: Williams and Norgate, 1873 2]). More recently, J. Munck (*Paulus und die Heilsgeschichte* [Copenhagen: Universitetsforlaget, 1954; ET *Paul and the Salvation of Mankind* [Atlanta: John Knox, 1959]) has urged a renewal of Baur's concern for historical context. For a review of the recent discussion, see J. C. Beker, *Paul the Apostle: The Triumph of God in Life and Thought* (Philadelphia: Fortress, 1980) 23-25.

[5]"Paul and Hellenism," 192.

the other. The result is a wide variety of incomplete and often mutually exclusive pictures of Paul's thought.

I. Paul and Apocalyptic Traditions[6]

Until the late nineteenth century, biblical scholars placed little stock in the Jewish apocalyptic features of early Christian theology. Critical interpreters of the NT, following the lead of dogmatic theologians, either relegated such ideas to the primitive Jewish religion which had been superseded by Christianity, or baptized them into theological respectability by treating them under the traditional Reformed *locus* of the Doctrine of the Last Things. J. Christiaan Beker observes that throughout church history,

> ...future eschatology was pushed out of the mainstream of church life and thus pushed into heretical aberrations. The impact of this spiritualizing process and the distaste for apocalyptic speculations made by sectarian groups have no doubt contributed to the overwhelmingly negative estimate of apocalyptic by biblical and theological scholarship since the Enlightenment.[7]

At the end of the century, Johannes Weiss attempted to alter that direction by calling attention to the apocalyptic content of Jesus' preaching.[8] Because his interpretation set Jesus' understanding of the

---

[6]The history of research on Paul's apocalyptic background is discussed in a number of works. A. Schweitzer, of course, made a scholar's attention to eschatology the acid test for determining the value of his work (*Paul and His Interpreters*). More recently, H. J. Schoeps (*Paulus: Die Theologie des Apostels im Lichte der jüdischen Religionsgeschichte* [Tübingen: J. C. B. Mohr (Paul Siebeck), 1959; ET Paul: *The Theology of the Apostle in the Light of Jewish Religious History* (Philadelphia: Westminster, 1961) 40-50]), E. Käsemann ("Die Anfänge christlicher Theologie," ET "The Beginnings of Christian Theology" in *New Testament Questions of Today*, tr. W. J. Montague [Philadelphia: Fortress, 1969] 109-110, n.2), and Beker (*Paul*, 138-143) have also chronicled the place of apocalyptic thought in Pauline studies; cf. also the chapter on "Consistent Eschatology" in Kümmel, *The New Testament*, 226-244. Given the fact that the territory is so well mapped, our own survey will be somewhat selective.

[7]*Paul*, 139.

[8]*Die Predigt Jesu vom Reiche Gottes* (Göttingen: Vandenhoeck and Ruprecht, 1882; rev., 1900; ET *Jesus' Proclamation of the Kingdom of God*, tr. R. H. Hiers and D. L. Holland [Philadelphia: Fortress, 1971]).

kingdom of God (transcendent, futuristic, and supernatural) at such a distance from the contemporary theological view (immanent, realized or realizable, and ethical), Weiss's conclusions caused a furor among NT scholars and church people alike. Even advocates of the nascent History of Religions school, such as Hermann Gunkel and Wilhelm Bousset, opposed this "consistently eschatological" picture of early Christianity.[9]

The die had been cast, however, and only a year later Richard Kabisch sought to demonstrate the influence of apocalyptic thought in Paul's letters as well.[10] In reaction to the portrait of Paul as a Hellenistic philosopher and theologian, Kabisch shows him to be a Pharisaic Jew whose apocalyptic longing for the coming of the Messiah has been fulfilled.

> [Paulus], der sicher als Jude, als Pharisäer brennender als alle anderen auf das Kommen des Messias gehofft hat,...hat sich mit lebendigster Seele in die ἔσχατοι καιροί mitten hineinversetzt gefühlt, als er es erfasste,dass der Messias bereits gekommen sei, und damit das Ende der Dinge begonnen habe. In diesem lebendigen Bewusstsein, einer von denen zu sein, die bis ans Weltende gekommen, predigte er nicht eine abstrakte Ethik oder eine das blosse schon jetzt beseligende Verhältnis des Menschen zu Gott umfassende Religion, sondern den Messias, Christus und sein Reich, d. h. Eschatologie.[11]

Paul's apocalyptic preaching, says Kabisch, is directly dependent on contemporary Jewish hopes, but is by no means a mere repetition of tradition. Paul's Christian consciousness of the Messiah's having arrived[12] forces him to modify those traditional expectations: the end times have begun, but the fulfillment of the kingdom is yet to be. Consequently, Paul sees the physical universe as belonging to the old aeon under bondage to sin and death, and utterly displaced for believers by the new order initiated by Jesus' death and resurrection. The Christian life, then, is literally life from the dead, rescue from the imminent judgment and destruction of the

---

[9]See the discussion in Kümmel, *The New Testament*, 226-232.

[10]*Die Eschatologie des Paulus in ihren Zusammenhängen mit dem Gesamtbegriff des Paulinismus* (Göttingen: Vandenhoeck and Ruprecht, 1893).

[11]*Ibid.*, 12.

[12] "Es ist ein höchst beachtenswerter Zug an der Entstehung des Christentums, der für die älteste Christenheit mit unabweisbar Notwendigkeit sich ergab dass des erschienene Christentum *bereits ein Stück ist von den letzten Dingen*" (*ibid.*, 317; emphasis his).

eschaton, and deliverance from the death that infects the creation. The believer's union with Christ through baptism is not merely a spiritual, but a decidedly corporeal experience that makes one a citizen of the heavenly realm even though continuing to reside in the earthly.[13] In short, the Apostle's whole doctrine of faith and ethics is a function of his apocalyptic eschatology and can only thus be rightly understood.[14]

Albert Schweitzer took up the crusade for "thoroughgoing eschatology," first in his *Von Reimarus zu Wrede*,[15] and then in his *Geschichte der paulinische Forschung*,[16] in which he praised Kabisch as the first to comprehend fully "the great paradoxes of Paulinism" and to describe clearly "their real eschatological essence."[17] Schweitzer locates the core of Paul's theology in what he calls the Apostle's "eschatological mysticism, expressing itself by the aid of the Greek religious terminology."[18]

Schweitzer intended his history of research to be just the introduction to a major work on Paul, but his medical career and other writing prevented publication of *Die Mystik des Apostels Paulus*[19] for another twenty-five years. In the interim, scholarly attitudes toward Jewish apocalypticism as an allegedly major source for early Christianity shifted from outright rejection to qualified acceptance.[20] When Schweitzer's *magnum opus* provided flesh and blood for the skeleton of Paul's apocalyptic thought as outlined in Kabisch's work and in *Geschichte der paulinische Forschung*, the result achieved wider acceptance.[21]

---

[13]*Ibid.*, 188-228.

[14]*Ibid.*, 183.

[15](Tübingen: J. C. B. Mohr, 1906; ET *The Quest of the Historical Jesus*, tr. W. Montgomery [London: SCM, 1910]).

[16]See above, n. 1, p. 4.

[17]*Paul and His Interpreters*, 60.

[18]*Ibid.*, 241.

[19](Tübingen: J. C. B. Mohr [Paul Siebeck], 1930; ET *The Mysticism of the Apostle Paul*, tr. W. Montgomery and F. C. Burkitt [New York: H. Holt, 1931]).

[20]See Kümmel, *The New Testament*, 243-244.

[21]Although the *religionsgeschichtliche Schule* tended to consider Christianity's Greco-Roman environment more decisive than its roots in Judaism (on this, see further below, pp. 10-12), it is clear that the growing emphasis on historical investigation prompted the change in attitude toward Schweitzer's picture of Paul. Kümmel cites laudatory reviews of *Mysticism* by Bultmann, Dibelius, and Goguel in *The New Testament*, 441, n. 315.

In Paul's mysticism the death of Jesus has its significance for believers, not in itself, but as the event in which the realisation of the Kingdom of God begins. For him, believers are redeemed by entering already, through the union with Christ, by means of a mystical dying and rising again with Him during the continuance of the natural world-era into a supernatural state of existence, this state being that which they are to possess in the Kingdom of God. Through Christ we are removed out of this world and transferred into the state of existence proper to the Kingdom of God, notwithstanding the fact that it has not yet appeared. This is the fundamental idea of the concept of redemption, which Paul worked out by the aid of the thought-forms of the eschatological world-view.[22]

The genius of Paul's system, according to Schweitzer, is that it embodies Jesus' eschatological preaching of the kingdom, but adds the notion of salvation by means of his death and resurrection.

The true continuation of the Gospel of Jesus is found only in the authentic Primitive-Christian eschatological Paulinism. This alone is the Gospel of Jesus in the form appropriate to the time subsequent to His death. So soon as Paulinism is made into any kind of doctrine of redemption, in which the concept of redemption is no longer attached to the belief in the Kingdom of God, it naturally comes into opposition with the Gospel of Jesus, which is wholly orientated to the Kingdom of God.[23]

Only this intimate connection in Paul's thought between salvation in Christ and the hope of the kingdom enables primitive Christianity to survive the delay of the Parousia and "become a possession of the faith of all times."[24] Later Christian tradition beginning with Ignatius would divide the two, separating redemption and eschatological expectation, and thus removing itself from its legitimate beginnings.

In the hearts in which Paul's mysticism of union with Christ is alive there is an unquenchable yearning for the Kingdom of God,

---

[22]Schweitzer, *Mysticism*, 380.
[23]*Ibid.*, 392.
[24]*Ibid.*, 381.

but also consolation for the fact that we do not see its fulfillment.[25]

Despite the strength with which Schweitzer marshalled his evidence, the impact of his conclusions was blunted somewhat by the work of the History of Religions school which highlighted Paul's relationship to Hellenistic popular piety.[26] For those who viewed Paul's debt to the mystery cults and pagan religion as decisive for his theology, Jewish apocalyptic expectation appeared to play a much less substantial role. Eventually the most influential scholar in this devaluation of Pauline apocalyptic eschatology was Rudolf Bultmann.

There is a certain irony in that because Bultmann, unlike some of his *religionsgeschichtliche* colleagues, recognizes clearly that early Hellenistic Christianity is substantially shaped by Jewish apocalyptic ideas.[27] Bultmann considers those ideas a stumbling block, however, because they have been empirically disconfirmed. "The mythical eschatology is untenable for the simple reason that the parousia of Christ never took place as the New Testament expected."[28] Paul's contribution consists in moving the interpretation of the earliest kerygma beyond mythology toward a more anthropologically construed doctrine of justification by faith.[29] The present

---

[25]*Ibid.*, 396.

[26]See, for example, P. Wendland, *Die hellenistische-römische Kultur in ihren Beziehung zu Judentum und Christentum* HNT I/2 (Tübingen: J. C. B. Mohr, 1907); H. Gunkel, *Schöpfung und Chaos in Urzeit und Endzeit: Eine religions-geschichtliche Untersuchung über Gen. 1 und Ap. Joh. 12* (Göttingen: Vandenhoeck and Ruprecht, 1895); W. Heitmüller, *Taufe und Abendmahl bei Paulus: Darstellung und religionsgeschichtliche Beleuchtung* (Göttingen: Vandenhoeck and Ruprecht, 1903).

[27]See his impressive treatment of Paul in *Theologie des Neuen Testaments* (Tübingen: J. C. B. Mohr [Paul Siebeck], 1953; ET *Theology of the New Testament*, tr. K. Grobel [New York: Charles Scribner's Sons, 1951-1955]) vol. 1, 74-92. Cf. also idem, "The New Testament and Mythology" in *Kerygma and Myth*, ed. H. W. Bartsch [New York: Harper and Row, 1961 (original, 1948)] 15: "The mythology of the New Testament is in essence that of Jewish apocalyptic and the Gnostic redemption myths."

[28]*Ibid.*, 5.

[29]"Paul's theology is, at the same time, anthropology.... Paul's christology is simultaneously soteriology" (*Theology of the New Testament*, 191).

reality of the believer's status *coram deo* replaces any notion of future redemption.

> The contrast between Paul and Judaism, then, is not that each has a different conception of righteousness as a forensic-eschatological entity. Rather the immediate contrast is that what for the Jews is a *matter of hope* is for Paul a *present reality.*[30]

For Paul, the eschatological moment of salvation is neither an event yet to occur nor a discreet event in the past, but a happening that takes place in each individual's confrontation with the claims of the gospel and consequent decision for faith.

> Now, this is eschatological existence; it means being a "new creature" (2 Cor.5.17). The eschatology of Jewish apocalyptic and of Gnosticism has been emancipated from its accompanying mythology, in so far as the age of salvation has already dawned for the believer and the life of the future has become a present reality. The fourth gospel carries this process to a logical conclusion by completely eliminating every trace of apocalyptic eschatology.[31]

This Pauline process of demythologizing, further advanced in the NT by the Fourth Gospel, Bultmann takes as a warrant for pursuing his own program of existential interpretation. "Myth should be interpreted not cosmically, but anthropologically, or better still, existentially."[32] He understands the apocalyptic eschatology still evident in Paul's letters to be a product of the Apostle's personal history rather than the essence of the gospel itself, and says that it essentially signifies the transcendence of God.

> However, it is not simply the idea of transcendence as such, but of the importance of the transcendent God, of God who is never present as a familiar phenomenon but who is always the coming God, who is veiled by the unknown future. Eschatological preaching views the present time in the light of the future and it says to [human beings] that this present world...is temporal and

---

[30]*Ibid.*, 278-279; emphasis his.
[31]"New Testament and Mythology," 20.
[32]*Ibid.*, 10.

transitory, yes, ultimately empty and unreal in the face of eternity.[33]

Behind Paul's apocalyptic thought and within it Bultmann discerns Paul's "explication of believing self-understanding,"[34] his doctrine of justification by faith. "To believe means not to have apprehended but to have been apprehended. It means always to be travelling along the road between the 'already' and the 'not yet', always to be pursuing a goal."[35]

Bultmann's anthropological interpretation of apocalyptic and Neoorthodox theology's transformation of eschatology into an aspect of christology, the ultimacy of God's revelation in Christ, defuses the element of future expectation in Paul that appears so similar to Jewish apocalyptic thought; eschatology's embarrassing 'foreignness' becomes palatable to modern sensibilities. As Beker has stated:

"Eschatology" in Neoorthodoxy becomes a term that no longer has any precise meaning.... When Karl Barth writes that "if Christianity be not altogether thoroughgoing eschatology, there remains in it no relationship whatever with Christ,"[36] the term "thoroughgoing eschatology" refers not to future eschatology, but to the Christ-event as God's transcendent revelation, which is and remains God's alone and touches history only tangentially.[37]

Publication of the documents discovered at Qumran,[38] however, and the undeniably apocalyptic force of their sectarian theology began to return students of the NT to Schweitzer's appreciation of the apocalyptic character of early Christianity.

The first advocate of this renaissance was Ernst Käsemann, whose study of the gospels led him to pronounce his well-known dictum, "die Apokalyptik ist...die Mutter aller christlichen Theologie gewesen."[39] In

---

[33]R. Bultmann, "The Interpretation of Mythological Eschatology" in *Jesus Christ and Mythology* (New York: Charles Scribner's Sons, 1958) 22-23.

[34]*Theology of the New Testament*, vol. 2, 251.

[35]"New Testament and Mythology," 21.

[36]K. Barth, *Der Römerbrief* (Munich: Chr. Kaiser, 1932[6]; ET *The Epistle to the Romans*, tr. E. C. Hoskyns [London: Oxford, 1933] 314).

[37]Beker, *Paul*, 142.

[38]*The Dead Sea Scrolls of St. Mark's Monastery*, 2 vols., ed. M. Burrows (New Haven: ASOR, 1950-1951).

[39]"Die Anfänge christlicher Theologie," 180.

succeeding articles and his commentary on Romans,[40] Käsemann argues against Bultmann's anthropocentrism and defends Schweitzer's thesis that Paul's apocalyptic world view is determinative for his thought. In one critical aspect, however, Käsemann disputes Schweitzer's conclusions. Whereas Schweitzer had claimed Paul's apocalyptic hopes relegated his doctrine of justification to the status of a "subsidiary crater,"[41] a mere polemical device against Judaizers, Käsemann counters that it is precisely God's justification of the ungodly by faith in Christ that is the mark of the new aeon.

> Paul's doctrine of justification...is the specific Pauline interpretation of Christology in its relation to [humanity] and the world.... I understand *all* the arguments of his theology from this starting point, and therefore feel bound to judge present-day Pauline interpretation by the degree to which it is able to bring this out[42]

A number of major monographs on Paul in the ensuing quarter-century have likewise considered Paul's apocalyptic background the most influential force behind his thought. The dissertation of Käsemann's student and successor at Tübingen, Peter Stuhlmacher,[43] locates the source of Paul's idea of God's righteousness in the Jewish apocalyptic notion of saving

---

[40]"Zum Thema der christlichen Apokalyptik," *ZThK* 59 (1962) 257-284; ET "On the Subject of Primitive Christian Apocalyptic" in *New Testament Questions of Today*, 108-137; "Eine Apologie der urchristlichen Eschatologie," *ZThK* 49 (1952) 272-296; ET "An Apologia for Primitive Christian Eschatology" in *Essays on New Testament Themes*, tr. W. J. Montague (London: SCM, 1964) 169-195; *An die Römer* (Tübingen: J. C. B. Mohr [Paul Siebeck], 1974; ET *Commentary on Romans*, tr. G. W. Bromiley [Grand Rapids: Eerdmans, 1980]).

[41]Schweitzer, *Mysticism*, 225.

[42]Käsemann, "Rechtfertigung und Heilsgeschichte im Römerbrief" in *Paulinische Perspektiven* (Tübingen: J. C. B. Mohr [Paul Siebeck], 1969) 136, n. 27; ET "Justification and Salvation History in the Epistle to the Romans" in *Perspectives on Paul*, tr. M. Kohl [Philadelphia: Fortress, 1971] 76-77, n. 27; emphasis added).

[43]*Gerechtigkeit Gottes bei Paulus* (Göttingen: Vandenhoeck and Ruprecht, 1965).

justice, found chiefly in the literature of Qumran, but also in other early Jewish writings[44] and even in the OT.[45]

> Gerechtigkeit Gottes ist...ein theologisches Grundthema der gesamten Apokalyptik. Es ist...die Frage nach der Beständigkeit von Gottes Recht, Gottes Treu und Schöpfertum in einer chaotischen Welt, welche die Apokalyptiker dennoch als Schöpfung zu begreifen suchen.[46]

This *Grundthema* Stuhlmacher identifies as the "Signatur und Abbreviatur der paulinischen Theologie."[47]

> Bei der Exegese von 2. Kor.5,21; Röm.1,17; 3,4f.; 3,21ff.; 10,3f. und Phil.3,9 haben wir festgestellt, dass δικαιοσύνη θεοῦ der Leitbegriff für die paulinische Eschatologie, für seine Christologie, sein Kirchenverständnis und natürlich für seine Rechtfertigungslehre ist.[48]

The proximity of Werner Georg Kümmel to Käsemann and Stuhlmacher is easy to miss because Kümmel claims that "there can be no doubt that Paul is basically molded in his thinking by the expectation of the imminent consummation of salvation."[49]

> ...neither the preaching of the cross and the resurrection of the Lord Jesus Christ nor the doctrine of justification by faith alone is the suitable point of departure for a historically appropriate presentation of Pauline theology. Both...can be rightly understood only when one recognizes that Paul fundamentally sees the present as the time of the beginning eschatological saving activity of God; in other words, when one recognizes that Paul, like Jesus, starts

---

[44]E.g., Jubilees, 1 Enoch, the Testaments of the Twelve Patriarchs, 4 Ezra, and 2 Baruch.

[45]Especially in Isaiah 24-27 and Daniel.

[46]*Gerechtigkeit Gottes*, 175.

[47]*Ibid.*, 203.

[48]*Ibid.*

[49]*Die Theologie des Neuen Testaments nach seinen Hauptzeugen: Jesus, Paulus, Johannes* (Göttingen: Vandenhoeck and Ruprecht, 1969; ET *The Theology of the New Testament According to Its Major Witnesses: Jesus, Paul, John*, tr. J. E. Steely [Nashville: Abingdon, 1973] 144).

out from the belief in the imminence of the eschatological consummation of salvation.[50]

But despite using what seems at first glance a different point of departure, Kümmel still identifies the *centrum Paulinorum* as the doctrine of justification:

> Thus Paul's message of the justification of the sinner by faith also describes the existence of the Christian in the present as the end-time in its inception, while the old aeon is hastening to its end. This is confirmed by *the juxtaposition of expressions about present and future* with respect to the justification event.[51]

Schweitzer's "thorough-going eschatology" is by no means left without advocates, however, as Käsemann, Stuhlmacher, and Kümmel argue for the centrality of justification by faith. The Jewish scholar Hans Joachim Schoeps sets the "Hellenistic," "Hellenistic-Judaic," and "Palestinian-Judaic" approaches to Pauline research beside the "Eschatological,"[52] and concludes that "all...are relatively right. The problem is only to decide correctly on their limits, to decide where and how they overlap."[53] In Schoeps's opinion, the single most important factor determining the proportions of those elements is Paul's conversion. In the moment at which Paul knows that Jesus is the Messiah and that the world is therefore in a post-messianic era, the apocalyptic eschatology of his pre-Christian Judaism becomes the most significant part of his background: "the personality of Paul himself...can be found only if we recognize the utter newness and uniqueness of his existence, which is...derivable...solely from the event of Damascus."[54] Schoeps's Paul is finally very much like Schweitzer's.

> That "consistent eschatology" has drawn a distorted sketch of Jesus seems to me to have been proved by criticism which has seldom been so unanimous in speaking from different points of view. But as far as Paul is concerned, this school seems to be right to a large extent.[55]

---

[50]*Ibid.*, 142.
[51]*Ibid.*, 202; emphasis his.
[52]*Paul*, 13-50. See above, n. 6, p. 6.
[53]*Ibid.*, 47.
[54]*Ibid.*, 48.
[55]*Ibid.*, 46.

So too, for Joseph A. Fitzmyer,[56] Paul's conversion occasions the decisive shift to a new eschatological perspective.

...the experience on the road to Damascus taught him that the Messianic age had already begun. This introduced a new perspective into his view of salvation history. The eschaton, so avidly awaited before, had already begun–although a definitive stage was yet to be realized.... The Messiah had not yet come in glory. Paul realized that he (with all Christians) found himself in a double situation: one in which he looked back to the death and resurrection of Jesus as the inauguration of the new age, and another in which he still looked forward to his coming in glory, his parousia.[57]

For no one, however, are Paul's conversion and call more significant than for Johannes Munck, who in his influential *Paul and the Salvation of Mankind*[58] argues that "Paul's apostolic consciousness in its eschatological form stands in the centre of his personality and theology."[59] On the basis of the reports in Acts 9, 22, and 26 and Galatians 1,[60] Munck determines that in Paul's view the prophetic nature of his apostolic commission places him—and the world—on the edge of the eschaton. As the Apostle to the Gentiles, he is responsible for fulfilling the divinely appointed requirement that Israel be saved before the end. In the apocalyptic scheme of things, the Gentiles must be evangelized before that can happen (τὸ κατέχον of 2 Thess 2:6; cf. Mark 13:10 and par.) and Paul himself is the agent of such evangelization (ὁ κατέχων of 2 Thess 2:7).[61]

Thus Paul, as the apostle to the Gentiles, becomes the central figure in the story of salvation.... The fullness of the Gentiles

---

[56]"Pauline Theology" in *The Jerome Biblical Commentary*, ed. R. E. Brown, J. A. Fitzmyer, R. E. Murphy (Englewood Cliffs: Prentice-Hall, 1963) vol. 2, 800-827; reprinted as *Pauline Theology: A Brief Sketch* (Englewood Cliffs: Prentice Hall, 1967).

[57]"Pauline Theology," 804.

[58]See above, n. 4, p. 5.

[59]Munck, *Paul*, 42.

[60]Munck sees the stories in Acts and Paul's own reports of his conversion to contain inherent similarities because "the accounts in Acts go back to Paul" (*ibid.*, 29).

[61]*Ibid.*, 36-44, following O. Cullmann, "Le caractère eschatologique du devoir missionaire et de la conscience apostolique de S. Paul: Etude sur le κατέχον(ων) de II Thess.2.6-7," *RHPR* 16 (1936) 210-245.

[Rom 11:25], which is Paul's aim, is the decisive turning-point in redemption history. With that there begins the salvation of Israel and the coming of Antichrist, and through it the coming of Christ for judgment and salvation, and so the end of the world.[62]

E. P. Sanders's massive treatment of Paul's relation to Palestinian Judaism[63] claims the "two...primary convictions which governed Paul's Christian life"[64] contain apocalyptic hope at their very center. Those convictions are:

(1) that Jesus Christ is Lord, that in him God has provided for the salvation of all who believe..., and that he will soon return to bring all things to an end;

(2) that he, Paul, was called to be the apostle to the Gentiles.[65]

Sanders, like Munck, considers that "Paul's role as apostle to the Gentiles is connected to the conviction that salvation is for all who believe, whether Jew or Gentile, and also to the nearness of the end of the age."[66]

The centrality of eschatological expectation in Paul's thought Sanders attributes, however, to Christian tradition rather than the Apostle's Jewish background.

The similarity between Paul's view and apocalypticism is general rather than detailed. Paul did not...calculate the times and seasons, he did not couch his predictions of the end in visions involving beasts, and he observed none of the literary conventions of apocalyptic literature. Since the conventions of apocalypticism had so little influence on him, the hypothesis might be put forward that before his conversion and call Paul was not especially apocalyptically oriented. This is one more reason for not supposing

---

[62]Munck, *Paul*, 49.

[63]*Paul and Palestinian Judaism: A Comparison of Patterns of Religion* (Philadelphia: Fortress, 1977).

[64]*Ibid.*, 441.

[65]*Ibid.*, 441-442.

[66]*Ibid.*, 442.

that Paul began with a set apocalyptic view and fitted Christ into it.[67]

Although Sanders simply prefers the term "participationist eschatology"[68] to "apocalyptic," his final picture of Paul's thought is substantially like Schweitzer's, and he repeatedly laments scholarly neglect of Schweitzer's insights.[69] While taking issue with Schweitzer's exaggeration of predestination in Paul, and his views on baptism and two resurrections, Sanders nevertheless whole-heartedly affirms the former's conclusions about the relative places of eschatology and justification in Paul's thought.[70] He describes the "content of Paul's preaching and his hearers' faith [as] the death and resurrection of Christ,"[71] which carries two implications:

First, resurrection implies Christ's lordship, his return, the judgment and the salvation of those who believe.... [Secondly]... what God is doing is of cosmic significance and affects 'all things', and it is this that Paul preaches about; but individuals will be affected differently, depending on whether or not they believe.[72]

J. Christiaan Beker has made the most spirited plea for the centrality of Paul's apocalyptic world view in his recent monograph, *Paul the Apostle*.[73] For Beker, the shape of Paul's thought is determined by a dialectical (or "dialogical"[74]) relationship between the coherent center of his theology and the contingent contexts of his apostolic ministry.

---

[67]*Ibid.*, 543. Cf. also, "if one is tallying differences and similarities, the expectation of the parousia counts as a *general* similarity between Paul and Palestinian Judaism" (*ibid.*; emphasis added).

[68]*Ibid.*, 552.

[69]*Ibid.*, 434-441.

[70]"...despite over-simplifications and errors in details, Schweitzer's arguments against considering the terminology of righteousness by faith to be the central theme of Paul's theology, and consequently the key to his thought, are, considered cumulatively, convincing; and they have never been effectively countered" (*ibid.*, 440).

[71]*Ibid.*, 445.

[72]*Ibid.*, 445-446.

[73]See above, n. 4, p. 5. Cf. also idem, *Paul's Apocalyptic Gospel: The Coming Triumph of God* (Philadelphia: Fortress, 1982).

[74]Beker, *Paul*, 18, 40-41.

Paul's center is not a theological proposition that is subsequently applied to sociological contingencies.... Rather, Paul's coherent center must be viewed as a symbolic structure in which a primordial experience (Paul's call) is brought into language in a particular way. The symbolic structure comprises the language in which Paul expresses the Christ-event. That language is, for Paul, the apocalyptic language of Judaism.... My claim...is that the *character* of Paul's contingent hermeneutic is shaped by his apocalyptic core in that in nearly all cases the contingent interpretation of the gospel points—whether implicitly or explicitly—to the imminent cosmic triumph of God.[75]

Unlike Sanders, for whom Paul's anticipation of an imminent eschaton is only generally a product of his Jewish heritage and more specifically a function of Christian tradition,[76] Beker insists, "No doubt Paul was an apocalypticist during his Pharisaic career."[77] Rather than limiting the characteristics of traditional apocalypticism as Sanders does, and thus being led to contrast it with Paul's thought, Beker takes a broader view of the outlines of Jewish apocalyptic thought and then isolates Paul's distinctive appropriation of it. He distills his working definition from the list of characteristics in Klaus Koch's handbook[78] and concludes:

...one can deduce that apocalyptic revolves around three basic ideas:
(1) historical dualism;
(2) universal cosmic expectation; and
(3) the imminent end of the world.[79]

---

[75]*Ibid.*, 15-16, 19; emphasis his.

[76]Sanders, *Paul*, 543.

[77]Beker, *Paul*, 143. "Paul's apocalyptic conviction was not initiated by his conversion to Christ but formed the background of his Pharisaic world view" (*ibid.*, 144).

[78]E.g., urgent expectation of impending doom and destruction, temporal dualism, the role of heavenly beings, the presence of a salvific mediator with royal functions, etc. (*Ratlos vor der Apokalyptik: Eine Streitschrift über ein vernachlässigtes Gebiet der Bibelwissenschaft und die schädlichen Auswirkungen auf Theologie und Philosophie* [Gütersloh: Gütersloher (G. Mohn), 1970; ET *The Rediscovery of Apocalyptic: A Polemical Work on a Neglected Area of Biblical Studies and Its Damaging Effects on Theology and Philosophy* SBT II/22 (London: SCM, 1972) 28-32], cited in Beker, *Paul*, 136).

[79]*Ibid*

For Beker, these three basic ideas that constitute the heart of Jewish apocalypticism also form the center of Paul's perspective on the coming glory of God, although Beker observes that in Paul's hands traditional Jewish apocalyptic thought undergoes "a profound modification."[80] Precisely those features of apocalypses that Sanders (and many others) find lacking in Paul's letters--calendrical speculation, vivid descriptions of heaven and hell, "kingdom of God" terminology, and so on--Beker explains as casualties of such modification. Paul's conviction of God's decisive act in Christ forces him to view the apocalyptic scenario more from the perspective of the "already" than the "not yet": because Christ has died and been raised, believers "can already rejoice, can already claim 'the new creation,' and can already live in the power of the Spirit."[81]

The present reality, however, by no means softens Paul's expectation; rather his confidence that the Christ-event marks the inauguration of the end times *intensifies* his longing for its consummation, his "hope of sharing the glory of God" (Rom 5:2).

> ...hope in Paul is not simply a component of faith.... Hope has also a specific content and signifies the hoped-for reality....the glory of the age to come (Rom 5:2; 8:18) or the redemption of the body (Rom 8:23) or the Parousia of Christ (1 Thess 1:10) or cosmic peace (Rom 5:1; cf. also Gal 5:5), that is, the specific blessings of the kingdom of God. Faith not only *is* hope but it *has* a hope; it cannot exist without the specific object of the hope.[82]

Although he resists the limitation of Paul's thought to any doctrinal core such as justification, sacramental participation, or even apocalyptic itself,[83] Beker's treatment in fact operates with a functional *Mitte* which he as much as concedes in his Preface to the First Paperback Edition: "the three apocalyptic motifs of Paul's gospel...are actually anchored in the *even-more-central* motif of the faithfulness of God."[84] Paul's 'modification of apocalyptic,' then, is this very focusing of hope in God's ultimate trust-worthiness to complete what he has begun in Christ, because Paul "views the Christ-event as a proleptic anticipation of God's final glory.... The

---

[80]*Ibid.*, 145.

[81]*Ibid.*, 145.

[82]*Ibid.*, 147; emphasis added.

[83]*Ibid.*, 14-17.

[84](Philadelphia: Fortress, 1984) xv; emphasis added.

Christ-event makes it possible for Paul to speak about the proleptic new in the present that is ushering in the full glory of God."[85]

Beker's insistence on the centrality of apocalyptic thought in Paul has prompted a number of further studies[86] which have added support to his conviction that, rather than being a single element of Paul's background or a dispensable feature of his cultural conditioning, such language is "the indispensable means for his interpretation of the Christ-event."[87]

Summary

Although all of these Pauline studies define the role of Jewish apocalyptic thought in Paul's theology differently, and each has its own peculiar nuance and intention, they all (except for Bultmann's) fundamentally affirm Schweitzer's basic insight. For each of these interpreters—and for the growing majority of contemporary scholars—it is impossible to do justice to Paul's theology without accounting for his pervasive use of Jewish apocalyptic language and ideas. The diversity among these scholars is due in large measure to a remarkable lack of consensus regarding the nature and dimensions of Jewish and Christian apocalyptic thought. Between the extremes of Sanders's precise "[calculation of] times and seasons...visions involving beasts...[and so on]"[88] and Beker's broad "vindication, universalism, dualism, and imminence"[89] lies a vast array of competing definitions. Each one seems to be tailored by its author to his own understanding of Paul. In an insightful assessment of the problem of Paul and apocalyptic theology, Leander Keck notes:

> The problem of Paul and apocalyptic would be more soluble if one could show that Paul had read an apocalypse (especially one we too can read), or if the presence in Paul's letters of ideas emphasized also in certain apocalypses (such as God's wrath) proved that his

---

[85]Beker, *Paul*, 150, 152.

[86]See, for example, L. E. Keck, "Paul and Apocalyptic Theology," *Int* 38 (1984) 229-241; K. P. Donfried, "Paul and Judaism: I Thessalonians 2:13 as a Test Case," *Int* 38 (1984) 242-253; M. A. Getty, "An Apocalyptic Perspective on Rom.10:4," *Horizons in Bibilical Theology* 4-5 (1982-1983) 79-131.

[87]Beker, *Paul*, 19.

[88]Sanders, *Paul*, 543.

[89]Beker, *Paul*, 30. In his review of the book, H. D. Betz notes that such a definition would hardly satisfy an historian of religion (*JR* 61 [1981] 458).

thought was apocalyptic, or if, conversely, the absence from Paul's letters of ideas common in apocalypses (e.g., portrayal of the saved and the damned) proved that Paul's thought was not apocalyptic. Unfortunately, these requirements cannot be met.[90]

Nevertheless, each of the advocates of an apocalyptic Paul concurs in some fashion with Keck's conclusion that "Paul's interpretation of the Christ-event is thoroughly apocalyptic, however many other theologies contributed to his Christology at points."[91]

Moreover—and even more significantly for our purposes here—these scholars share a common disregard for the place of Jewish wisdom traditions in Paul. They mention the presence of sapiential thought in passing in their discussions of 1 Corinthians 1-3,[92] and they note wisdom features of individual arguments here and there throughout the Pauline corpus.[93] There is almost no consideration, however, of the possible influence of the wisdom tradition on the Apostle's interpretation of the gospel.

Because they do not comment on the matter, one can only speculate that the reason these scholars ignore Paul's use of wisdom thought is that they see differences between it and apocalypticism that are admittedly nothing short of remarkable. Wisdom thought is reflective, this-worldly, and common-sensible, concerned with social relations and natural phenomena, and notably unconcerned with cultic or traditionally 'religious' matters. Apocalyptic theology, on the other hand, is thoroughly 'religious'—visionary, other-worldly, and revelatory, concerned with redemption that will occur beyond the realm of human history, and therefore obsessed with the course of previous history. No two books in the canon could appear so far apart as, say, Proverbs and Revelation. They obviously represent two very different ways of looking at the world, and the natural (and understandable)

---

[90]Keck, "Paul and Apocalyptic Theology," 231.

[91]*Ibid.*

[92]E.g., "It would be as erroneous to define Paul's own soteriological goal by the term 'righteousness', which he employs in debates with Jews and Judaizers, as it would be to define it by the term 'wisdom'" (Sanders, *Paul*, 505-506); and "The symbol of 'righteousness,' for example, is proper for the situation in Galatia and Rome, but it does not meet the needs in Corinth, where 'wisdom' is employed" (Beker, *Paul*, 18).

[93]E.g., Käsemann's *Romans* (284-291, 318-321), which notes the sapiential character of the *pesher* on Deut 30:11-14 in Rom 10:6-8 and the hymn in praise of God's wisdom in Rom 11:33-36, but even then claims "Paul stands here in an apocalyptic-enthusiast tradition" (*ibid.*, 320).

assumption that arises from perceiving such drastic distinctions is that a given writer must surely stand in one camp or another.

Those who argue the case for Paul's apocalyptic background are so convinced of its profound impact on his thought that there is scant room for any other options. None of these interpreters denies that occasional sapiential motifs appear in Paul's letters, but it is clear they consider such motifs largely peripheral to the center of the Apostle's theology.

II. Paul and Wisdom Traditions

The same can scarcely be said for the second group of scholars we examine—the investigators of Paul's wisdom thought. To be sure, very few of them postulate the wisdom tradition as the single most significant source of his theological vocabulary and perspective,[94] thereby offering extreme alternatives to Schweitzer's "thorough-going eschatology." More typically, scholars engaged in the search for Paul's reliance on Jewish wisdom consider that sapiential traditions substantially inform a *part* of his theology— generally a significant part such as his christological or sacramental speculation. They do not attribute to the wisdom tradition the same crucial role in shaping Paul's thought that others have credited to apocalypticism. Still, those who search for wisdom in Paul in even this relatively restrained manner do not, as a rule, consider apocalyptic language and ideas very significant to Paul's theology at all; and therein lies the greatest difference between exponents of an apocalyptic Paul and a sapiential Paul. There are a few exceptions, as will be evident, but the twentieth century has largely witnessed a schism between those who investigate the Apostle's apocalyptic and wisdom backgrounds. This half of the divided quest for Paul's heritage has not been nearly so coherent as the other, and it is probably for this reason that no one has yet attempted a critical history of research on the subject of wisdom in Paul.

Only three years after Schweitzer introduced his apocalyptic Paul, Hans Windisch opened the door to a sapiential Paul.[95] Windisch claims that Paul's christology—indeed most of NT christology—derives largely from late Jewish expectation that had merged the figures of the Messiah and personified Wisdom. Beginning with the assumption that Paul's

---

[94] As do W. L. Knox, H. Conzelmann, and D. Georgi (see below, pp. 26 and 34-37).

[95] "Die göttliche Weisheit der Juden und die paulinische Christologie" in *Neutestamentliche Studien für Georg Heinrici*, ed. H. Windisch (Leipzig: J. C. Hinrichs, 1914) 220-234.

understanding of Christ is "ein viel komplizierteres Gebilde,"[96] not limited to traditional Jewish messianic expectations, Windisch looks for the source of the Pauline concept of the Messiah's pre-existence. Of all the elements making up Paul's christology—the Messiah, Wisdom, Spirit, Logos, and so on—Windisch claims only Wisdom carries with it the notion of pre-existence. The figure of Dame Wisdom familiar from Proverbs 8, Sirach 24, and Wisdom 9, therefore, despite her gender,[97] lies behind Paul's descriptions of Christ as the Wisdom of God (1 Corinthian 1-3), the following rock (1 Cor 10:4), the first-born of creation (Col 1:15-20), the head of the church (Eph 1:19-21), and the word of righteousness that is near (Rom 10:6-9).

Windisch is careful to distinguish the personification of divine Wisdom from any mythological speculation on Paul's part:

> Der Begriff der jüdischen Weisheit ist ja doch ein sehr mannigfaltiger; die Weisheit, die er hier [i.e., in 1 Corinthians 1-3] mit Christus deckt, ist nicht das selbständige hypostatische Wesen, das vor Zeiten gezeugt, Gottes Ebenbild trägt, die Schöpfung vermittelt und durch die Wüste gezogen ist, sondern das göttliche Wissen und Planen an sich, oder das den Gläubigen mitgeteilte göttliche Wissen, der Inbegriff aller apokalyptischen Geheimnisse s. Eph.1,8ff., 17ff.[98]

He is nevertheless confident

> dass Paulus den Messias Jesus mit dem Strahlenkranz der judischen "Weisheit" umkleidet hat, ist zweifellos.... Der präexistente Christus des Neuen Testaments, insbesondere des Paulus, ist die göttliche Weisheit der Juden.[99]

There are several respects in which Windisch's essay sets the stage for future discussions of Paul's wisdom background. First, Windisch focuses exclusively on the issue of christology. The question which provokes his study is how Paul comes to affirm Christ's pre-existence. What that entails is looking for evidences of wisdom influence in texts referring to the person and work of Christ and in those texts alone; his choice of Col 1:15-20, 1

---

[96]*Ibid.*, 221.
[97]"Paulus wird Scheu getragen haben, den *Kurios* mit einem weiblichen Prädikate auszustatten" (*ibid.*, 227).
[98]*Ibid.*, 226.
[99]*Ibid.*, 225, 232.

Corinthians 1-3, 1 Cor 10:4, Eph 1:19-21, and Rom 10:6 establishes the agenda for many of the studies that follow.

Secondly, Windisch assumes that Col 1:15-20 represents the most mature expression of Pauline christology, so that its obvious similarities to Proverbs 8 confirm his hypothesis. This argument presupposes three further notions: that Paul wrote Colossians, that he composed 1:15-20, and that the pericope argues a christological point in its literary context. These are the most problematic features of Windisch's study. The authorship of Colossians is by no means certain; the pre-Pauline or even pre-Christian sources of the hymnic material in 1:15-20 are equally unclear; and the passage appears to serve a more ecclesiological or parenetic function in the argument than an explicitly christological one.[100] It is methodologically precarious to interpret one unknown by means of another, and the subsequent searches for wisdom christology in Paul, insofar as they relied on the hymn in Colossians 1, were therefore flawed from the outset. Once Pauline scholarship began to treat the relationship between Colossians and the *Hauptbriefe* more gingerly, the search for wisdom in Paul was forced to take another route.

Thirdly, having once determined that Paul's understanding of Christ derives from "die göttliche Weisheit der Juden," Windisch then assumes that the very complicated argument about true and false wisdom in 1 Corinthians 1-3 is largely christological in nature. Once that decision achieved the status of common presupposition, 1 Corinthians 1-3 then began to serve along with—or even instead of—Col 1:15-20 as prooftext for Paul's wisdom christology.

These three major assumptions were to remain essentially unchallenged and to govern investigations into Paul's use of Jewish wisdom traditions for nearly the next half-century. The net effect, as the following survey shows, was to limit unnecessarily the search for evidences of wisdom influence in Paul. Not until Hans Conzelmann's watershed "Paulus und die Weisheit"[101] did scholars think to look for sapiential thought in Paul's letters except where Windisch had, and few considered its influence except on the Apostle's christological speculation.

---

[100]See the discussions in E. Lohse, *Die Briefe an die Kolosser und an Philemon* (Göttingen: Vandenhoeck and Ruprecht, 1968; ET *Colossians and Philemon*, tr. W. R. Poehlmann and R. J. Karris [Philadelphia: Fortress, 1971]); and *Conflict at Colossae: A Problem in the Interpretation of Early Christianity*, ed., F. O. Francis and W. A. Meeks (Missoula: Scholars, 1975).

[101]*NTS* 12 (1965) 231-244. See below, pp. 34-35.

One significant insight of Windisch's "Die göttliche Weisheit der Juden" was unfortunately ignored for the most part in succeeding attempts to demonstrate Paul's dependence on wisdom language and thought. Windisch, as we have mentioned, had sharply opposed any attempt to define Pauline christology in mythological terms, and had asserted instead that for the Apostle God's Wisdom consists of the divine plan of salvation, "the essence of all apocalyptic mysteries."[102] Not for another fifty years would the words "wisdom" and "apocalyptic" again be used in such a mutually informative fashion. After Windisch, wisdom and apocalyptic modes of discourse came to be seen as so drastically dissimilar as to preclude any relationship of the one to the other. Moreover, once the methodological weaknesses of Windisch's case for Pauline wisdom christology were unmasked, scholars argued the opposition of wisdom to apocalypticism even more strongly.

Wilfred L. Knox popularized Windisch's contention of wisdom christology in Paul in his own *St. Paul and the Church of the Gentiles*,[103] invoking the same texts, and developing the argument with further appeal to apocryphal literature, Philo, and rabbinic tradition. Rather than claiming any direct literary influence of Sirach, Wisdom, or Philo on Paul's letters, though, Knox argues that a common tradition of interpretation lies behind all these different first-century discussions of the Wisdom of God, and that indeed such sapiential speculation is central to the Hellenistic Judaism of the time.[104] Because Paul is a Hellenistic rather than a Palestinian Jew, Knox claims, surely wisdom rather than apocalyptic priorities dominate his theology.

The important feature of that wisdom speculation in Knox's view is just that Greco-Roman provenance. Paul's use of wisdom categories marks a shift in early Christianity from a Palestinian apocalyptic to a Hellenistic sapiential focus and identity. Paul's wisdom christology, then, functions as part of his missionary strategy. Apocalyptic thought is particular and Jewish; wisdom thought, universal.

> [Paul's] transformation of Christianity from a system of Jewish apocalyptic, with a purely local and temporary appeal, into a religion of salvation by faith in the historical Jesus as the first-born of all creation was essential if Christianity was to survive and to conquer the world.[105]

---

[102]"Die göttliche Weisheit der Juden," 226.
[103](Cambridge: University, 1939) 55-89, 111-124.
[104]*Ibid.*, 113-114.
[105]*Ibid.*, 181.

A decade later, W. D. Davies revised Windisch and Knox's picture by locating the supposed source of Paul's wisdom christology in the Apostle's identification of Jesus with the Torah, which itself was already understood as the pre-existent σοφία of God active in creation and redemption (e.g., Sir 24:23, Bar 3:37-4:1).[106] Davies buttresses the case for wisdom christology in Paul with an elaborate patchwork of ideas that equates Wisdom, Torah, and Messiah, to the end that pre-existence, instrumentality in creation, and redemptive activity are seen as natural and obvious correlates. Once Paul has replaced the law with Christ, says Davies, he must automatically attribute to Christ the characteristics of Dame Wisdom. Already with Davies, Windisch's distinction between the Wisdom of God and the myth of Wisdom was being lost, and his definition of the Wisdom of God as the sum total of apocalyptic mysteries was left behind in favor of a more mythological picture of Sophia. Davies hardly denies the place of apocalyptic thought in Paul, especially as it informs Paul's attitude toward the law's inability to save, his conviction of God's transcendence, and his "mysticism."[107] But he discerns no relationship between apocalyptic ideas and Paul's wisdom christology.

Shortly thereafter, Lucien Cerfaux[108] expressed some reservations about the possibility of discerning clear evidence of wisdom influence in Paul's christology. Yes, the Apostle makes allusion to sapiential texts and traditions, and Cerfaux examines all the standard pericopes. In each case, however, he finds alternative interpretations for the christological points previously scored. He suggests that Knox's too hasty assumption of mythological speculation on Paul's part has unduly influenced his conclusions. Although Paul is certainly familiar with Jewish wisdom traditions, and employs those traditions to explain the nature of Christ, he nowhere expressly equates Christ with the mythological figure of Wisdom.[109] Cerfaux acknowledges a measure of wisdom content to Paul's christology, but the most he is willing to concede is that

> ...we may perhaps conclude that [Paul] saw in Wisdom a type of the divine Christ, but we are not entitled to say that he made this equation in his mind. And we should remember that insofar as he

---

[106]*Paul and Rabbinic Judaism* (New York: Harper and Row, 1948) 147-176.

[107]*Ibid.*, 9-16.

[108]*Le Christ dans le Théologie de S. Paul* (Paris: du Cerf, 1951 2 ; ET *Christ in the Theology of St. Paul*, tr. G. Webb and A. Walker [New York: Herder and Herder, 1959]).

[109]*Ibid.*, 271.

follows the example of the sapiential books in representing Wisdom as personified, he has yet kept it sufficiently distinct from Christ to enable him to consider it as a type.[110]

For Cerfaux, the real center of Paul's christology is his affirmation of Jesus' divinity, and all the christological titles and images he employs—including those of sapiential origin—serve to support that basic premise.[111]

Although Andre Feuillet's *Le Christ Sagesse de Dieu d'Après les Epîtres Pauliniennes*[112] appeared nearly twenty years after Davies's work, and fifteen after Cerfaux's, and although at the time it was the most extensive monograph devoted to the subject, it simply executes in greater detail the program laid out by Windisch. The book's organization is somewhat deceptive. The chapter on Col 1:15-20 (nearly a third of the book)[113] does not appear until after five chapters have been devoted to the Corinthian correspondence. Nevertheless, the first reference to the Colossians text is in the initial chapter, and the hymn and its wisdom character are never far from the author's attention. Although the structure of the study appears to proceed from another methodological starting point (i.e., the debate about wisdom in 1 Corinthians 1-3), Feuillet actually repeats Windisch's procedure, proving wisdom christology by reference to Col 1:15-20.

> A lire nombre d'exégètes, la littérature de sagesse n'exerce pour la première fois son influence sur la christologie paulinienne que dans l'hymne de l'Epître aux Colossiens.... Si l'enquête que nous verons de faire est solide, il convient d'accorder à cette influence une place beaucoup plus grande.[114]

Convinced that the christology of Col 1:15-20 derives from the myth of Sophia, Feuillet points to the presence of similar ideas and themes in the *Hauptbriefe*, and concludes that the same image of personified Wisdom that informs the Colossians text shapes all of Paul's christological speculation. The study functions therefore not only to examine wisdom influence in

---

[110]*Ibid.*, 274.

[111]*Ibid.*, 509-520.

[112](Paris: J. Gabalda, 1966). Cf. also Feuillet's earlier "L'énigme de I Cor.ii.9," *RB* 70 (1963) 52-74.

[113]*Ibid.*,163-274.

[114]*Ibid.*, 361.

Paul's christology, but to argue for the authenticity of Colossians as well.[115]

Feuillet finds three basic aspects to Pauline wisdom christology: Christ as the image of God, as the saving Wisdom of God, and as the creative Wisdom of God.[116] He argues, as Knox had, that the Apostle's purpose in such preaching is to communicate the gospel effectively to the philosophically sophisticated Greek world.[117] Far from having parochial apocalyptic content, the Wisdom of God is a universal image that appeals beyond the narrow confines of Jewish religious language.

> En l'occurrence, le recours aux données de l'Ancien Testament lui a été particulièrement précieux. Voulant faire saisir à des gens fiers de la culture grecque que le Christ était une sagesse supérieure, dépassant infiniment toute sagesse humaine, le Sagesse même de Dieu, désireux de leur faire contempler en lui en quelque sorte le *principe suprême d'intelligibilité* de la réalité totale, univers visible et mode invisible, il a décrit l'être et le rôle du Saveur à l'aide des grands développements de la Bible sur la Sagesse divine hypostasiée.[118]

In 1963, Myles M. Bourke produced something of a landmark study by moving a step beyond the position Windisch had initiated, arguing that the presence of wisdom christology can be discerned in 1 Corinthians not only in the polemic against false wisdom in chapters 1-3, but in the eucharistic material in the letter as well.[119] Furthermore, he claims, Paul shares such wisdom interpretation of the sacrament with those responsible for the Bread of Life discourse in John 6.

> ...the nature of the epistle seems to make it unlikely that the thematic unity of Word and Sacrament found in John 6 (union with Christ through faith in his word, a union which is the requisite and preparation for union with him through reception of the sacrament of his flesh and blood) is to be found also in I Corinthians. Yet,...there are several considerations which suggest a similarity of concept between that chapter of John on the one hand and I Cor

---

[115]*Ibid.*, 361-399.

[116]*Ibid.*, 359-360.

[117]*Ibid.*, 396-399.

[118]*Ibid.*, 398-399; emphasis his.

[119]"The Eucharist and Wisdom in First Corinthians," *AnBib* 17 (1963) 367-381.

1,17-3,4 and 10,1-4 on the other. Both the gospel and the epistle have associations with the sapiential literature of the Old Testament....[120]

Although he concedes that "the most important eucharistic section of the epistle, 11,17-34, has no such sapiential reference,"(!)[121] Bourke claims the midrash on the exodus found in Wisdom 10-19 lies behind several of the epistle's important features: the entire typology of the sacraments in 10:1-13, the statement that "all have been made to drink of one Spirit" in 12:13, and the reference to the "life-giving Spirit" in 15:45. Since Paul identifies Christ with Wisdom in 1 Corinthian 1-3, and since the wisdom tradition had already equated Wisdom and Spirit (especially Wis 1:4,6; 7:21-22, 25), the eucharistic texts which mention πνεῦμα point not only to Christ, but to Christ the Wisdom of God.[122] So also, since Paul equates Christ with Wisdom, in his discussion of the eucharist he must be referring to the traditions about Wisdom's feeding those who love her (e.g., Sir 15:3; 24:19-21; Prov 9:1-6).[123] Windisch's conclusions about the wisdom background of the following-rock tradition in 1 Cor 10:4[124] simply provide Bourke further reason to claim that Paul interprets the Lord's Supper by means of wisdom traditions.

While marked by an initial methodological caution regarding the use of Colossians,[125] Bourke's study nevertheless presupposes a genetic relationship between the christologies of Colossians and the undisputed letters. The connection between the two Bourke sees in Paul's description of Christ as one who effects "new creation" (e.g., 2 Cor 5:17, Gal 6:15). Because Paul attributes creative activity to Christ and the sapiential literature similarly credits Dame Wisdom, the Apostle must intend an equation of the two figures.

---

[120]*Ibid.*, 367.

[121]*Ibid.*, 368.

[122]*Ibid.*, 379.

[123]*Ibid.*, 368.

[124]In Philo's commentary on Deut 8:15 (Leg.All. II.86), Wis 10:17, and Sir 15:3, 24:19-21 (*ibid.*, 377). Cf. Windisch, "Die göttliche Weisheit der Juden," 223.

[125]"Admittedly, because of...the problem of the authenticity of Colossians, the fact that Col.1,15-20 is so closely related to Prv.8,22-36 does not, by itself, settle the question of the origin of the concept expressed in I Cor.1,24. 30" ("The Eucharist and Wisdom," 369).

It would seem, then, that although in certain respects it would be a fault of method to explain I Corinthians by Colossians, the antecedents of Colossians in the sapiential literature and the similarity of those antecedents with the Pauline "new creation" idea --an idea which is already expressed in the "great epistles",--make it entirely probable that at the time of writing I Corinthians Paul had already made the connection between Jesus and the Wisdom of the Old Testament.[126]

Despite the claim not to be relying on the Colossians hymn, Bourke follows precisely the train of thought Windisch had begun, leading from Colossians 1 to 1 Corinthians 1-3, and from there throughout the letter to Corinth. Bourke never questions the *existence* of wisdom christology in 1 Corinthians, he merely looks for *evidence* of it beyond the first three chapters. Any apocalyptic features of 1 Corinthians 1-3 and 10-11 either are not apparent to him or not considered worthy of mention. For one who seeks from the beginning to demonstrate a theological relationship between Paul and the Fourth Gospel, however, the failure to note any apocalyptic tone in 1 Corinthians is less than surprising.

Ulrich Wilckens's classic study of wisdom in Paul[127] takes a somewhat different tack, addressing the issue from the argument in 1 Corinthians 2-3 itself rather than from the general question of christology, and thus turning Windisch's approach on its head. Wilckens self-consciously engages in a comparative religions approach in his investigation, looking for just the sort of mythology in Paul's letters that Windisch and Cerfaux had denied,[128] and working out the implications of Rudolf Bultmann's hypothesis of gnosticism in Corinth and its impact on Paul's thought.[129]

---

[126]*Ibid.*, 172.

[127]*Weisheit und Torheit: Eine exegetisch-religions-geschichtliche Untersuchung zu I Kor. 1 und 2* BHT 26 (Tübingen: J. C. B. Mohr, 1959). See also idem, "σοφία" in *TDNT*, 7 (1964) 517-522.

[128]On Wilckens's relationship to the History of Religions school, see E. E. Ellis, "'Wisdom' and 'Knowledge' in I Corinthians" in *Prophecy and Hermeneutic in Early Christianity* WUNT 18 (Grand Rapids: Eerdmans, 1978) 45-62.

[129]R. Bultmann, "γινώσκω" in *TDNT* 1 (1966, original 1933) 708-713; cf. also idem, *Theology of the New Testament*, vol. 1, 295-299. The theory was first proposed at the turn of the century by W. Lütgert (*Freiheitspredigt und Schwarmgeister in Korinth* [Gütersloh: Gütersloher, 1908]).

Wilckens decides on the basis of gnostic references to the myth of Sophia that Paul's wisdom language stems not, as Windisch had claimed, directly from Jewish speculation about personified Wisdom, but indirectly from the Corinthians' Valentinian gnostic language which is itself dependent on the Jewish myth of Sophia.[130] Paul appropriates that language for the situation of debate and redefines it according to the distinctively Pauline categories of cross and resurrection.[131] It is the Corinthians who employ σοφία as a christological title, drawing it in large measure from the gnostic Redeemer myth.

> Die Vorstellung der *personhaften* Weisheit wie sie einerseits im hellenistischen Judentum unter immer deutlicher vorhertretended gnostischen Einfluss und andererseits in der ausserjüdischen, vor- und nachchristlichen Gnosis geprägt worden ist, hat im Urchristentum in verschiedener Weise auf die Gestaltung der Christologie eingewirkt. Dabei spielen der Mythos von der Herabkunft und dem Wiederaufstieg der Weisheit [e.g., in Enoch 42], die kosmologischen Sophia-Spekulation sowie besonders die Vorstellung von der Sophia als Offenbarer und Erlöser eine besondere Rolle.[132]

This exalted spiritual Christ, the Wisdom of God, who initiates Christians by baptism into the divine Wisdom, is the same as the κύριος τῆς δόξης (1 Cor 2:8) of 1 Enoch 63.[133] Christ removes the gnostic τέλειοι into an exalted heavenly state like his own, beyond judgment, on the far side of the eschaton, where they regain their true places in the Pleroma.[134] The implications for ethical and community life of this image

---

[130]"...die personhafte Weisheitsgestalt im Judentum und die gnostische Sophia ursprünglich denselben religionsgeschichtlichen Hintergrund hätten" (*ibid.*, 195). Further on the Jewish roots of the gnostic myth, see G. W. Macrae, "The Jewish Background of the Gnostic Sophia Myth," *NovT* 12 (1970) 86-101.

[131]Wilckens, *Weisheit und Torheit*, 5-96. Similarly, M. Winter, *Pneumatiker und Psychiker in Korinth* (Marburg: N. G. Elwer, 1975) 12-41, and W. Schmithals, *Die Gnosis in Korinth* FRLANT 66 (Göttingen: Vandenhoeck und Ruprecht, 1969; ET *Gnosticism in Corinth*, tr. J. E. Steely [Nashville: Abingdon, 1971]) 151-155.

[132]Wilckens, *Weisheit und Torheit*, 205; emphasis his.

[133]*Ibid.*, 73; cf. idem,"σοφία,"519.

[134]*Weisheit und Torheit*, 205-213.

of Christ are party strife, flagrant immorality, and denial of a future resurrection.

Paul's response to the Corinthians' wrong-headed christology is not to reject it outright but to redefine it. Yes, Christ is the Wisdom of God, the Lord of Glory; but he is above all the Crucified (1 Cor 2:2). Christ's coming as Wisdom in the garb of Foolishness (i.e., the cross) is the means whereby God tricks the ἄρχοντες τοῦ αἰῶνος τούτου (2:8) and achieves salvation for the world. By emphasizing the apocalyptic dimensions of Christ's identity as the Lord of Glory, Paul counters the Corinthians' realized eschatology and reasserts the essential futurist dimension of redemption.[135] The crucial element of Paul's christology for Wilckens, then, is not the sapiential--which, after all, is only borrowed from his opponents--but the apocalyptic.

Wilckens's thesis has come under a good bit of criticism,[136] first because his exegetical decisions about the Corinthians' christology cannot be sustained,[137] secondly because he fails to produce any complete gnostic myth contemporary to 1 Corinthians and relies instead on second-and-third-century sources for parallels, and thirdly because he cannot demonstrate the independence of those later gnostic texts from Paul himself.[138] His conclusion about Paul's indirect and polemical use of wisdom language has nevertheless had substantial currency.[139] Even many of those outside the so-

---

[135]*Ibid.*, 214-224.

[136]E.g., H. Koester's review in *Gnomon* 33 (1961) 590-595; Ellis, "'Wisdom' and 'Knowledge'," 47; Scroggs, "Paul: ΣΟΦΟΣ and ΠΝΕΥΜΑΤΙΚΟΣ," *NTS* 14 (1967) 33-35; R. Hamerton-Kelly, *Pre-Existence, Wisdom, and the Son of Man: A Study of the Idea of Pre-Existence in the New Testament* (Cambridge: University, 1973) 112-119.

[137]Particularly his claims that ἐγὼ δὲ Χριστοῦ (1:12) alone of the four slogans denotes a theological affirmation rather than a faction, and that the κύριος τῆς δόξης is equivalent to θεοῦ σοφία (2:7, 8). See especially Koester's review.

[138]E.g., A. D. Nock ("Gnosticism," *HTR* 57 [1964] 278): "Certainly it is an unsound proceeding to take...texts, full of echoes of the New Testament, and reconstruct from them something supposedly lying back of the New Testament".

[139]E.g., Wilckens's teacher Günther Bornkamm, for whom "the apostle [in 1 Cor 2:6-16] is drawing on the style of preaching favored by his 'gnostic' opponents in Corinth and taking up a body of already current ideas...in order to amend both...." (*Paulus* [Stuttgart: W. Kohlhammer,

called mythological school of interpretation have concurred with his contention that in 1 Corinthians Paul opposes rather than espouses a straight-forward equation of Christ with Wisdom.[140] For a majority of interpreters, Paul's christology is only indirectly influenced by traditional Jewish wisdom language, and that in a negative fashion. It is rather the Apostle's reliance on apocalyptic categories that is most evident in his christological dispute with the Corinthians and their realized eschatology.

The first significant advance over Windisch's program came in 1965. In "Paulus und die Weisheit" Hans Conzelmann takes up the question of Paul's relationship to the Jewish wisdom tradition from an altogether different direction, limiting it neither to the issue of christology nor to the letter to Corinth.[141] Although Conzelmann essentially concurs with Wilckens's theory that Paul uses Corinthian vocabulary in 1 Corinthians 2-3, he denies that Paul's discussion partners are gnostics, and maintains instead that they have misunderstood the Apostle's own wisdom teaching. Conzelmann suggests that in Paul's theological background there stands a consciously organized "Schulbetrieb, eine 'Schule des Paulus' ...wo man 'Weisheit' methodisch betreibt bzw. Theologie als Weisheitsschulung treibt."[142] This Jewish-Christian wisdom training can be discerned not only behind its distortion in the Corinthian pursuit of σοφία, but throughout the Pauline corpus in the reworking of traditional wisdom language and thought.

Pointing to Acts 19:9-10, Conzelmann suggests Ephesus as the probable site for Paul's school, and claims that the deutero-Pauline letters represent the clearest products of such a school, since it likely continued after the Apostle's death.[143] To demonstrate the effects of such school activity in Paul himself, Conzelmann finds traditional wisdom themes and arguments not only in 1 Corinthians (1:18ff, 2:6ff, 10:1ff, 11:2ff, and 13:1ff), but in 2 Cor 3:7-18 and Rom 1:18ff as well,[144] and suggests a

---

1969; ET *Paul*, tr. D. M. G. Stalker (New York: Harper and Row, 1971) 162]).

[140]E.g., Ellis, "'Wisdom' and 'Knowledge'," 59-62; B. A. Pearson,*The Pneumatikos-Psychikos Terminology in I Corinthians: A Study in the Theology of the Corinthian Opponents of Paul and Its Relation to Gnosticism* SBLDS 12 (Missoula: Scholars, 1973) 27.

[141]"Paulus und die Weisheit," 231-244. The same argument is made *in nuce* in Conzelmann's essay on "Wisdom in the NT" in *IDBS* (1976) 959-960.

[142]Conzelmann, "Paulus und die Weisheit", 233.

[143]*Ibid.*, 233-234.

[144]*Ibid.*, 235-244.

number of other texts that might prove fruitful for similar investigation: 1 Thess 5:1ff, Gal 3:1ff, and Romans 9-11.[145] The criteria he suggests for isolating such traditions are essentially among those commonly used for locating any traditional material—the presence of unusual words or ideas, or passages that disrupt their literary contexts.[146] Here for the first time the search for wisdom in Paul moves beyond the allegedly christological texts Windisch employed, but Conzelmann's insight was not destined for widespread acceptance.

Although he concedes that "a synthesis between wisdom and the temporal concepts of Apocalypticism could occur (Enoch 42; Wisdom of Solomon),"[147] Conzelmann decrees that "as forms of thought they are fundamentally different."[148] Here the dichotomy 'wisdom or apocalyptic' is stated with force and conviction, and Conzelmann leaves no doubt as to which alternative he chooses.

> Es ist einseitig, den Abschnitt [Rom 1:18ff] als 'apokalyptisch' zu charakterisieren...Abgesehen davon, dass Weisheit und Apokalyptik sich berühren, kommt bei dieser Charakteristik weder die Begrifflichkeit noch der Einschlag an hellenistischen Gedanken...noch die relative Eliminierung der Zeit zu ihrem Recht. Der Gebrauch des Verbums ἀποκαλύπτειν beweist natürlich gar nichts für 'apokalyptischen' Stil.[149]

It was in the same year as Conzelmann's essay that Dieter Georgi published his dissertation on Paul's collection for Jerusalem.[150] Georgi argues, among other things, that a "Schultradition"[151] of wisdom speculation common to Paul and Philo (Rer.Div.Her. 141-206) lies behind Paul's use of ἰσότης in 2 Cor 8:13ff. Paul's notion of equality, says Georgi, has its roots in wisdom convictions about divine power immanent in and ordering the creation, the cosmic glue holding the world together. The wisdom of God assures that the cosmos is balanced, and this sapiential

---

[145]*Ibid.*, 244.

[146]*Ibid.*, 234-35. There are a number of other useful criteria for determining the presence of traditional material, not all named by Conzelmann but clearly implied.

[147]Conzelmann, "Wisdom in the NT," 957.

[148]*Ibid.*

[149]"Paulus und die Weisheit," 243, n.2.

[150]*Die Geschichte der Kollekte des Paulus für Jerusalem* (Hamburg: Herbert Reich, 1965) 62-67.

[151]*Ibid.*, 62.

background informs the theological basis of Paul's collection: Gentile support of the Jewish church provides a balance to the Jewish-Christian mission to Gentiles. Furthermore, ἰσότης and δικαιοσύνη are closely related in the wisdom "Überlieferungsstück"[152] on which Paul draws, so his preaching of justification--and therefore the center of his thought--is itself deeply indebted to the wisdom school tradition. The righteousness of God which 'right-wises' all on the same basis of divine grace is evidence of this traditional wisdom concern for balance and equality.[153]

Like Conzelmann, Georgi claims that wisdom rather than apocalyptic language and ideas play the more important role in Paul's thought. Rather than posing the stark dichotomy Conzelmann does,[154] though, he suggests a dialectic.

Doch wäre es falsch, zu meinen, das Apokalyptische sei dem Zentrum der paulinischen Theologie näher als das Denken der hellenistisch-jüdischen spekulativen Mystik. Beide stehen bei Paulus vielmehr in einem dialektischen Verhältnis zueinander.... Dieser Ansatz aber ist weisheitlich orientiert.[155]

Georgi's treatment of the christological hymn in Phil 2:5-11 also assigns a sapiential background to that text, although its author is not the Apostle but someone from the "Stephanuskreis".[156] This pre-Pauline hymnwriter, according to Georgi, derives his christology from the myth of the humiliation and exaltation of the wise man in Wisdom 2-3, a theme which itself already interprets the Isaianic Suffering Servant to be one in whom pre-existent Wisdom dwells. The ἐκένωσεν of Phil 2:7 therefore refers to Wisdom's relinquishing pre-existence to become human. Unlike

---

[152]*Ibid.*, 64
[153]*Ibid.*, 64-65.
[154]But cf. Georgi's footnote to the cited paragraph: "Wäre Paulus wirklich Apokalyptiker gewesen, so hätte schon der 1. Thessalonicherbrief anders ausgesehen, vor allem wäre 5,1ff nie geschrieben worden. Erst recht hätten wir dann von 1. Korintherbrief ausser dem 15. Kapitel nur wenige Sätze. 2.Kor. 4 und 5 besässen wir dann genauso wenig wie Phil. 3,7ff und Röm. 10. Aber Paulus ist nie, auch nicht als Jude, reiner Apokalyptiker gewesen, ebenso wie er auch nie nur Gnostiker gewesen ist" (*ibid.*, 66).
[155]*Ibid.*
[156]D. Georgi, "Der vorpaulinische Hymnus Phil 2,6-11" in *Zeit und Geschichte: Dankesgabe an Rudolf Bultmann zum 80. Geburtstag* ed. E. Dinkler (Tübingen: J. C. B. Mohr [Paul Siebeck], 1964) 263-293; 292.

others who have sought to discern a wisdom background to the hymn,[157] Georgi insists on the presence of the pre-existence motif by seeing the image of the wise man merged with the idea of transcendent Wisdom. Although he thus dissents from Käsemann's view of the hymn's hellenistic background,[158] he agrees that Paul uses the hymn to argue a christological and soteriological point in Philippians rather than a paraenetic one. The composition of the hymn with its wisdom myth transformed to christological ends is not Pauline, but Paul's appropriation of the hymn continues the wisdom emphasis.

As in 2 Corinthians 8, so in Philippians 2 Georgi sees wisdom language and thought to be constitutive of Paul's theology, even if--as in the latter--such sapiential background comes to the Apostle second hand. In a later essay on another subject, Georgi goes so far as to say:

The influence of the wisdom-movement on Paul is so thorough and the use of specific terms and patterns so precise that the assumption of a formal training in a wisdom school is inevitable. In Phil.3, Paul uses the form of the Jewish testament, thereby not only showing his knowledge of it but also telling us that he is using the school-pattern for organizing his work too.... All this means that Paul is our first literary evidence for an encounter between wisdom-schools and Pharisaism, scribal training and Pharisaic piety.[159]

Robin Scroggs's study of 1 Cor 2:6-16[160] followed Conzelmann's "Paulus und die Weisheit" and Georgi's *Die Geschichte der Kollekte* by only two years, but was apparently submitted for publication too soon to take account of them. Scroggs argues a remarkably similar case, but with some significant differences. The aim of his exegesis of 1 Cor 2:6-16 is

---

[157]See J. Murphy-O'Connor, "Christological Anthropology in Phil., II,6-11," *RB* 83 (1976) 25-50, and the literature cited there.

[158]E. Käsemann, "Kritische Analyse von Phil. 2:5-11" in *Exegetische Versuche und Besinnungen* (Tübingen: J. C. B. Mohr [Paul Siebeck], 1964) vol. 1, 51-95.

[159]"The Records of Jesus in the Light of Ancient Accounts of Revered Men" in *SBL Proceedings*, 1972, ed. L. C. McGaughy (SBL, 1973) vol. 2, 532.

[160]"Paul: ΣΟΦΟΣ and ΠΝΕΥΜΑΤΙΚΟΣ," 33-55. See above, n. 136, p. 33.

to demonstrate that Paul must have had an esoteric wisdom teaching entirely separate from his kerygma; that one must judge he drew his teaching *directly* from Jewish and Christian apocalyptic-wisdom theology; and that the main motifs revealed in these verses, so far from indicating a concession to foreign ideas [*contra* Wilckens], are consistent with his theology as a whole.[161]

Whereas Conzelmann starkly distinguishes wisdom from apocalyptic thought, Scroggs fuses the two into what he calls "Jewish and Christian apocalyptic-wisdom theology." He makes repeated reference to this alleged apocalyptic-wisdom theology, but never defines it, except for pointing vaguely in a footnote to "such a union [which]...is of course common to many Jewish materials--Daniel, the parables in Enoch, the Qumran writings, and Wisdom of Solomon."[162]

Furthermore, Conzelmann considers Paul's wisdom teaching to underlie his basic preaching, but Scroggs distinguishes between the Apostle's "esoteric wisdom teaching" and his kerygma. He preaches the gospel to everyone, but reserves his apocalyptic-wisdom message "for a select few,"[163] the τέλειοι. Only occasionally do his letters reveal fragments of that esoteric teaching, particularly when he makes reference to divine μυστήρια (e.g., 1 Cor 2:1, 7; 15:51; Rom 11:25). The most Scroggs can conclude about the content of Paul's σοφία is that it is "not simply about Christ himself, but about the whole eschatological drama of the final time,"[164] and that it has a place in Paul's ministry "in addition to, but not in place of, faith called forth by the kerygma."[165] Although Scroggs does not participate in the search for wisdom christology, his study affirms for the first time in fifty years Windisch's opinion about the apocalyptic content of Paul's notion of the Wisdom of God.

Twelve years later, James M. Reese picked up on Scroggs's argument in a brief popular essay on 1 Corinthians 1-2,[166] calling the passage "the most developed picture of apocalyptic wisdom in the New Testament".[167]

---

[161]*Ibid.*, 35; emphasis his.

[162]*Ibid.*

[163]*Ibid.*, 37.

[164]*Ibid.*, 46.

[165]*Ibid.*, 55.

[166]"Paul Proclaims the Wisdom of the Cross: Scandal and Foolishness," *Biblical Theology Bulletin* 9 (1979) 147-153.

[167]*Ibid.*, 149. Reese credits Jesus with a similar "apocalyptic wisdom" in Matthew's Sermon on the Mount which "unfolds the lifestyle of the Kingdom with a series of apocalyptic maxims or wisdom proverbs...(Mt

Although Scroggs never defines "apocalyptic wisdom," Reese offers this
general description:

> Paul seldom speaks of the earthly life of Jesus, except for his death
> on the cross, which he treats as an apocalyptic event that
> anticipates his return in glory.... An apocalyptic event calls for a
> new form of insight which we can call apocalyptic wisdom. This is
> the wisdom needed to believe in the power of the cross and to live
> by the destiny it offers.[168]

Reese does not explain how such "a new form of insight" differs from
traditional wisdom except to call it "transcendent wisdom" and contrast it
with "human wisdom."[169] At this point, he appears to side with Wilckens
against Scroggs by implying that Paul's Corinthian opponents have set the
sapiential agenda and Paul has borrowed–and modified–their wisdom
vocabulary. In contrast to the Corinthians' pursuit of "immortality and
perfection,"[170] Paul holds up the wisdom of the cross, that is, Jesus'
"perfect loyalty to God's will."[171]

5:1-12)" (*ibid.*, 147). For a similar assessment of Matt 11:25-30, cf. J. P.
Meier, *The Vision of Matthew* (New York: Paulist, 1979) 78: "The whole
passage...is suffused with the terminology of apocalyptic revelation and
wisdom theology. Indeed, Matthew gives us here a fine example of that
fusion of apocalyptic and sapiential themes which is characteristic not only
of his gospel but also of a large part of the New Testament." So also, P.
H. Davids observes of σοφία in Ephesians and Colossians: "the believer's
wisdom is the new, eschatological life-style of the Christian rather than
God's past deeds: wisdom is the way the believer must live to please God
and to accord with [the believer's] knowledge of God's future
consummation. One could almost call it skill in living in the light of the
eschaton" (*The Epistle of James: A Commentary on the Greek Text* [Grand
Rapids: Eerdmans, 1982] 54).

[168]Reese, "Paul Proclaims the Wisdom of the Cross," 147. Cf. also
"Apocalyptic wisdom enables believers to embrace the lifestyle of the
Cross, which is a life of freedom and of witness to the saving presence of
the risen Lord within the lives of members of his church" (*ibid.*, 151).

[169]*Ibid.*, 149.

[170]*Ibid.*

[171]*Ibid.*, 150.

Reese notes that the mystery (1 Cor 2:7) of "God's saving plan in Christ"[172] has "deep roots in the apocalyptic development of Jewish wisdom tradition"[173] and suggests that there are "many natural links" between apocalyptic and wisdom literature "because both were seeking to answer the place of humans in the creation and the saving plan of God."[174] Like Scroggs before him, Reese does not discuss what those links might be, he attempts no historical or linguistic investigation of the connections between the apocalyptic and wisdom traditions, nor does he finally say what is so distinctively sapiential or apocalyptic about speculation on "the place of humans in the creation and the saving plan of God." His essay nevertheless revives, by supporting Scroggs, Windisch's turn-of-the-century view that Paul's wisdom thought is somehow apocalyptic in nature.

M. Jack Suggs's contribution to the John Knox *Festschrift*[175] seeks to vindicate both Windisch's initial observations about the sapiential background of Rom 10:6-9[176] and Davies's syllogism Torah = Wisdom, Christ = Torah, therefore Christ = Wisdom.[177] Suggs finds in Bar 3:29-30 a wisdom interpretation of Deut 30:13 parallel to Paul's own use of it in Rom 10:6-7, and concludes that "Baruch affirms of the Torah what Paul affirms of Christ: that by this instrument 'the word is near to you.'"[178]

> The importance of establishing a link between Paul and the wisdom tradition is not merely that the apostle is thereby acquitted of gross mishandling of Deut. 30:11-14. The greater significance lies in his appropriation of that tradition in relation to the continuing problem of Gospel and Law. In Rom. 10:6-10 Paul has taken up the familiar identification of Wisdom and Torah and added a third term: Jesus Christ. The tension between Gospel and Law is

---

[172]*Ibid.*, 151.

[173]*Ibid.*

[174]*Ibid.*, 147.

[175]"'The Word Is Near To You': Romans 10:6-10 Within the Purpose of the Letter" in *Christian History and Interpretation: Studies Presented to John Knox*, ed. W. R. Farmer, *et al.* (Cambridge: University, 1967) 289-312.

[176]"Die göttliche Weisheit," 224.

[177]*Paul and Rabbinic Judaism*, 147-176. Suggs assumes with Davies and J. Fichtner (*Die altorientalische Weisheit in ihrer israelitisch-jüdischen Ausprägung* [Giessen: A. Töpelmann, 1933] 95) that "there is no *nomismusfrei* wisdom writing later than Ecclesiasticus" ("'The Word Is Near To You'," 307).

[178]Suggs, "'The Word Is Near To You'," 309.

resolved by the identification of Christ with Wisdom-Torah.... The righteousness based on faith does not annul the law but brings it to its true goal, for 'the word of faith which we preach' is Jesus Christ, incarnate wisdom, τέλος νόμου (10:4).[179]

What sets Suggs's conclusions apart from his predecessors' in the search for wisdom christology is the purpose for which he claims Paul identifies Christ and Sophia. Knox and Feuillet had argued that the myth of Wisdom provides the culturally appropriate package for preaching about Jesus to a philosophically sophisticated Hellenistic audience, and Paul's wisdom christology is therefore a function of his missionary strategy. Suggs, on the other hand, says Paul's interpretive paraphrase of Deut 30:13 is designed as much to make a point about the law as about Christ, "to mollify (if not to pacify) the Jewish opposition [to his Gentile mission] and thus to satisfy the needs and feelings of the Jewish-Christian community in Jerusalem."[180] Whereas in 1 Corinthians 1-3 his wisdom christology functions to combat "a Gnosticizing spiritualism,"[181] its purpose in Romans 10 is to defend before Jewish adversaries his preaching of a law-free gospel to Gentiles.

My own response to the particulars of Suggs's interpretation of Romans 10 is properly left to the exegetical section of this study,[182] but here is it well to point out that his essay demonstrates the resilience of Windisch's early hypothesis of Pauline wisdom christology. Suggs's is the first significant study of alleged wisdom christology in Paul in a text outside of 1 Corinthians. Moreover, the essay provides the first test of Conzelmann's proposed Pauline "Weisheitschule."[183]

More than a third of R. G. Hamerton-Kelly's major monograph on the NT concepts of pre-existence addresses the Pauline and deutero-Pauline letters.[184] It examines all the texts formerly invoked in support of wisdom

---

[179]*Ibid.*, 311.

[180]*Ibid.*, 299.

[181]*Ibid.*, 304.

[182]See below, Chapter Three.

[183]Although it appeared too late for Suggs to consider it at length, he says in a footnote of Conzelmann's "Paulus und die Weisheit": "If the thesis could be established, it would serve our understanding of Rom. 10:6-10 well" ("'The Word Is Near To You'," 305).

[184]*Pre-Existence, Wisdom, and the Son of Man*, 103-196. See above, n. 136. F. B. Craddock's earlier *The Pre-Existence of Christ in the New Testament* (Nashville: Abingdon, 1968) deals with a number of the same texts, but is limited to the specific notion of Christ's pre-existence and is

christology and a number of others, as well. Hamerton-Kelly concludes that
the figure of hypostatized Wisdom does contribute to the early Christian
picture of Christ, but Paul modifies that traditional christology substantially
by means of Jewish apocalyptic categories. Paul affirms the "protological
pre-existence" of Christ which is central to the tradition, but places that pre-
existence "within the framework of apocalyptic eschatology."[185]

> Paul accepts the idea that Christ is the original mediator of creation
> (I Cor. 8:6), but distinguishes him from the original man, and
> from the true humanity potentially present in [human beings]. He
> does this by means of eschatology. Jesus Christ, who pre-existed
> the world, and mediated the creation, will, nevertheless, be fully
> manifested only at the end of time.... [I]t is important for [Paul]
> that the one who appears at the end be the one who has existed
> from the beginning.[186]

The notion of pre-existence that Windisch had found in wisdom
traditions Hamerton-Kelly finds in apocalyptic literature as well: "the
earliest Christian theology [and, therefore, Paul] used the Jewish apocalyptic
scheme of things existing in heaven before their eschatological
manifestation."[187] The Son of Man in 4 Ezra, the law, the heavenly
Jerusalem, and personified Wisdom are all described in apocalyptic literature
as pre-existent, and each informs a facet of Paul's Christian theology.[188]

In Hamerton-Kelly's view, Paul does not construe the wisdom of God
primarily as Christ, but as the whole apocalyptic plan of God for

---

addressed to a popular audience. Craddock eschews *religionsgeschichtliche*
methods of interpreting wisdom language and thought in Paul, at least
wherever he finds them in conjunction with pre-existence christology. He
prefers instead to ask how any given statement about pre-existence functions
psychologically or sociologically in its supposed historical context.
Unfortunately, he seldom considers as seriously the literary contexts of a
number of passages—notably the hymns in Philippians 2 and Colossians 1
and the image of the rock in 1 Cor 10:4--and his exegesis suffers
accordingly. See Hamerton-Kelly's responses to Craddock in *Pre-Existence,
Wisdom, and the Son of Man*, 4-5 and *passim*.

[185]*Ibid.*, 195.
[186]*Ibid.*, 193-194.
[187]*Ibid.*, 105.
[188]*Ibid.*, 106-107.

salvation.[189] For reasons different from those of Windisch, and with a different outcome, Hamerton-Kelly does view wisdom and apocalyptic ideas as operating together in Paul. But in the final analysis, Paul's adaptation of the wisdom elements in traditional "Hellenistic-Jewish-Christian"[190] christology by means of Jewish apocalyptic categories removes it several stages from the fairly explicit equation of Christ with Wisdom in the Colossians hymn. Only in what he labels pre-Pauline texts (e.g., 1 Cor 8:6 and 10:4) does Hamerton-Kelly discern anything close to such a simple equation, and each is significantly altered by its context so that its impact is soteriological rather than christological.[191]

Hamerton-Kelly claims against Wilckens that Paul's reference to Christ as the κύριος τῆς δόξης (1 Cor 2:8) equates him not with pre-existent Wisdom, but only with the heavenly Son of Man in 1 En 63:11.

> The secret wisdom...is that the humiliated one is indeed the apocalyptic redeemer, and that the crucifixion was part of the divine plan, which could also be called the divine 'wisdom'.[192]

The σοφία θεοῦ, far from being a christological title, is Paul's description of God's apocalyptic plan of salvation. His calling Christ the Wisdom of God (1:24, 30) is simply his synecdochic shorthand for all the salvific blessings present and yet to be revealed (2:9).[193] Not only does Paul not adopt any allegedly gnostic terminology from the Corinthians, the Corinthians themselves are not gnostics, but are rather influenced by a type of Philonic anthropology and mysticism.[194]

One significant observation Hamerton-Kelly makes regarding wisdom influence in Paul has nothing to do with christology at all. According to Hamerton-Kelly, the Jewish wisdom tradition has its most profound impact not on Paul's christology but on his ecclesiology. And here, too, the wisdom influence is intimately tied up with Paul's reliance on apocalyptic categories.

---

[189]*Ibid.*, 117. Cf. also Scroggs, "Paul: ΣΟΦΟΣ and ΠΝΕΥΜΑΤΙΚΟΣ," 46.

[190]*Pre-Existence, Wisdom, and the Son of Man*, 193.

[191]*Ibid.*

[192]*Ibid.*, 117.

[193]*Ibid.*, 115.

[194]*Pre-Existence, Wisdom, and the Son of Man*, 114-123. Although Hamerton-Kelly cites only an abstract of it (122), his conclusions on this point foreshadow those of the dissertation of B. Pearson discussed below, pp. 45-47.

The main pre-existent entity,...as far as Paul is concerned, is the Church. It is the heavenly city or heavenly temple, to be revealed at the end but pre-existent now in heaven.... Paul's unique contribution...to early Christian thought about pre-existence is not in the realm of Christology, but in the doctrine of the Church.[195]

In 1974, A. Van Roon undertook an earnest, often plodding polemic against any sort of wisdom christology in Paul.[196] Essentially a point-by-point response to Windisch and Feuillet, Van Roon's essay takes no note of the studies by Conzelmann, Scroggs, or Suggs, and engages in only sporadic conversation with Wilckens's. As Feuillet had sought to demonstrate the universality of wisdom traditions in Paul, Van Roon proposes the opposite, repeatedly offering alternative religio-historical sources for Paul's language. For example, in his discussion of 1 Cor 10:4, he dismisses the parallels in Wis 10:17 and Philo as lacking precise verbal correspondence with 1 Cor 10:4, and asserts instead:

the fact that the OT refers time and time again to Israel's God as the rock and that in Ps. Lxxviii 35, too, he is the rock "of their fathers" offers a more convincing explanation. Thinking which is so deeply influenced by the OT as is this passage in I Cor. x 1-14 makes a connection between the rock and God more natural than that between the rock and wisdom. The idea of accompanying, which is brought out in the expression ἀκολούθουσα πέτρα, also accords very well with the picture of God in Ps. lxxviii and the OT as a whole.[197]

So also, the other titles previously claimed to be sapiential in origin—mediator or first-born of creation, image of God, and so on—Van Roon explains as attributes of God applied by Paul to Christ. "Paul uses divine predicates for Christ and considers him equal to God. This opinion is consistent with his christology."[198] That christology, according to Van Roon, is based on Paul's "idea of the pre-existence of the Messianic Son of God" derived from Ps 110:3 and Mic 5:2.[199] What appears to have connections with sapiential thought in Paul's language about Jesus (e.g., 1

---

[195]*Pre-Existence, Wisdom, and the Son of Man*, 193, 196.
[196]"The Relation Between Christ and the Wisdom of God According to Paul," *NovT* 16 (1974) 207-239.
[197]*Ibid.*, 230.
[198]*Ibid.*, 233.
[199]*Ibid.*, 234.

Cor 1:24, 30) reflects no more than the traditional Jewish attribution of wisdom to the messiah.[200] Van Roon's essay serves to demonstrate the extent to which conclusions about the shape of Paul's christology are able to control the search for his theological background if given free reign, for Van Roon disputes even the clearest evidence of wisdom thought in the Colossians 1 hymn (which he takes to be Pauline).[201] When he denies the presence of wisdom christology, he also rejects any but the slightest influence of sapiential thought on Paul.

The next contribution to the debate about Paul's reliance on wisdom came, as had so many others, from a study on 1 Corinthians. Birger Pearson's dissertation[202] seeks to answer directly the claims by Bultmann, Wilckens, *et al.* of gnosticism in Corinth, and arrives at a scenario much like that hinted at by Hamerton-Kelly.[203] Pearson pursues the Jewish exegetical tradition that interprets Gen 2:7 to explain human nature as composed of σῶμα from the earth, ψυχή, a vital principle shared by animals and humans alike, and a πνεῦμα granted by God at creation. It is this divine "inbreathing" that gives human beings the unique capacity to know God and experience God's wisdom.[204]

According to Pearson, the Corinthians have just such a Jewish (not gnostic) anthropology, and they see their glorying in σοφία to be entirely appropriate to their spiritual nature. It is Paul's redefinition of πνευμάτικος, with apocalyptic and ethical modifications, rather than his redefinition of σοφία or Christ, that initiates the polemic of 1 Corinthians 2. For Paul, being spiritual is a function not of human nature or potential, but of the gift of God in Christ.[205] As a result, Pearson sees the direct influence of wisdom traditions in 1 Corinthians not on Paul but on his opponents, while it is Paul's own apocalyptic heritage that is most evident in his response.

> The opponents were operating on a non-eschatological plane in dividing [humanity's] present existence into a duality of heavenly-earthly, spiritual-psychic, incorruptible-corruptible, immortal-mortal levels. Paul can use the *same* terminology, but employs it

---

[200]*Ibid.*, 237.
[201]*Ibid.*, 233-235.
[202]*The Pneumatikos-Psychikos Terminology*; see above, n. 140, p. 34.
[203]See above, n. 194, p. 43.
[204]*The Pneumatikos-Psychikos Terminology*, 17-24.
[205]*Ibid.*, 24-25.

in a completely eschatological fashion, in which a dualism of "the present age" and "the age to come" are the principle factors.[206]

Pearson pursues his argument about 1 Corinthians 2 further in a later essay in which he also responds to Conzelmann's proposal of a Pauline "Weisheitschule."[207] As in the earlier work, Pearson claims that Paul's wisdom language in 1 Corinthians is indeed that of his opponents, but is neither gnostic nor particularly christological in content. Nor is Paul's revision of their language specifically christological: the "wisdom of God" for Paul is "the wisdom of God's salvific plan."[208]

> The error of the Corinthians, from Paul's point of view, would not have been in christology itself--with which he is in basic agreement--but the conclusions they were drawing from it vis-à-vis their own self-understanding: they were applying the exalted state of Christ to themselves, considering that they were "already reigning" with Christ (cf. 4:8), and in possession of such things as "eye has not seen, nor ear heard, nor has occurred to the heart of man."[209]

Paul's correction of the Corinthian heresy consists of his "historical realism and...'eschatological reservation'."[210] Although he is certainly familiar with wisdom teaching and probably did have a 'school of theology,'[211] Paul thinks of himself not primarily as a sage, but as an apostle, and

---

[206]*Ibid.*, 26; emphasis his.

[207]"Hellenistic-Jewish Wisdom Speculation and Paul" in *Aspects of Wisdom in Judaism and Early Christianity*, ed. R. L. Wilken (Notre Dame: University of Notre Dame, 1975) 43-66.

[208]*Ibid.*, 51. Cf. "the content of Paul's version of the wisdom of God is nothing else than the salvatory crucifixion of Christ as the center of God's salvific plan" (*The Pneumatikos-Psychikos Terminology*, 31).

[209]"Hellenistic-Jewish Wisdom Speculation," 56-57.

[210]*Ibid.*, 58. The phrase "eschatological reservation" is Käsemann's ("On the Subject of Primitive Christian Apocalyptic," 132).

[211]Although he questions the image of Paul as a wisdom teacher, Pearson is most impressed with Conzelmann's school theory as an explanation for the existence of the deutero-Pauline letters ("Hellenistic-Jewish Wisdom Speculation," 44).

his own theology [is] *critical* of 'Hellenistic-Jewish wisdom speculation'...[and rather reflects] the influence of an apocalyptically-oriented Pharisaism...at home in the apocalyptic Christianity of the primitive Palestinian church.[212]

Once again, wisdom and apocalyptic influences in Paul are set against each other, particularly as wisdom christology is denied.

Despite this growing skepticism about Pauline wisdom christology, Martin Hengel attempted in 1975 to explain all of early Christian language about Jesus--and particularly Paul's--from Jewish wisdom traditions.[213] Taking as his point of departure the title Son of God, Hengel examines the historical antecedents to what he calls "the thought patterns involved with [the title]: pre-existence, mediation at creation, and sending into the world."[214] Eduard Schweizer had earlier suggested in a brief essay[215] that the traditional affirmation "God sent his Son"[216] reflects the myth of Wisdom's seeking out those she saves (e.g., Prov 8:1-12; Wis 9:10-18). Hengel pursues Schweizer's hypothesis, and adds to it his own opinions about the religio-historical background of other christological titles and confessions. His conclusion is essentially a revision of that of Davies.

The confession of the exaltation of Jesus as Son of Man and Son of God in the resurrection and his appointment as God's eschatological plenipotentiary immediately posed for earliest Christianity the question of the relationship of Jesus to other intermediary figures, whether the supreme angels or Wisdom-Torah, which was at least partially thought of as a personification.... Once the idea of pre-existence had been introduced, it was obvious that the exalted Son of God would also

---

[212]*Ibid.*, 59; emphasis his.

[213]*Der Sohn Gottes: Die Entstehung der Christologie und die jüdische-hellenistische Religionsgeschichte* (Tübingen: J. C. B. Mohr [Paul Siebeck], 1975; rev., 1977; ET *The Son of God: The Origin of Christology and the History of Jewish-Hellenistic Religion*, tr. J. Bowden [Philadelphia: Fortress, 1976]).

[214]*Ibid.*, 57.

[215]E. Schweizer, "Zum religionsgeschichtlichen Hintergrund des 'Sendungsformel' Gal 4:4f. Rm 8:3f. John 3:16f. I Joh 4:9," *ZNW* 57 (1966) 199-210. Cf. also idem, "υἱός, κ.τ.λ." in *TDNT* (1972) vol. 8, 374-376.

[216]The verb for sending can be either (ἐξ)αποστέλλω, πέμπω, or δίδωμι" ("υἱός, κ.τ.λ.," 374-375).

attract to himself the functions of Jewish Wisdom as a mediator of creation and salvation.[217]

On what he believed to be the strength of Hengel's conclusions, Anthony Tyrell Hanson renewed the search for both wisdom christology in Paul and gnosticism in Corinth.[218] He searches first for the source of the enigmatic quotation in 1 Cor 2:9:

> What no eye has seen, nor ear heard, nor the human heart conceived, what God has prepared for those who love him.

Hanson finds antecedents to the citation throughout early Jewish exegetical tradition, and sees the clearest parallel in the *Biblical Antiquities* of Pseudo-Philo.[219] He concludes that its function in 1 Corinthians is to show that what the ἄρχοντες τοῦ αἰῶνος τούτου of v 8 do not recognize is the wisdom of God revealed to Christians by the Spirit, namely "the whole design of God apprehensible in the life, death, and resurrection of Jesus Christ, but centrally in his death on the cross."[220] In one respect, Hanson shares Windisch's (and Hamerton-Kelly's) opinion that the Wisdom of God includes the plan of salvation. That plan of salvation, however, is for Hanson focused in christology and not materially conditioned by its apocalyptic horizon. Hanson decides next that the quotation from Isa 40:13 in 1 Cor 2:16 ("For who has known the mind of the Lord so as to instruct him?") is the proof-text for Paul's claim to have the νοῦς Χριστοῦ.[221] That text, too, has a long history of wisdom interpretation, in which it is combined with a line from the Targum on Job 41:3 and referred to the pre-existent Torah or Wisdom of God.[222] Consequently, both of Paul's uses of the citation—in its complete form in Rom 11:34-35 and partially in 1 Cor 2:16—are intended to make the same "implicitly christological"[223] point: Christ is God's agent in creation, God's counsellor "to whom God disclosed

---

[217]Hengel, *The Son of God*, 67, 72.

[218]"A Quasi-Gnostic Pauline Midrash: I Corinthians 2.6-16" in *The New Testament Interpretation of Scripture* (London: S.P.C.K., 1980) 21-96.

[219]*Ibid.*, 58-62.

[220]*Ibid.*, 64.

[221]*Ibid.*, 69-78.

[222]*Ibid.*, 78-89.

[223]*Ibid.*, 91.

his whole mind and in whom his whole plan for the redemption and justification of [humanity] has been carried out."[224]

Hanson neglects to mention just how the "proto-gnostic"[225] Gentile Corinthians might know the Jewish exegetical tradition that presumably lies behind Paul's quotations from scripture in 1 Corinthians 2, nor does he explain how the passages from Isaiah 40 and Job 41 make any christological point--implicit or otherwise—in their literary context at the end of Romans 11. He does, however, make a rather convincing case for the sapiential background of the conflated citation.[226] He assumes the existence of Paul's wisdom christology without demonstrating it, and as Bourke had done, attempts to demonstrate its presence elsewhere in Paul's interpretation of scripture.

Summary

This diffuse search for wisdom influence in Paul allows very few generalizations. The early work was marked by the quest in Colossians and 1 Corinthians for wisdom christology which later methodological advances made unpopular; but as Hanson's recent essay demonstrates, even that has not been given up totally. The Pauline texts Windisch surveyed—and others, as well—have continued to impress some scholars as sapiential in nature, but the source of that wisdom character has been variously assigned to Paul, his opponents, and early Christian tradition. Conzelmann, Georgi, Scroggs, and Hamerton-Kelly have attempted to move beyond the obvious texts in 1 Corinthians 1-3 for further evidence of wisdom traditions in the Pauline corpus, but only Scroggs and Hamerton-Kelly take any serious note of the engagement of those sapiential traditions with the apocalyptic content of Paul's thought. For most, the differences between the wisdom and apocalyptic traditions—and their respective influences on Paul—have appeared too drastic to permit anything but a forced choice: Paul is *either* an apocalypticist *or* a wisdom thinker.

III. The Confluence of Apocalyptic and Wisdom Traditions

Impetus for the continued distinction between the two modes of thought probably comes also from reaction against Gerhard von Rad's thesis about apocalyptic and wisdom literature in *Die Theologie des Alten*

---

[224]*Ibid.*

[225]*Ibid.*, 96.

[226]Further on the exegesis of Romans 11, see below, Chapter Three.

Testaments.[227] Von Rad revives and expands Gerhard Hölscher's contention that Jewish apocalyptic thought derives not from prophecy but from the degenerate wisdom tradition.[228] The theory has not been well received,[229] despite several revisions of it in succeeding editions of the *Theologie*, and as a result the distance between apocalyptic and wisdom thought in scholarly minds has grown. When no genetic historical relationship between the apocalyptic and wisdom movements can be demonstrated, the differences between the two become all the more apparent. Von Rad's proposal has nevertheless prompted a few investigations into the possible relationships between the two in various early Jewish writings, and the debate has by no means been abandoned.[230] The quest has been undertaken for the most part, however, in early Jewish rather than in Christian or specifically Pauline

---

[227]Vol. 2 (Munich: Chr. Kaiser, 1960; ET, *Old Testament Theology*, tr. D. M. G. Stalker [New York: Harper and Row, 1965] vol. 2, 301-315). The same thesis is expounded further in von Rad's *Weisheit in Israel* (Neukirchen-Vlyun: Neukirchener, 1970; ET, *Wisdom in Israel*, tr. J. D. Martin [Nashville: Abingdon, 1972] 263-283).

[228]"Die Entstehung des Buches Daniel," *Theologische Studien und Kritiken* 92 (1919) 113-138.

[229]The strongest criticism has come from P. von der Osten-Sacken, *Die Apokalyptik in ihrem Verhältnis zu Prophetie und Weisheit* Theologische Existenz Heute 157 (Munich: Chr. Kaiser, 1969). H.-P. Müller offers support with a revised proposal that apocalyptic is the child of mantic wisdom ("Mantische Weisheit und Apokalyptik" in *Congress Volume Uppsala* Supplement to *VetT* 22, ed. G. W. Anderson, et al. [Leiden: Brill, 1972] 268-293). See the detailed discussion below, Chapter Two.

[230]E.g., J. J. Collins, "The Court Tales in Daniel and the Development of Apocalyptic," *JBL* 94 (1975) 218-234; idem, "Cosmos and Salvation: Jewish Wisdom and Apocalyptic in the Hellenistic Age," *HR* 17 (1977) 121-142; M. A. Knibb, "Apocalyptic and Wisdom in 4 Ezra," *JSJ* 13 (1981) 56-74; J. Z. Smith, "Wisdom and Apocalyptic" in *Religious Syncretism in Antiquity: Essays in Conversation With Geo Widengren,* ed. B. A. Pearson (Missoula: Scholars, 1975) 131-156; J. G. Gammie, "Spatial and Ethical Dualism in Jewish Wisdom and Apocalyptic Literature," *JBL* 93 (1974) 356-385; S. J. De Vries, "Observations on Quantitative and Qualitative Time in Wisdom and Apocalyptic" in *Israelite Wisdom: Theological and Literary Essays in Honor of Samuel Terrien*, ed. J. G. Gammie, et al. (New York: Union Theological Seminary, 1978) 263-276; N. Perrin, "Wisdom and Apocalyptic in the Message of Jesus" in *SBL Proceedings 1972*, ed. L. C. McGaughy (SBL, 1972) vol. 2, 543-572. See the discussion below, Chapter Two.

literature. The one exception has been the work of the OT scholar Hartmut Gese.

Gese attempts in three major essays[231] to expand von Rad's thesis by seeing the process of wisdom's growth into apocalypticism extend into the NT. As a self-described tradition historian in the mold of von Rad,[232] Gese seeks to explain not only how all of NT christology derives from the confluence of the Jewish wisdom and apocalyptic traditions, but how the Old and New Testaments relate to one another historically and theologically. Paul occupies only one place in the overall picture, but since the Apostle is supposedly characteristic of the process of early Christian theologizing, and his letters are products of that process, Gese's proposal merits discussion in this survey.

According to Gese, the ideal world envisioned by 'late theological wisdom,'[233] combined with its failure to be achieved, sets up a yearning in Judaism for its fulfillment, a yearning that gives birth to the apocalyptic world view.

> Precisely the ideal nature of the conceptuality of late wisdom opens the vista of apocalyptic consummation. The wisdom of Sir 24 and the apocalyptic hope are by no means a contradiction since exactly from this picture of Sophia the longing for its realization had to arise, i.e. the event of a new creation.[234]

---

[231]"Natus ex Virgine" in *Vom Sinai zum Zion* (Munich: Chr. Kaiser, 1974) 130-146; "Der Johannesprolog" in *Zur biblischen Theologie* (Munich: Chr. Kaiser, 1977) 152-201, ET "The Prologue to John's Gospel" *Essays on Biblical Theology*, tr. K. Crim (Minneapolis: Augsburg, 1981) 167-222; and "Die Weisheit, der Menschensohn und die Ursprünge der Christologie als konsequente Entfaltung der biblischen Theologie," *SEA* 44 (1979) 77-114, ET "Wisdom, Son of Man, and the Origins of Christology: The Consistent Development of Biblical Theology," tr. U. Mauser, *Horizons in Biblical Theology* 3 (1981) 23-57.

[232]"It is the task of theology...to penetrate by interpretation into the nature of revelation as it manifests itself in its tradition.... It is the task of biblical theology to understand by reflection that tradition in its historical development..." ("Wisdom, Son of Man, and the Origins of Christology," 23).

[233]The phrase is von Rad's (*Old Testament Theology*, vol. 1, 441-453; and idem, *Wisdom in Israel, passim*).

[234]Gese, "Wisdom, Son of Man, and the Origins of Christology," 37.

In the NT, Gese says, this relationship between sapiential idealism and apocalyptic hope is most obvious in the development of christology.

To begin with, Gese views all early Christian language about Jesus as essentially unified: the same traditioning process results in John 1:1-18,[235] Matthew 1 and Luke 1-2,[236] 1 Cor 8:6, Gal 4:4ff, and Rom 8:3ff,[237] Col 1:15-20,[238] and even the Nicene Creed.[239] Secondly, all these primitive Christian writers use as their basic theological resources the notions of a hypostatized Wisdom (Job 28, Proverbs 8, Sirach 24, Wisdom 9),[240] a pre-existent Torah identified with Wisdom (Psalm 119, Sirach 24),[241] and a martyred Davidic Messiah (Zechariah 13) identified with the heavenly Son of Man (Daniel 7, 1 Enoch 37-71, 4 Ezra) and the Son of God (Psalm 2, 2 Samuel 7).[242] It does not trouble Gese that he cannot demonstrate direct NT use of the Enochic Son of Man traditions,[243] since

> this late tradition, located at the border of the Old Testament, displays at any rate the necessity which conjoins the universality of the Son of Man-Messiah and the universality of wisdom.[244]

Thirdly, when Jesus of Nazareth arrives, teaching like a wise man (e.g., Matt 11:25ff//Luke 10:21) and arrogating to himself Wisdom's revelatory discourse language (Matt 11:28-30),[245] Christians automatically recognize who he is: Wisdom = Torah = Messiah = Son of Man = Son of God = everything-else-first-century-Jews-are-expecting-by-way-of-salvation. Even Jesus' resurrection is interpreted in the light of this homogenized anticipation:

---

[235]Gese, "The Prologue to John's Gospel;" idem, "Wisdom, Son of Man, and the Origins of Christology," 51-55.

[236]Gese, "Natus ex Virgine."

[237]Gese, "Wisdom, Son of Man, and the Origins of Christology," 46.

[238]*Ibid.*, 47-51.

[239]*Ibid.*, 55-56.

[240]*Ibid.*, 28-34.

[241]*Ibid.*, 35-37.

[242]*Ibid.*, 38-40.

[243]The Similitudes are notoriously difficult to date. See the discussion of E. Isaac in *The Old Testament Pseudepigrapha*, ed. J. H. Charlesworth (Garden City: Doubleday, 1983) vol. 1, 6-7.

[244]"Wisdom, Son of Man, and the Origins of Christology," 40.

[245]*Ibid.*, 41-43.

In line with the *Davidic-Messianic tradition*, the resurrection is the
enthronement as Son of God [Rom 1:3ff].... In line with the *Son
of Man tradition*, the Risen is the exalted Messiah appointed to be
the Son of Man [Acts 7:56].... But only in line with the *wisdom
tradition* the full christological perspective becomes evident: Jesus
is the manifestation of wisdom itself because he is the revelation of
complete transcendence.[246]

Gese's analysis of the origins of christology bears a striking
resemblance to the rabbinic interpretive principle which allows one to
develop complex doctrine from the conjoining of (originally) disparate
texts.[247] He nowhere demonstrates that the numerous passages from the
OT, Apocrypha, or Pseudepigrapha are actually cited (or even consulted) by
NT writers, but rather puts together a collection of ideas and images, a
selective assortment of traditional threads which he weaves into a tapestry
bearing Jesus' image. Rather than buttressing von Rad's case for the genetic
development of apocalypticism from wisdom, Gese instead makes a
theological affirmation about the unity of the Christian canon. Moreover,
with his uncritical generalizations about the broad phenomenon of early
christology, Gese contributes almost nothing to the question of Paul's
relationship to the wisdom and apocalyptic traditions.

IV. Conclusions

Several observations should be made regarding this sketch of Pauline
research. In the main, when scholars have investigated wisdom influence on
Paul's thought, they have done so for one of two reasons: either they have
been convinced that the figure of Wisdom stands behind Paul's
understanding of Christ,[248] or they have been trying to make sense of the

---

[246]*Ibid.*, 45; emphasis his.

[247]See H. L. Strack, *Einleitung in Talmud und Midras* (Munich: Beck,
1887; 5th ed., 1921; ET *Introduction to Talmud and Midrash* [Philadelphia:
Jewish Publication Society of America, 1931] 94).

[248]It is not difficult to imagine that R. Bultmann's influential studies
of Johannine Logos christology have provided some of the impetus for this
line of reasoning ("Der religionsgeschichtliche Hintergrund des Prologs zum
Johannesevangelium" in *EYXAPIΣTHPION: Studien zur Religion und
Literatur des Alten und Neuen Testaments* FRL 36, ed. H. Schmidt
[Göttingen: Vandenhoeck and Ruprecht, 1923] vol. 2, 3-26; "Die
Bedeutung der neuerschlossenen mandäischen und manichäischen Quellen für
das Verständnis des Johannesevangeliums," *ZNW* 24 [1925] 100-146; and

very abstruse argument of 1 Corinthians 1-3. If the motivation is the latter, they are still, for the most part, intent on claiming or denying the presence of wisdom christology in the passage and thus in Paul generally. Only Conzelmann's "Paulus und die Weisheit" departs from this pattern, and his call for programmatic study of wisdom in Paul has gone surprisingly unanswered. The time has come to search for wisdom influence in Paul beyond the obvious passage in 1 Corinthians.

Secondly, scholars have viewed wisdom influence in Paul largely in isolation from his debt to Jewish apocalyptic thought. Evidence for the magnitude of that debt has been so convincingly argued so frequently of late that there has been scarcely any incentive to respond to Conzelmann's provocative thesis that the wisdom tradition also played a significant role in shaping Paul's thought. As with the religion-theology and Jewish-Hellenistic dichotomies of prior generations of scholars, much of this generation seems to have fallen prey to an alternative of 'wisdom or apocalypticism.' Conzelmann himself shared the assumption; almost no one has risen to challenge it.

There are three notable exceptions to this trend: Gese's less than persuasive explanation of all NT christology as the product of fused wisdom and apocalyptic traditions; Scroggs's uncritical merging of "apocalyptic-wisdom theology" and Reese's further popularization of that phrase; and Hamerton-Kelly's observations regarding the joint influence of the two traditions on Paul's understanding of pre-existence. Although Hamerton-Kelly makes no explicit reference to Scroggs's hypothesis, his work may be seen as a preliminary test of it, successful enough to provoke further study of the phenomenon and its possible impact on Paul's thought.

The next task, then, is to investigate representative early Jewish literature to see how a confluence of sapiential and apocalyptic thought might have functioned in those contexts. If Scroggs's "apocalyptic-wisdom theology" can be demonstrated among Paul's contemporaries, then the same might reasonably be postulated for him.

Das Evangelium des Johannes [Göttingen: Vandenhoeck and Ruprecht, 1941]).

2

The Confluence of
Apocalyptic and
Wisdom Traditions in
Early Jewish
Literature

I. Historical and Methodological Considerations

A. History of Research

Although only a few scholars have considered the relationship between apocalyptic and wisdom thought in Paul's theology, the same cannot be said with regard to the OT and early Jewish literature. In fact, Robin Scroggs's provocative phrase "apocalyptic-wisdom theology" was foreshadowed some thirty years previously by Johannes Fichtner's characterization of the Wisdom of Solomon as "ein apokalyptisches Weisheitsbuch."[1] The contemporary discussion, however, has largely taken the form of varied responses to Gerhard von Rad's hypothesis about the origins of OT apocalyptic literature.

In 1919, Gerhard Hölscher had suggested that apocalyptic thought owed a large debt to the OT wisdom literature.[2] After being roundly ignored for

---

[1]"Die Stellung der Sapientia Salomonis in der Literatur- und Geistesgeschichte ihrer Zeit," *ZNW* 36 (1937) 124. Further on the Wisdom of Solomon, see below, pp. 74-79.

[2]"Die Entstehung des Buches Daniels;" see above, n 228, p. 50. The notion of a link between wisdom and apocalyptic thought had had brief

forty years, Hölscher's proposal was restated and expanded in von Rad's *Theologie des Alten Testaments* and *Weisheit in Israel*.[3] Von Rad argues not only that apocalyptic literature's debt to wisdom was substantial, but that the entire late sapiential tradition was singularly responsible for the rise of apocalypticism. The prophetic and apocalyptic attitudes toward history, he claims, are too drastically dissimilar for the one to have led to the other, as the prevailing assumption held. Israel's prophetic theology views history as the arena within which God acts meaningfully to judge and to save; the apocalypticist looks at human history as increasingly evil, as no longer the medium of divine actions but rather as a series of predetermined events in the lives of people and nations.

> The prophetic message is specifically rooted in the saving history...in definite election traditions.... Now, contrast this with the accounts of the history of God's people as we met them throughout the apocalyptic literature—they are really devoid of theology! This view of history lacks all confessional character; it no longer knows anything of those acts of God on which salvation was based and in the light of which previous accounts of the nation's history had been constructed.... Indeed, we may even ask whether apocalyptic literature had any existential relationship with history at all, since it abandoned the approach by way of the saving history.[4]

The apocalyptic notion that salvation transpires "outside" of human history, according to von Rad, has most in common with the wisdom emphasis on universal belief in God and proper understanding of the created order.

> We understood Wisdom as the effort made by the people of Israel to grasp the laws which governed the world in which she lived, and to

---

currency nearly a hundred years prior to Hölscher's article, suggested by L. Noack and H. Ewald. See J. M. Schmidt, *Die jüdische Apokalyptik: Die Geschichte ihrer Erforschung von den Anfängen bis zu den Textfunden von Qumran* (Neukirchen-Vlyun: Neukirchener, 1976[2]) 13-21.

[3]See above, n. 227, p. 50. It is curious that von Rad nowhere expressly mentions Hölscher's essay, despite the striking similarities between their arguments.

[4]von Rad, *Old Testament Theology*, vol. 2, 303-304.

systematize them.... And are not the matters with which apocalyptic literature is occupied expressly those of wisdom and its science?... Can we not interpret this interest in time and in the secrets of the future shown by the apocalyptic writers in the light of Wisdom teaching that everything has its times, and that it is the part of Wisdom to know about these times (Ecc. III.1ff.)?[5]

Initial negative reaction to von Rad's theory forced him to defend it in succeeding editions of his *Theology* by enumerating specific similarities between wisdom and apocalyptic thought: the apocalyptic seers are frequently called wise men; both traditions attend more to nature than to history; both contain the concept of determinism, relate interpretations of dreams and oracles, employ the stylistic device of question and answer, and (most importantly) concern themselves with the problem of evil. Finally, both traditions tend to be encyclopedic, cataloguing either the natural phenomena of the world and human behavior (wisdom *Listenwissenschaft* [6]) or the events of past and future as signs of imminent judgment and salvation (apocalyptic periodizations of history).[7]

Despite revisions of his thesis, von Rad has still met with a storm of protest, most of it focusing on the wisdom literature's utter disregard for eschatology and imminent expectation—perhaps the most readily identifiable characteristic of apocalyptic literature[8]—and von Rad's distinction between so-called prophetic and deterministic views of history.[9]

---

[5]*Ibid.*, 306-307.

[6]The word coined by A. Alt, "Die Weisheit Salomos," *TLZ* 76 (1951) 139-143.

[7]von Rad, *Old Testament Theology*, vol. 2, 306-315.

[8]See especially the response by P. Vielhauer, "Introduction," 598.

[9]P. von der Osten-Sacken (*Die Apokalyptik in ihrem Verhältnis zu Prophetie und Weisheit*, 18-34) demonstrates that the determinism of Daniel (both he and von Rad consider it the earliest apocalyptic work) derives not from wisdom, which is concerned with the fates of *individuals* and *nature*, but from Second Isaiah and the enthronement Psalms, which deal with God's determination of *history* and *nations*.

P. D. Hanson interprets von Rad's hypothesis to be theologically rather than historically motivated. He contends that von Rad's view of the apocalyptic movement as derivative of wisdom witnesses to a desire to return to the "prophetic connection theory [between the Old Testament and the New] of nineteenth-century German scholarship" by "leap [-ing] over the dark period of post-exilic Judaism to Christianity" ("Prolegomena to the Study of Jewish Apocalyptic" in *Magnalia Dei: The Mighty Acts of God*,

58   *Function of Apocalyptic and Wisdom Traditions*

The rebuttal of his claim that apocalypticism derives solely from wisdom has been very nearly decisive, but because there nevertheless remain numerous indications of some measure of wisdom influence on many early Jewish apocalypses, the question is hardly a settled one. If nothing else, von Rad's list of characteristics common to both styles of discourse continues to provoke study of the relationship between them. Paul Hanson gives voice to the majority opinion in the wake of von Rad's overstated case:

> That wisdom was drawn into apocalyptic and given a prominent position within that literature cannot be denied. That wisdom, however, accounts for the origin and circumscribes the essence of apocalyptic is an untenable hypothesis.[10]

---

ed. F. M. Cross, W. E. Lemke, P. D. Miller [Garden City: Doubleday, 1976] 401). Cf. also the call for *religionsgeschichtlich* investigation of the origins of apocalypticism by H. D. Betz, who thinks the net should be flung much more widely than over Jewish wisdom traditions alone ("Zum religionsgeschichtlichen Verständnis der Apokalyptik," *ZTK* 63 [1966] 391-409; ET "On the Problem of the Religio-historical Understanding of Apocalypticism," *Journal for Theology and the Church* 6 [1969] 134-156).

[10]Hanson, "Prolegomena," 401. Similarly, M. E. Stone: "The recent emphasis upon the speculative material in the apocalypses serves to highlight certain points of contact and connection between them and biblical wisdom literature; it still does not demonstrate von Rad's claim" ("Apocalyptic Literature" in *Jewish Writings of the Second Temple Period: Apocrypha, Pseudepigrapha, Qumran Sectarian Writings, Philo, Josephus*, ed. M. E. Stone [Compendia Rerum Iudaicarum ad Novum Testamentum II; Assen and Philadelphia: Van Gorcum/Fortress, 1984] 388). Cf. also M. Hengel's assessment: "The modern approach which wants to derive apocalyptic one-sidedly from wisdom or prophecy would have been almost incomprehensible to Ben Sira or to the Hasidic apocalypticists.... One might perhaps say that Hasidic apocalyptic combined the systematic view of history held in priestly wisdom with an eschatology determined by the prophetic tradition" (*Judentum und Hellenismus: Studien zu ihrer Begegnung unter besonderer Berücksichtung Palästinas bis zur Mitte des 2. Jh.s. v. Ch.* WUNT 10 [Tübingen: J. C. B. Mohr (Paul Siebeck), 1973; ET *Judaism and Hellenism: Studies in Their Encounter in Palestine During the Early Hellenistic Period*, tr. J. Bowden (Philadelphia: Fortress, 1974) vol. 1, 206-207, 189]).

The ensuing twenty-five years have seen three different lines of research in response to von Rad's failure to prove that apocalypticism sprang full-grown from the head of Sophia. Some scholars have persisted in pursuing von Rad's notion of genetic historical development, although on a greatly reduced scale.[11] The positions are more cautious, the conclusions more restricted. These investigations, however, bear only peripherally on the present study, since their aim is exclusively historical: to understand the origins of apocalypticism. Still other scholars have concentrated on literary characteristics and theological themes shared by apocalyptic and sapiential literature.[12] Their work fuels the suspicion of confluence, and documents

---

[11]H.-P.Müller ("Mantische Weisheit und Apokalyptik," *Congress Volume Uppsala VT* Sup 22 [Leiden: Brill, 1972] 268-293) argues that mantic wisdom, rather than traditional educational wisdom, provided the background for much of the apocalyptic material in the Old Testament. He claims that the figure of Daniel in Daniel 2, 4, and 5 is a wise man of mantic character, and that Isa 19:11-13, 44:25, 47:13; Jer 50:36; Esth 1:13; and Gen 41:8 suggest the prevalence of mantic wisdom in Israel after 587 B.C.E. Such mantic wisdom, he says, was continued in apocalyptic notions of eschatology and determinism.

J. Z. Smith ("Wisdom and Apocalyptic" in *Religious Syncretism in Antiquity: Essays in Conversation With Geo Widengren*, ed. B. A. Pearson [Missoula: Scholars, 1975] 131-156) looks not to Jewish but to Babylonian and Egyptian apocalyptic sources, and concludes that the development of apocalyptic expectations is the product of wisdom speculation about the ideal human ruler after the cessation of native kingship.

J. J. Collins ("The Court Tales in Daniel and the Development of Apocalyptic," *JBL* 94 [1975] 218-234) reaches remarkably similar conclusions to Smith's. Collins claims that the tales of Daniel as the *international* wise courtier (Daniel 1-6) were transformed into the apocalyptic visions of chapters 7-12 under the pressure of Antiochus Epiphanes's persecution of *Palestinian* Jews.

[12]Typical are the following: J. G. Gammie ("Spatial and Ethical Dualism in Jewish Wisdom and Apocalyptic Literature," *JBL* 93 [1974] 356-385) claims that the absolute distances between heaven and earth and between the righteous and the unrighteous are common to both traditions. S. J. DeVries ("Observations on Quantitative and Qualitative Time in Wisdom and Apocalyptic" in *Israelite Wisdom: Theological and Literary Essays in Honor of Samuel Terrien*, ed. J. G. Gammie, W. A. Brueggemann, W. L. Humphreys, J. M. Ward [New York: Union Theological Seminary, 1978] 263-276) suggests that both share an idealized perspective on time, and that "the essential bond tying apocalyptic to

some of those aspects of wisdom thought that were, in Hanson's words, "drawn into apocalyptic[ism]."[13] But here again, the results tend to contribute more to the discussion of the religio-historical ancestry of apocalyptic literature than to the functions in specific documents of a coalescence of traditions. Recognition of themes common to apocalyptic and

---

wisdom...is its timelessness," although "apocalyptic departs from wisdom ...in abandoning empirical observation for esoteric speculation" (270, 272). J. J. Collins ("Cosmos and Salvation: Jewish Wisdom and Apocalyptic in the Hellenistic Age," *History of Religions* 17 [1977] 121-142) finds that both wisdom and apocalyptic thought share a "cosmological conviction" that sees the "way to salvation...in understanding the structure of the universe and adapting to it" (142).

[13]Hanson, "Prolegomena," 401. On the basis of cursory examination of some 30 passages from apocalyptic literature, M. Küchler even goes so far as to summarize what he calls "die Weisheit der Apokalyptiker": (1) The apocalypticists explicitly connect Torah with Wisdom; (2) Apocalyptic wisdom is therefore revealed rather than discerned; (3) Accordingly, apocalyptic wisdom is starkly contrasted with mere human wisdom and knowledge; (4) Despite its concern for cataloguing all heavenly and earthly phenomena, apocalyptic wisdom has essentially one single object: divine secrets or mysteries; (5) Finally, the ground for the intensification and radicalization of wisdom in apocalypticism is hope in God's imminent intervention to save his people and to end the current period of "Unheilsgeschichte" (*Frühjüdische Weisheitstraditionen: Zum Fortgang weisheitlichen Denkens im Bereich des frühjüdischen Jahwehglaubens* OBO 26 [Göttingen: Vandenhoeck and Ruprecht, 1979] 52-87, 87). Provocative as Küchler's conclusions are, they rest more on intuition and generalization than detailed exegesis, and there is no attempt to differentiate the functions of given wisdom traditions in apocalyptic contexts. The result is a two-dimensional picture of "apocalyptic wisdom" that blurs the distinctions among such diverse texts as 1 Enoch, 4 Ezra, and Jubilees, and says very little about the peculiar contributions of wisdom thought to these apocalyptic works. To say, for example, that the apocalypticists equate Wisdom with Torah scarcely distinguishes them from Sirach. So also C. Rowland, who rightly observes that all of apocalyptic literature "seems essentially to be about the revelation of divine mysteries" (*The Open Heaven: A Study of Apocalyptic in Judaism and Early Christianity* [London: SPCK, 1982] 70). How then is it reasonable to say that revelation of divine mysteries is a *distinctive* concern of "apocalyptic wisdom"?

wisdom literature is important for locating some of these intersections, but does not go far enough to ask what such intersections accomplish in their individual literary contexts.

The most helpful studies for our purposes, therefore, have been those which approach specific texts with focused questions, asking the particular function of apocalyptic language and thought in traditionally "wisdom" literature, and the role of sapiential themes in texts commonly designated "apocalyptic."[14] Although as a rule these studies avoid making broad generalizations which would soften important distinctions among diverse texts, they otherwise operate with few shared methodological assumptions. "Wisdom" and "apocalyptic" are words used as both nouns and adjectives in a myriad of senses by scholars. Does "apocalyptic" describe a literary genre, a socio-religious movement, a theological world view, or (more likely) all three?[15] So also, is "wisdom" a genre, a school (or schools), an intellectual tradition, or again, all three?[16]

Since this dissertation is an exegetical and literary-theological investigation, rather than a purely traditio-historical one, questions of origin and derivation, as well as exhaustive definition and "explanation" of the wisdom and apocalyptic movements may be bracketed. Our search consists only of the uses by one sort of literature of motifs from the other. Consequently, the words "apocalyptic" and "wisdom" themselves will be employed only as adjectives, since in this context it is more helpful to be descriptive than definitive. The following criteria for identifying wisdom and apocalyptic motifs have been isolated on the basis—so far as possible—of what is distinctive about each type of literature, rather than what is generally characteristic. The results therefore represent critically minimal rather than historically maximal pictures. The function of each set of criteria is not to

---

[14]The literature is discussed in the treatments of individual documents below, pp. 74-106.

[15]P. D. Hanson rightly distinguishes among apocalypses, apocalypticism, and apocalyptic eschatology (*The Dawn of Apocalyptic* [Philadelphia: Fortress, 1975; rev., 1979] 1-37; idem., "Apocalypticism" in *IDBS* [1976] 28-34).

[16]Thus R. N. Whybray, *The Intellectual Tradition in the Old Testament* BZAW 135 (Berlin: de Gruyter, 1974). See also J. L. Crenshaw, "Method in Determining Wisdom Influence Upon 'Historical' Literature," *JBL* 88 (1969) 129-142. Cf. DeVries's hunch that "it must be more than coincidence that apocalyptic and wisdom share the formal characteristics of structural complexity and the material characteristics of encompassing comparable [form-critical] subelements" ("Quantitative and Qualitative Time," 264).

identify a given document as either sapiential or apocalyptic, but to locate variant traditions in texts already determined to be one type or the other.

B. Descriptive Criteria: Wisdom Traditions

Outlining what constitutes a wisdom passage or idea presents no small challenge, since the classical wisdom corpus—Proverbs, Job, Qoheleth, Sirach, and Wisdom—is itself so diverse. James L. Crenshaw sets von Rad's broad characterization ("practical knowledge of the laws of life and of the world, based on experience"[17]) and his distinction between didactic and theological wisdom against his own more nuanced categorization of four "kinds" of wisdom ("juridical, nature, practical, and theological"[18]). Crenshaw suggests that most other attempted descriptions fall somewhere between the two.[19] But recent research into Jewish wisdom of the Hellenistic period tends to expand still further the number of possible definitions, particularly as the distinctiveness of later from earlier wisdom thought becomes clearer. John E. Worrell speaks of a pervasive "sapiential milieu" that he says characterized all of post-biblical Judaism;[20] and Max

---

[17]Von Rad, *Old Testament Theology*, vol. 1, 418, 428.

[18]Crenshaw, "Prolegomenon" in *Studies in Ancient Israelite Wisdom*, ed. J. L. Crenshaw (New York: KTAV, 1976) 3; cf. idem, "Method in Determining Wisdom Influence," 130. R. E. Murphy listed precisely the same four types two years before ("Assumptions and Problems in Old Testament Wisdom Research," *CBQ* 29 [1967] 410). Cf. also Murphy's bibliographic review essay, "Hebrew Wisdom," *JAOS* 101 (1981) 25-26.

[19]Crenshaw, "Prolegeomenon," 4.

[20]"The essence of this 'milieu' is that it is not a movement, restricted to a formal group or sect. It is an understanding of life which has existed from antiquity, but which only in the post-exilic and Hellenistic periods scored a major breakthrough in acceptance to the point of becoming a major determinative in shaping things sacred as well as secular, theological as well as practical. As such it became the spirit of the times" ("Concepts of Wisdom in the Dead Sea Scrolls" [Ph.D. Dissertation, Claremont Graduate School, 1968] 108). Cf. the similar opinion of M. Küchler: "Einmal zeigte sich, dass der Anspruch auf Weisheitsbesitz ein Charakteristikum *aller* frühjüdischen Bekenntnisgruppen war. Der Weise ist eine allegegenwärtigen Gestalt. Die weisheitliche Terminologie geht quer durch alle Schul- und Meinungsrichtungen. Der Anspruch auf die entscheidende Weisheit wird sowohl von den angesehenen *soferim* von Gesetz und Sitte als auch von den apokalyptischen *hasidim* aller Schattierungen—eingeschlossen die Extremisten in Qumran und die Jesuaner in Galiläa und Jerusalem—,

Küchler differentiates nearly as many types of wisdom within that milieu as there are documents of the period.[21] Some definitions rely almost solely on vocabulary and form-critical criteria,[22] while others focus on a single notion as constitutive of "late theological wisdom."[23] The problem becomes doubly difficult in this period of early Judaism, because the search for the character of wisdom thought goes beyond the traditional corpus. Although he perhaps overstates the problem, Crenshaw laments: "wisdom has ceased to have any distinctive meaning. Like Sheol in proverbial lore, its definition is constantly expanding."[24]

In an effort to be as descriptive as possible without presuming to settle the larger disputes over the nature of wisdom thought in general, we will operate with the following three criteria for judging a passage in an apocalyptic document to be sapiential:

---

sowohl von den Pharisäischen Schulen Hillels und Shammais als auch von den christlichen Theologen und Predigern erhoben" (*Frühjüdische Weisheitstraditionen*, 15; emphasis his).

[21]*Ibid., passim.* The primary representatives are Torah Wisdom, Apocalyptic Wisdom, and Qumran Wisdom, but he finds also poetic, musical, midrashic, scientific, and traditional gnomic types.

[22]Such as R. A. Coughenour's pursuit of wisdom influence in 1 Enoch ("Enoch and Wisdom: A Study of the Wisdom Elements in the Book of Enoch" [Ph.D. Dissertation, Case Western Reserve University, 1972] 31-32). See further below, p. 79.

[23]The phrase is von Rad's (*Old Testament Theology*, vol. 1, 441-453) and has been nearly universally adopted, despite the plethora of attendant definitions. Crenshaw, for example, defines theological wisdom by saying it "moves in the realm of *theodicy*, and in so doing affirms God as ultimate meaning" ("Method in Determining Wisdom Influence," 132; emphasis added). Others, like Küchler, locate the theological focus in the equation of wisdom with *Torah* (*Frühjüdische Weisheitstraditionen*, 67).

[24]Crenshaw, "Prolegomenon," 13. Cf. also R. Murphy's oft-quoted quip: "The phrase 'wisdom literature' is too small an umbrella for all that has been brought under it" ("Assumptions and Problems," 410).

1. *Vocabulary*[25] characteristic of the wisdom corpus,[26] such as *bînāh*[27] and *nābôn*;[28] *bāᶜar*; *hākām* and *hokmāh*; *kĕsîl, lēṣ, leqaḥ, ᶜārôm*, and *śākal*. Obviously the many languages of early Jewish apocalyptic literature render these Hebrew terms in diverse and fluid ways, but as a rule, words that refer to wisdom or folly, insight, knowledge, understanding, and perception will be considered reflective of wisdom

---

[25]The list is essentially that of Whybray (*The Intellectual Tradition*, 71-76, 142-149), which is substantially included in the more extensive lists of Coughenour ("Enoch and Wisdom," 30) and R. B. Y. Scott (*The Way of Wisdom in the Old Testament* [New York: Macmillan, 1971] 121-122). Whybray's selection criteria are both statistical and interpretive: to qualify as distinctively sapiential, a word must not only occur predominantly among the OT books of Proverbs, Job, and Qoheleth (he thus restricts the scope of the wisdom corpus further even than does Crenshaw), but the word must also "express a concern with the main interests of the intellectual tradition: that is, with the problems faced by [human beings] in society or as individuals" (*The Intellectual Tradition*, 122). Whybray summarizes those wisdom interests: "i. Wisdom and folly; virtue and wickedness; human conduct in general. ii. The consequences of the possession of these qualities, e.g., prosperity, happiness, friendship; disaster, poverty, punishment. iii. The search for knowledge and for prosperity: intelligence, knowledge, education, advice, thought, planning" (*ibid.*, 123).

[26]It seems reasonable, with Crenshaw ("Prolegomenon," 5), to limit that corpus to Proverbs, Job, Qoheleth, Sirach, and Wisdom, "and a few psalms," if only for the sake of manageability. Several other documents have also been suggested as candidates for the wisdom corpus: Ruth, Esther, Song of Solomon, Tobit, Ahikar, and so on (see, e.g., R. E. Murphy, *Wisdom Literature: Job, Proverbs, Ruth, Canticles, Ecclesiastes, and Esther* [The Forms of the Old Testament Literature 13; Grand Rapids: Eerdmans, 1981]). But Crenshaw wisely counsels "defin[ing] wisdom literature as narrowly as possible so as to retain the distinctiveness of that body of texts" ("Wisdom" in *Old Testament Form Criticism*, ed. J. H. Hayes [San Antonio: Trinity University, 1974] 227).

[27]Whybray determines that "there is reason to suppose that *bina* was virtually interchangeable with *hokma*, and so an item in the specific and exclusive vocabulary of the intellectual tradition" (*The Intellectual Tradition*, 145).

[28]"This word appears to be virtually a synonym of *hakam*: it appears in parallelism with it, or joined to it by the copula, or otherwise associated with it or with *hokma*, in no less than 18 of its 21 occurrences" (*ibid.*, 147).

interests. Because they are the least ambiguous or susceptible to diverse translation, occurrences of "wisdom" or "wise" will be given primary consideration.[29]

2. *Ideas and Themes* found primarily among wisdom writers,[30] particularly concerning correct human social behavior and relationships, the order of the social and natural worlds, questions of theodicy and the purpose of human life,[31] and the divine origin of Wisdom and its essentially revelatory nature.[32] Although these concepts are of course also found scattered throughout legal, historical, and prophetic literature, they are particularly central to sapiential books. The presence of such ideas and themes in apocalyptic literature can be considered indicative of wisdom influence when they appear to carry similar import.[33]

---

[29]In his concluding remarks, Whybray observes that "vocabulary is by no means the only valid criterion for identifying the literature of [Israel's intellectual] tradition. On the other hand it is equally true that no method yet devised is entirely satisfactory: all are subject to a considerable degree of subjectivism" (*ibid.*, 155). Rather than despair totally of any usable method, though, he counts his own cautious results supportive of some conclusions reached on other grounds about the wisdom influence in some OT passages. It is therefore legitimate to use his method in conjunction with other criteria to examine texts outside the canon, too.

[30]Cf. Whybray's summary cited above (n. 25), and Crenshaw's definition of wisdom: "Wisdom, then, may be defined as the quest for self-understanding in terms of relationships with things, people, and the Creator. This search for meaning moves on three levels: (1) nature wisdom which is an attempt to master things for human survival and well-being, and which includes the drawing up of onomastica and study of natural phenomena as they relate to [human beings] and the universe; (2) juridical and *Erfahrungsweisheit* (practical wisdom), with the focus upon human relationships in an ordered society or state; and (2) theological wisdom, which moves in the realm of theodicy, and in so doing affirms God as ultimate meaning" ("Method in Determining Wisdom Influence," 132).

[31]Understood narrowly, in the sense of Job's dispute with God and Qoheleth's skepticism.

[32]E.g., the hypostatic portraits in Proverbs 8, Sirach 24, Job 38, and Wisdom 9; and the identification of Wisdom with Torah in Sirach.

[33]Crenshaw cautions that "whenever a wisdom phrase or motif is found outside wisdom literature the scholar must determine whether or not the meaning has been changed" ("Method in Determining Wisdom Influence," 133). What Crenshaw means is that mere similarity of common phrases or words (that is, words not exclusively from the wisdom tradition) may be

3. *Forms* typical of the wisdom literature, such as proverbs, riddles, fables and allegories, hymns and prayers, disputations and dialogues, autobiographical narratives and confessions, lists, and didactic poetry and narratives.[34] Clearly none of these forms is found exclusively in wisdom books; there are examples of each throughout the rest of the Hebrew Bible and early Jewish literature. Moreover, it is notoriously difficult with wisdom forms to ascertain their *Sitze im Leben*,[35] one of the primary aims of form-critical research. But because these forms—particularly proverbs, riddles, and lists—are so characteristic of wisdom literature, their presence in other types of literature may be considered reflective of wisdom interests when sapiential language and ideas are also present.

These verbal, conceptual, and formal features common to the wisdom corpus can be most helpful for detecting wisdom traditions beyond that body of literature when they are used in conjunction with one another. Although the wisdom vocabulary isolated by Whybray is distinctive, neither the typical wisdom themes nor forms are unique to the genre. Consequently, the clearest indications of wisdom influence in apocalypses will be demonstrated by multiple criteria.

C. Descriptive Criteria: Apocalyptic Traditions

The debate over what constitutes an apocalyptic text is even more far-ranging than that over wisdom,[36] and the challenge to find a definition

---

deceptive. If a motif has a radically different meaning in an otherwise non-wisdom context, the chances are that it has little sapiential heritage. The example Crenshaw offers is the motif of silence in Egyptian and Israelite wisdom: silence is a familiar epithet for the Egyptian sage ("the truly silent one"), but in Israel silence is considered simply "a means of combatting slander and gossip, and depicts proper reverence before the Holy one" (*ibid.*).

[34]The eight categories are suggested by Crenshaw, "Wisdom," 229.

[35]Cf. Crenshaw's judgment: "In view of this remarkable variety of forms and sociological-theological settings, the composition of a literary history of the genres is virtually impossible. So long as the date of the literary complexes eludes scholarly pursuit, and the precise form of each genre cannot be discerned, real confidence in the results of form-critical analysis will be wanting" (*ibid.*, 263).

[36]See the variety of definitions offered in the handbooks on the subject, particularly H. H. Rowley, *The Relevance of Apocalyptic* (New York: Association, 1964); D. S. Russell, *The Method and Message of Jewish*

therefore greater. But here again, rather than enter into the larger discussion, we will set up descriptive criteria for locating apocalyptic material in otherwise sapiential texts. Just as "wisdom characteristics" were earlier determined by what is in wisdom books, so "apocalyptic features" will be understood as those found in apocalypses.[37] The Apocalypse Group of the SBL Genres Project has made a systematic, inductive search into the nature of this type of literature, and offers the following definition:[38]

"Apocalypse" is a genre of revelatory literature[39] with a narrative framework, in which a revelation[40] is mediated by an otherworldly being to a human recipient, disclosing a transcendent reality which is both temporal,[41] insofar as it envisages eschatological salvation, and spatial,[42] insofar as it involves another, supernatural world.[43]

Apocalyptic (Philadelphia: Westminster, 1964[3]); Klaus Koch, *Ratlos vor der Apokalyptik* (Gütersloh: Gütersloher [G. Mohn], 1970; ET *The Rediscovery of Apocalyptic*, tr. M. Kohl [London: SCM, 1972]); Hanson, *The Dawn of Apocalyptic* 1-31; and C. Rowland, *The Open Heaven*, 193-267.

[37]"Apocalyptic literature" is by no means hereby to be circumscribed by the genre apocalypse. Obviously a great body of literature shares the perspective of apocalyptic eschatology. This limitation of apocalyptic characteristics to those found in apocalypses, while resulting in a critically minimal description rather than an exhaustive definition, has the advantage of avoiding the morass of trying to determine what is "characteristic" in texts of diverse literary genres.

[38]J. J. Collins, "Introduction: Toward the Morphology of a Genre," *Semeia* 14 (1979) 9; cf. idem, *The Apocalyptic Vision of the Book of Daniel* Harvard Monograph Series 16 (Missoula: Scholars, 1977) 26.

[39]"Pseudonymity [is] a feature which is universal in Jewish and Gnostic apocalypses and very common in the Christian ones..." (*ibid.*, 11).

[40]The revelation may come by vision, epiphany, audition, discourse of the otherworldly mediator, dialogue with that mediator, an otherworldly journey, or a writing (*ibid.*, 6).

[41]The content of the revelation on the "temporal axis" may be any of the following, singly or in combination: protology or pre-history; theogony or cosmogony; review of history (either explicit recollection or prophecy *ex eventu*); present salvation through knowledge; eschatological crisis, judgment, and salvation; cosmic transformation, personal salvation; and resurrection or other form of afterlife (*ibid.*, 6-7). Note also that "all

This will serve as our working understanding of what what constitutes
an apocalypse,[44] and the literary and theological features of such documents
will determine the criteria for assessing the presence of apocalyptic motifs in
wisdom texts. Unlike the wisdom corpus, this body of literature admits of
no exhaustive list of characteristic vocabulary, since the languages and
unique settings of the individual texts are so diverse.[45] These documents do

---

apocalypses which do not have an otherworldly journey contain an *ex eventu*
prophecy of history" (Collins, "Jewish Apocalypses," *Semeia* 14 [1979]
22).

[42]The "spatial axis" includes such elements as otherworldly regions and
beings (Collins, "Morphology of a Genre," 7).

[43]Other elements sometimes present are paraenesis (which Collins
notes is "relatively rare") and instructions to the recipient of the revelation
(ibid., 8). Contrast the generalization of P. Vielhauer (largely on the basis
of 1 Enoch) that "all Apocalypses include paraenesis, both exhortations to
repentance and conversion in view of the imminent end and of judgment, and
also paraenesis in the form-critical sense of the word, i.e., traditional
exhortations in the form of maxims and series of aphorisms which are
sometimes arranged thematically" ("Introduction," 587). Collins explains
his phrase "relatively rare": "Paraenesis by the mediator to the recipient
occurs very rarely. It is noted in the paradigm, however, because it is a
significant element. There is little doubt that all apocalypses seek to
influence the lives of their readers and many imply exhortation to a specific
course of action. The hortatory purpose is usually *implicit* in the work as a
whole, but it is expressed *explicitly* in the few works which contain
paraenesis" ("Morphology of a Genre," 9; emphasis added).

[44]On the basis of this definition, Collins identifies fifteen Jewish
apocalypses from the period 250 B.C.E. to 150 C.E.: Daniel 7-12, the
Animal Apocalypse (1 Enoch 83-90), the Apocalypse of Weeks (1 Enoch
93, 91:12-17), Jubilees 23, 4 Ezra, 2 Baruch, the Apocalypse of Abraham
15-32, 1 Enoch 1-36, the Similitudes of Enoch (1 Enoch 37-71), the Book
of the Heavenly Luminaries (1 Enoch 72-82), 2 Enoch, the Testament of
Levi 2-5, 3 Baruch, the Testament of Abraham 10-15, and the Apocalypse
of Zephaniah ("Jewish Apocalypses," 22).

[45]K. Koch's designation of "the catchword *glory*" as distinctive of
apocalyptic literature (*The Rediscovery of Apocalyptic*, 32) is perhaps as
specific as is possible under the circumstances. Verbs for seeing, revealing,
and so on are of course commonplace in visions, but in themselves hardly

have formal and conceptual traits that are distinctive of them, though, and these may be summarized as follows:[46]

1. *Ideas and themes* found primarily in apocalypses, such as concern with history and pre-history, presented either as records of the past or *vaticinia ex eventu*; awareness of imminent eschatological crisis, bringing cosmic and personal judgment and salvation; and stark distinctions between the righteous and the ungodly, this age and the age of salvation, benevolent and malevolent spiritual beings, heaven and earth.

2. *Forms* common to apocalypses, particularly revelations—by means of visions, epiphanies, auditions, conversations with otherworldly beings, otherworldly journeys, or heavenly writings—and ethical and religious exhortations grounded in the expectation of imminent judgment and redemption.

These conceptual and formal traits common to apocalypses, although by no means providing an exhaustive description of apocalyptic literature, do offer manageable criteria for discerning apocalyptic traditions in other

---

constitute uniquely "apocalyptic" vocabulary. It may be argued that the thematic and conceptual traits common to apocalypses imply a certain vocabulary of judgment, repentance (or lack of it), shame, reward, vindication, restoration, and so on. But here again, no statistical evidence is possible because the "corpus" of apocalypses—such as it is—comes in so many different languages, often several times removed by translation from the originals.

[46]The list is compiled substantially from the SBL Apocalypse Group genre paradigm (see above, nn. 38-43, p. 67-68). Cf. also the lists of apocalyptic characteristics suggested by P. Vielhauer ("Introduction," 582-600), K. Koch (*The Rediscovery of Apocalyptic*, 28-32), and D. S. Russell (*Method and Message*, 104-139). Each of these lists includes traits found in one or some of the apocalypses, but not necessarily in all of them. The list of forms compiled by Vielhauer, for instance ("Introduction," 586-587), includes symbolic utterances, blessings, wisdom sayings, sacred sayings, prayers, and hymns, which are neither common to all apocalypses nor uniquely characteristic of the genre. The list chosen here is descriptive of the genre more than of select examples from it, and therefore attempts to be less prejudiced by any predetermined definition of apocalypticism or apocalyptic theology.

types of literature. As with the criteria for locating wisdom traditions, these indicators of apocalyptic traditions will be most reliable when used together. A distinction between the wicked and the righteous, for example, is made by wisdom writers unaffected by apocalyptic thought. But if such a distinction—or its consequences—is revealed as part of a heavenly mystery or discussed in the context of eschatological judgment, the theme can be said to be marked by apocalyptic influence.

D. The Thesis

Such descriptions of the constitutive aspects of wisdom and apocalyptic traditions throw into sharp relief the remarkable differences between these two kinds of religious literature. Viewed in their "ideal" forms, these ways of looking at God and the world stand at opposite ends of a scale with regard to immanence and transcendence.[47]

(1) For the "ideal" sage, the meaning of life is immanent; accessible in the present, the mundane, the human experiences of God and nature. For the archetypal seer, meaning is virtually absent from those spheres, and is rather located in the future, the supramundane, the transcendent realms.

(2) The wisdom writer finds meaning in the proper conduct of this life—social relations, personal integrity, the pursuit of happiness and prosperity. The apocalyptic writer, on the other hand, finds meaning in divine activity yet to occur and his own preparation for that activity.

(3) Wisdom is available to all who seek it; revelations are granted only to specific persons. The sage finds wisdom by observation and active study; the seer receives revelations passively from other-worldly beings.

(4) The wisdom writer experiences boundless confidence in the order, balance, and harmony of God's creation and his own rightful and appropriate place in that creation. His life can make sense if he aligns himself with the world's God-given order: virtue is rewarded, sin is punished. The writer of an apocalypse, on the other hand, despairs of all order this side of the eschaton: the godly seem to be punished and the wicked rewarded, and creation itself is decaying. His life makes no sense apart from his hope that God will soon break into human history and rescue him from his plight. For the sage, the present has great potential for experience of the good, and this life carries with it responsibility for faithful ethical action that can bear fruit. For the

---

[47]Not in the strict philosophical sense of divine immanence and transcendence, but as a measure of the value accorded human experience in the world. See the discussion of M. Weber's "pure-type" analysis and its value for historical research in M. Hill, *A Sociology of Religion* (London: Heinemann Educational, 1973) 147-151.

seer, only the eschatological future is potentially good, and this life is a matter of (none-too-patient) waiting in which one's primary responsibility is to discern the signs of the times and prepare for divine visitation and redemption.

Despite these startling discontinuities between apocalyptic and wisdom literature, however, there remain undeniable points of continuity: the seers frequently refer to themselves as wise men and label their works wisdom books, and both traditions share a number of similar theological concerns.[48] Thus a growing scholarly concensus grants the presence of wisdom material in apocalypses.[49] Although the religio-historical question of apocalypticism's ancestry will continue to provoke important research, what is necessary for the present study is an analysis of the *function* of such intersections of these diverse traditions in specific documents.

Given the sharp distinctions between the "ideal" forms of apocalyptic and wisdom literature and the simultaneous points of contact between them, it is reasonable to hypothesize between the two poles a spectrum along which such literature might be plotted.[50] Presumably texts lie closer to and farther from either of these poles to varying extents; that is, the wisdom books that employ apocalyptic traditions do so to greater and lesser degrees, and apocalypses make use of wisdom themes in varying measures. Some books are clearly wisdom books with no use of apocalyptic traditions: Proverbs is such a book. Other books, such as the Apocalypse of Abraham, are manifestly apocalypses with no evident reliance on wisdom language or thought. But still other books appear to fall somewhere between the two ends of the spectrum: wisdom literature that uses apocalyptic motifs, and apocalypses that employ wisdom traditions. The clearest examples of these are 1 Enoch, the Wisdom of Solomon, 4 Ezra, 2 Baruch, and the sectarian library found at Qumran.[51] The challenge is to discover where each one of

---

[48]See particularly the list of common characteristics enumerated by von Rad (above, p. 57).

[49]See, for example, Hanson's position noted above, p. 58.

[50]It should be noted from the outset that this is not an historical or chronological continuum; the categories are purely conceptual, and intended to relate documents to one another in terms of their content rather than their historical settings or possible direct literary relationships.

[51]The literature of Qumran is rightfully considered in this study together with the apocalypses, not because it adds to their number, but because the Qumran covenanters were patently an apocalyptic community, treasuring particularly the Enochic apocalypses and being governed in their life and thought by the conceptual world common to apocalypse writers.

these stands in relation to the others on the continuum between the "ideal" poles of apocalypse and wisdom book.

In this investigation we will (1) limit our consideration to the two groups of texts defined on external grounds as the classical wisdom corpus and the body of Jewish apocalypses written between 250 B.C.E. and 150 C.E.;[52] (2) determine the presence of wisdom and apocalyptic traditions in those texts by means of the criteria outlined above; and (3) inquire about the functions of such confluent traditions in their literary contexts. If documents of two so divergent sorts employ one another's motifs, such borrowing ought to affect the ways they look at God and the world. Corresponding to the points of variance between the "ideal" types of wisdom and apocalyptic traditions set forth above, the following questions seek to uncover the distance from "ideal" positions at which given documents stand when they combine motifs from both traditions.

(1) Where is wisdom to be located? Is it immanent or transcendent?
(2) Once discerned, what is the content of that wisdom?
(3) Who has access to wisdom?
(4) What is the means of access?
(5) What potential exists for ordered and meaningful life before the eschaton? What is the value of the present for human life?

The five texts or groups of texts—Wisdom of Solomon, 1 Enoch, 4 Ezra, the Qumran library, and 2 Baruch—are chosen because each clearly comes from one tradition or the other.[53] Wisdom of Solomon is part of the

---

Pace P. R. Davies, "Qumran Beginnings" in *SBL Seminar Papers*, ed. K. H. Richards (Atlanta: Scholars, 1986) 361-368.

[52] See above, nn. 26 and 44, pp. 64, 68.

[53] Although it was the mixed character of the book of Daniel, containing both apocalyptic and wisdom traits, that first drew von Rad's attention to the phenomena he tried to explain with his genetic argument, the book is not discussed here for two reasons. First, the stories of chapters 1-6, while attached to the visions of chapters 7-12, are literarily distinct from them. Secondly, the sapiential nature of the stories is not touched by apocalyptic language or thought forms, nor are the revelations themselves marked by substantial wisdom language or thought. Admittedly, the seer is exhorted to "understand" his visions (8:17; 9:23; 10:1, 12), Gabriel grants him "wisdom" for the task (9:22), and "the wise" are singled out as those who will survive the destruction of the end times (11:33; 12:3) and

classical wisdom collection, 1 Enoch represents redaction of five apocalypses, 4 Ezra and 2 Baruch are apocalypses, and the Qumran covenanters valued apocalypses and wrote their own sectarian literature from a perspective shared by apocalypse writers. Each apocalyptic writer, however, makes clear and abundant use of terminology, images, and ideas from the wisdom tradition; Wisdom of Solomon employs apocalyptic traditions.

Discussion of these texts[54] is presented in the order that best demonstrates the relative location of each on our spectrum of immanent to transcendent wisdom. Wisdom of Solomon comes first, as it represents one end of the spectrum: a book that clearly comes from the wisdom tradition but also makes use of apocalyptic language and imagery. At the opposite pole stands 1 Enoch, an apocalyptic document marked by frequent use of sapiential ideas. To highlight the contrast we treat it next. After 1 Enoch come 4 Ezra, Qumran, and 2 Baruch, as each of them stands at greater remove from the "ideal" apocalyptic perspective.

---

understand Daniel's prophecy (12:10). Nowhere, however, are these wise described nor is the content of their wisdom defined. We will argue below (p. 84) that the writers of 1 Enoch, 4 Ezra, and 2 Baruch, for whom it is also "the wise" who are granted revelations, have taken their cue in this matter from Daniel, but they specify the identity of "the wise" in a way that Daniel does not. For discussions of the genre(s) of Daniel, see Collins, "The Court Tales in Daniel;" idem, *The Apocalyptic Vision of the Book of Daniel*; idem, *Daniel, First Maccabees, Second Maccabees: With An Excursus on the Apocalyptic Genre* (Wilmington, DE: Michael Glazier, 1981); J. A. Montgomery, *The Book of Daniel* ICC (New York: Charles Scribner's Sons, 1927) 88-104; N. W. Porteus, *Daniel: A Commentary* (London: SCM, 1965).

[54]The discussions of these documents are part of a broad survey with only one point of analysis: the intersection of apocalyptic and wisdom themes. They are obviously heavily indebted to the exegesis of specialists in early Jewish literature, and make their contribution by presenting a wide-ranging comparative overview of the texts and previous studies of them rather than by attempting to break new exegetical ground. Given the wide diversity of detailed research into the discreet apocalyptic and wisdom elements in these individual texts, it is important to stand back a step from what is known about them to ask how the general stylistic and thematic features they share function in their individual literary contexts.

II. The Texts

A. Wisdom of Solomon

Although in genre it is not an apocalypse, the "Book of Eschatology"[55] that opens the late first-century B.C.E. Wisdom of Solomon (1:1-6:11) contains a number of apocalyptic features. In fact, those features are sufficiently prominent that Nickelsburg says of the whole book, "the sage *combines* the wisdom and apocalyptic traditions of Israel, synthesizing them with an eclectic use of Greek philosophy and religious thought,"[56] and Fichtner labels it "ein apokalyptisches Weisheitsbuch."[57]

The subject of the first six chapters is God's righteous judgment of the godly and the ungodly.[58] Human beings are created for wisdom,

---

[55]So named by W. Weber to distinguish it from the Book of Wisdom (6:12-9:18) and the Book of History (10:1-19:21) ("Die Composition der Weisheit Salomo's," *Zeitschrift für wissenschaftliche Theologie* 47 [1904] 168). J. M. Reese further refines the structure by identifying the Book of Eschatology (1:1-6:11, 6:17-20), the Book of Wisdom Proper (6:12-16, 6:21-10:21), the Book of History (11:1-14, 16:1-19:22), and the Book of Divine Justice and Human Folly (11:15-15:19). The entire composition is a *logos protreptikos* or hortatory discourse (*Hellenistic Influence on the Book of Wisdom and its Consequences* AnBib 41 [Rome: Biblical Institute, 1970]). Reese classifies the Book of Eschatology as a diatribe, on grounds of content (judgment is used as warrant for exhortation, logical appeal is made for moral uprightness, the author makes use of "the Cynico-Stoic witness theme") and style (parallelism, gnomic phrasing, use of imaginary opponent, apologetic intent) (*ibid.*, 109-113).

[56]Nickelsburg, *Jewish Literature* 175; emphasis added. Cf. also *ibid.*, 178-179 for Nickelsburg's rationale.

[57]"Die Stellung der Sapientia Salomonis," 36 (see above, n. 1, p. 55). Fichtner's footnote (23a) backs off a bit, almost as an afterthought, with "oder vorsichtiger: apokalyptisierendes." On the presence of apocalyptic characteristics in Wisdom see also C. Larcher, *Le Livre de la Sagesse ou La Sagesse de Salomon* EBib, n.s. 1 (Paris: J. Gabalda, 1983) 179-261; Reese, *Hellenistic Influence*, 109-113; Collins, "Cosmos and Salvation," 138-142.

[58]M. Gilbert summarizes the results of several studies that discern a chiastic structure to the passage:

A   Address to rulers and description of wisdom as avenger [1:1-15]
B   Speech of the ungodly--'enjoy life, persecute the just man' [2:1-20]

righteousness, and immortality (1:1-15), but the wicked live carelessly, and deny responsibility for their actions because they do not believe there is anything after death (1:16-2:5). As a result, they carouse wildly and oppress the righteous (2:6-12), mocking the confidence of the righteous in immortality and divine justice (2:13-20). The righteous appear to be bereft (cf. ἔδοξαν, 3:2) while the wicked seem to prosper. But appearances are deceptive, because God is nevertheless in control of all destinies, and will reward people according to their deserving. Not even the just who die prematurely, who are barren, or who are eunuchs are deserted by God; but the wicked who live long lives and have many children ultimately lose everything (3:1-5:1).

A clear distinction between the earthly and heavenly worlds stands behind this contrast between appearance and reality, a dualism more spatial than temporal at points. The author's doctrine of ἀθανασία (3:4; 4:1; 8:13, 17; 15:3)[59] is sufficiently personal[60] that time and history are somewhat flattened out. The setting of judgment and vindication is not so much the

---

C   Three types of the just life, and three types of the ungodly life [3:1-5:1]

B[1]   Second speech of the ungodly, in the afterlife [5:2-23]

A[1]   New address to rulers, description of the benefits of wisdom; plan of the rest of the discourse [6:1-11]

("Wisdom Literature" in *Jewish Writings*, 283-324; 302). Cf. A. G. Wright, "The Structure of the Book of Wisdom," *Bib* 48 (1967) 168-173; J. M. Reese, "Plan and Structure in the Book of Wisdom," *CBQ* 27 (1965) 394-396; idem, *The Book of Wisdom, Song of Songs* Old Testament Message 20 (Wilmington, DE: Michael Glazier, 1983) 26-27; D. Winston, *The Wisdom of Solomon: A New Translation With Introduction and Commentary* AB 43 (Garden City: Doubleday, 1979) 10.

[59]On Wisdom and immortality, see F. C. Porter, "The Pre-Existence of the Soul in the Book of Wisdom and in the Rabbinical Writings," *American Journal of Theology* 12 (1908) 53-118; J. P. Weisengoff, "Death and Immortality in the Book of Wisdom," *CBQ* 3 (1941) 104-133; G. W. E. Nickelsburg, *Resurrection, Immortality; and Eternal Life in Intertestamental Judaism* (Cambridge: University, 1972) 88-89; Reese, *Hellenistic Influence*, 62-71.

[60]"Immortality for man is not a quality of his nature as such but of a particular condition, whether he receives it as a gift or as a recompense. In either case its origin is God, who bestows it only upon the just and the wise" (Reese, *Hellenistic Influence*, 64).

end of the created order as it is the end of individuals' lives. "Let us test what will happen," the wicked propose, "at the end of *his* [that is, the righteous one's] life" (2:17). Although it seems clear that Pseudo-Solomon anticipates God's final judgment on the righteous and the wicked, it is not so clear from the rest of the book that he expects such judgment to occur at the eschaton. Judgment is most often seen in terms of traditional measure-for-measure retribution: "one is punished by the very things by which he sins" (11:16; cf. 12:23). Here in the Book of Eschatology, however, the promise is of "unexpected salvation" (5:2) and God's "terrible and swift" visitation on the ungodly (6:5).

The tension between those two ways of perceiving judgment—in the context of this life for nations, and in the afterlife for individuals—appears to be a function of Pseudo-Solomon's awareness that, while history provides illustrations of God's just retribution against Israel's national enemies,[61] no such assurances can be made on behalf of individuals. The present world fails to conform to the affirmation that God rewards righteousness and punishes sin, but the heavenly world rights all wrongs and balances the cosmic scales. God's wisdom, "the Spirit of the Lord," is "that which holds all things together" (1:7), and ultimately it restores the order that seems missing in a chaotic world where bad people prosper and good people suffer. Whereas Job's debate with God on this subject arrives at no real conclusion—except a reassertion of divine sovereignty and right—Wisdom finds consolation in the distinction between earth and heaven. The example of Enoch, "who pleased God ...while living among sinners" (4:10-14), offers a guarantee that God takes care of his own by rescuing them from earthly pain and suffering and crowning them with heavenly grace and mercy.

Enoch's righteous life and assumption to heaven are not his only means of assisting the Sage to make this point, and here the traditional apocalyptic notion of the age to come is more evident. The description in 4:20-5:23 of the "unexpected salvation" of the just (5:2) shows contact with a similar description in 1 Enoch 62. Both are dependent on images from Second Isaiah's Servant (Isa 49:7ff, 52:13ff, 59:16-17), and both contrast the seeming failure of the righteous one's life with his final vindication by God.[62] Those who have tormented him see the wickedness of their ways with terrible clarity and they repent of their cruelty and scorn (Wis 5:3-14; 1 En 62:1-11). Both scenes aim at shaming civil authorities for their

---

[61]Particularly Egypt; note 15:18-19:22.
[62]See M. J. Suggs, "Wisdom of Solomon 2.5-5.1: A Homily Based on the Fourth Servant Song," *JBL* 76 (1957) 26-33.

treatment of God's people (Wis 1:1, 1 En 62:1) and promise an eschatological turning of the tables to comfort the faithful.

> This whole opening polemic—directed against unbelieving Hellenists whom the Sage equates with the ungodly—serves as an apologia for the Jewish faith, which reveals God's saving justice to the world.[63]

At 5:15 the scene shifts to the rewards of the righteous. Although not properly an apocalyptic vision[64], 5:15-23 do detail a scene familiar from numerous apocalypses. The royal status of the righteous sufferers (Wis 5:16) echoes the exaltation of the Elect One in 1 En 62:6 (cf. 46:4-8, 48:4) and the elevation of the saints in Dan 7:18. The eschatological reversal of fortunes runs like a thread throughout all apocalyptic literature, and here in Wisdom serves the Sage as a warrant for his concluding exhortation to the kings (6:1) to rule as God does: with righteous impartiality (6:7; cf. 5:18).

The motifs of God's impartial judgment and human impartiality are common in the wisdom tradition.[65] Proverbs frequently urges impartial treatment of rich and poor (18:15; 24:23-25; and 28:21) and Job and his friends argue about whether or not God abides by impartial retributive justice (cf. 34:19). Sirach affirms God's impartial judgment (35:12-14), as does the Testament of Job (4:7; 43:5-13), and 3 Ez 4:39 similarly lauds God's Truth. But because the notion also appears so frequently in so many other canonical (2 Chron 19:6-7, Deut 10:17, 16:19; Ps 82:1-4) and noncanonical (Jub 5:12-16, 21:3-5; PsSol 2:15-18, 32-35; 2 Bar 13:8-10, 44:2-5; 1 En 63:6-9) contexts, Jouette Bassler concludes that throughout Judaism divine impartiality was an axiomatic attribute of God adapted to the changing historical needs of the people of God:

> Contributing to its axiomatic status was the development of an *eschatological* dimension for the concept of God's impartial justice... With a new framework which permitted other-worldly recompense, the doctrine of impartial justice was rescued as a valid

---

[63]Reese, *The Book of Wisdom*, 27; cf. R. A. Kraft, "Philo (Josephus, Sirach and Wisdom of Solomon) on Enoch," *SBL Seminar Papers*, ed. P. J. Achtmeier (Missoula: Scholars, 1978) vol. 1, 253-257.

[64]The passage lacks any narrative framework that describes the seeing, hearing, or being shown; there is no review of history or prophecy *ex eventu*; and so on. *Contra* Winston, *The Wisdom of Solomon*, 146.

[65]See particularly J. M. Bassler, *Divine Impartiality: Paul and A Theological Axiom* SBLDS 59 (Chico: Scholars, 1982) 13-16, 18-44, 193.

way of describing God's relationship to his people and to other nations as well. In fact, with this new dimension divine impartiality acquired heightened importance in providing a theological explanation for Israel's fate...an explanation which also pointed beyond the present circumstances to offer a measure of future hope.[66]

This trend is particularly evident in the Wisdom of Solomon, where the apocalyptic motifs of last judgment and reversal of fortunes serve to buttress the conviction of God's impartial and sovereign ordering of the universe by means of wisdom.

Summary

As might perhaps be expected, the Wisdom of Solomon ranks at the end of the immanence-transcendence scale closest to the "ideal" wisdom stance. The Sage says explicitly that wisdom inheres in the creation (1:7) and that all who love and seek wisdom have access to it (6:12-13). Although the older conception of the ubiquity of God's wisdom permeates the book, Pseudo-Solomon also adds a revelatory note to wisdom's nature: "I would not possess wisdom unless God gave her to me" (8:21; cf. 9:17).[67] The content of wisdom is closest to the classical definition—social order, righteousness, and the good life—but to it the Sage has added assurance of immortality for the wise/righteous. But the modified apocalyptic tradition of last judgment in chapters 1-5 places Pseudo-Solomon a step away from the "ideal " wisdom perspective to the extent that he can affirm wisdom's traditional ordering role despite the suffering of righteous individuals. Not only do the wise know how to live this life wisely, they know how to attain the next life as well. Wisdom teaches ὅσα τέ ἐστιν κρυπτὰ καὶ ἐμφανῆ (7:21).

Pseudo-Solomon holds out great hope for meaningful human life before the eschaton. His book is addressed to earthly rulers (1:1; 6:1) whom he expects in some measure to influence on behalf of his people. And he uses the apocalyptic motifs of judgment and reversal of fortunes to ensure that his exhortations to pursue, love, and study wisdom will not be ignored by Jews who might despair in the face of persecution. The value of the present, therefore, is great: one can and ought to become wise to gain both wisdom's

---

[66]*Ibid.*, 43-44; emphasis added.

[67]This thought, too, has antecedents as old as Solomon's prayer for wisdom in 1 Kgs 3:6ff, but gains heightened emphasis in Wisdom.

present benefits and the blessings of immortality, for "a multitude of wise men is the salvation of the world " (6:24).

B. 1 Enoch

The composite nature of 1 Enoch poses numerous critical problems.[68] Robert A. Coughenour, whose dissertation seeks to trace the wisdom elements in the book,[69] follows R. H. Charles in claiming the language of chapters 1-5 indicates a final redactor of 1 Enoch composed that section as an introduction to the entire work.[70] Coughenour then attributes what he calls "the wisdom orientation of the Book of Enoch "[71] to this final editor, whose sapiential language and theology are traced throughout the rest of the five sections. But the fact that 4QEn[a] and 4QEn[b], which come from the third century B.C.E., seem never to have contained any more than chapters 1-36 suggests that the "introduction " of chapters 1-5 introduces only the Parable of Enoch (6-36). This makes Charles's—and therefore Coughenour's—thesis of a "sapiential redactor " for all of 1 Enoch untenable.[72] In light of this, it is preferable to view 1 Enoch as five independent though related works[73] dating from the third century B.C.E. through the first C.E.,[74] and to

---

[68]The issues involved are summarized briefly and a select bibliography provided by E. Issac in *The Old Testament Pseudepigrapha*, vol. 1, 5-12. See also the discussion in J. H. Charlesworth, *The Pseudepigrapha and Modern Research* (Septuagint and Cognate Studies 7s; Chico: Scholars, 1981) 98-103; M. Black, *The Book of Enoch or I Enoch: A New English Edition With Commentary and Textual Notes* (Leiden: Brill, 1985) 12-23.

[69]"Enoch and Wisdom. " See above, n. 22, p. 63.

[70]*Ibid.*, 34; cf. Charles, *The Book of Enoch* (Oxford: Clarendon, 1912²) 2.

[71]Coughenour, "Enoch and Wisdom, " 175-187.

[72]See Stone, "Apocalyptic Literature," 400; cf. idem, "The Book of Enoch and Judaism in the Third Century B.C.E., " *CBQ* 40 (1978) 486; and G. W. E. Nickelsburg, "Revealed Wisdom as a Criterion for Inclusion and Exclusion: From Jewish Sectarianism to Early Christianity" in *To See Ourselves As Others See Us: Christians, Jews, "Others" in Late Antiquity*, ed. J. Neusner, E. S. Frerichs (Chico: Scholars, 1985) 77.

[73]The Books of the Watchers (1-36), Similitudes (37-71), Heavenly Luminaries (72-82), and Dream Visions (83-90), and the Epistle of Enoch (91-108).

[74]J. T. Milik's late dating of the Similitudes (*The Books of Enoch: Aramaic Fragments of Qumran Cave 4* [Oxford: University, 1976]) has been seriously disputed. See M. A. Knibb, "The Dating of the Parables of Enoch:

examine the wisdom traits of each one separately. The greatest concentration of these traits is in the first three books: the Parables of Enoch, the Similitudes, and the Book of the Heavenly Luminaries.

Book I (1 Enoch 1-36)

After his initial description of God's arrival on earth with his holy ones to execute judgment on all (1:3b-9), Enoch invites the reader, in typical wisdom fashion,[75] to consider the creation an appropriate illustration of the reliability of his forecast. Chapters 2-5 repeatedly urge one to "examine all the activities which take place in the sky " (2:1), "examine and observe everything—and the trees " (3:2), "examine the days of summer " (4:1), "observe...the verdant trees " (5:1), "pay attention concerning all things " (5:1), "look at the seas " (5:3). These object lessons about the orderliness and dependability of nature are designed to show that "all the work of God as being manifested does not change " (2:3), and that "everything functions in the way in which God has ordered it " (5:3). Although apocalyptic literature often views the natural order as part of the old aeon, i.e., as former things that are passing away (cf. 4 Ez 5:55: "already...aging and passing the

---

A Critical Review, " *NTS* 25 (1979) 345-359. Current decisions on the date of the Similitudes range from the late first century B.C.E. (G. W. E. Nickelsburg, *Jewish Literature Between the Bible and the Mishnah: A Historical and Literary Introduction* [Philadelphia: Fortress, 1981] 221-223) to the late first century C.E. (Knibb, "The Dating of the Parables, " 358). A certain concensus may be discerned among the SNTS Pseudepigrapha Seminar, reported by J. H. Charlesworth in *The Old Testament Pseudepigrapha and the New Testament: Prolegomena for the Study of Christian Origins* SNTS Monograph Series 54 (Cambridge: University, 1985) 106-110.

[75]Cf. Sir 16:26-28; 43:1-12; PsSol 18:11-14; TNaph 3. That creation theology is central to wisdom thought has been widely held since W. Zimmerli's well-known pronouncement that "Wisdom thinks resolutely within the framework of a theology of creation " ("The Place and Limit of Wisdom in the Old Testament Theology," *SJT* 17 [1964] 146). For cautions, see H. J. Hermisson, "Observations on the Creation Theology in Wisdom " in *Israelite Wisdom*, 43-57. On the wisdom style of 1 Enoch 1-5, see Nickelsburg, *Jewish Literature*, 49, and Black, *The Book of Enoch*, 25-40.

strength of youth "), Enoch considers the orderliness of creation a witness to God's consistency and righteousness.[76]

This consistency of the cosmic order is in stark contrast to the sinners who have *not* fulfilled their created roles (5:4-6).[77] The conclusion to the introductory vision is a prediction of the judgment day, relating in lurid detail the sufferings planned for the wicked who have not learned their lessons from the creation. The elect, however, will be granted wisdom (5:8) so that the wise will "be humble and not return again to sin." The sinners are primarily guilty of disobeying "the commandments of the Lord " (5:4), indicating that this revealed wisdom that saves the elect also has to do with God's Torah. In the Epistle (chapters 91-108), which "in language and viewpoint" is parallel to this section,[78] the "wise" are those who are "given the Scriptures of joy " (104:12), and who "give heed to all the words of this [i.e., Enoch's] book " (100:6; cf. 98:1, 9). Much as for Sirach— "If you desire wisdom, keep the commandments " (1:26; cf. 15:1; 19:20; 24:23; 39:1)—revealed, salvific wisdom for Enoch is identified with Torah.[79] But Enoch goes a significant step beyond Sirach to claim that his particular *interpretation* of Torah constitutes the wisdom of God necessary for salvation.[80] And his interpretation of Torah rests on a conviction of God's all-embracing sovereignty and maintenance of cosmic order. To obey Torah is not simply to keep certain commandments, but to align oneself with the Creator's intentions for the universe. Meinrad Limbeck observes of 1 Enoch:

---

[76]Cf. Collins's observation cited above (n. 12, p. 59) that both the wisdom and apocalyptic world views understand cosmic order as testimony to God's sovereignty.

[77]Even elements of the creation that refuse their intended functions suffer judgment. Sheol is the "prison house for the stars which roll over upon the fire; they are the ones which have transgressed the commandments of God from the beginning of their rising because they did not arrive punctually " (18:14).

[78]Nickelsburg, "Revealed Wisdom, " 77.

[79]The connection of wisdom with Torah goes back to the Pentateuch itself, even though the explicit identification represents later tradition: "Behold, I have taught you statutes and ordinances, as the Lord my God commanded me, that you should do them in the land which you are entering to take possession of it. Keep them and do them; for that will be your wisdom and your understanding in the sight of the peoples, who, when they hear all these statutes, will say, 'Surely this great nation is a wise and understanding people' " (Deut 4:5-6).

[80]At 104:10-13 the sinners are even accused of altering the text of scripture as well as its interpretation.

Der Glaube an Gottes *alles* umfassenden und bestimmenden Willen hatte in ihnen vielmehr die Überzeugung hervorgerufen, dass sie nur durch die Übernahme dieser alles umspannenden Ordnung der Wirchlichkeit, das heisst Gott selbst gerecht werden könnten,— nicht in einem formalen Legalismus freilich, sondern in einem Gehorsam, der im dankbaren Lobpreis seinen entsprechendsten Ausdruck findet.[81]

The revelation of wisdom is not without its ambiguities for Enoch. The secrets of heaven, including specifically God's wisdom, are clearly for the elect in the last days. But premature and inappropriate revelation of at least some of those secrets is given as the reason for the fall of the heavenly beings in chapters 7-9: "they revealed secrets which are performed in heaven (and which) man learned" (9:6).[82] This dual nature of wisdom—for good and evil—is also reflected in the description of the garden Enoch sees on his journey to the east (chapters 28-33). Eden is called the "garden of righteousness" (32:3), and in it grows the tree of wisdom

> from which your old father and aged mother....ate and came to know wisdom; and (consequently) their eyes were opened and they realized they were naked and (so) they were expelled from the garden (32:6).

Raymond Brown discerns three types of heavenly mysteries in 1 Enoch:[83] evil mysteries such as those revealed by the fallen Watchers, cosmic mysteries that generally also have moral dimensions, and divine mysteries concerning God's will and human behavior.[84] The OT background to these mysteries lies primarily in the notion of God's council or assembly,

---

[81]*Die Ordnung des Heils: Untersuchungen zum Gesetzverständnis des Frühjudentums* (Düsseldorf: Patmos, 1971) 72; emphasis his.

[82]At 16:3 Enoch is instructed to say to the Watchers: "not all the mysteries (of heaven) are open to you, and you (only) know the rejected mysteries. Those ones you have broadcast to the women in the hardness of your hearts and by those mysteries the women and men multiply evil deeds upon the earth. " When essentially the same story is recounted later in the Similitudes, Noah is accounted pure and kindhearted becaused he "detest[s] the secret things " that are none of his business and that result in sin (65:11).

[83]R. E. Brown, *The Semitic Background of the Term "Mystery" in the New Testament* FBBS 21 (Philadelphia: Fortress, 1968).

[84]*Ibid*, 14-19.

where prophets are invited to gain knowledge of otherwise secret divine decrees. In post-exilic literature beginning with Daniel those decrees or mysteries increasingly concern the future and God's plan for the salvation of the world, and in Sirach and Wisdom the wisdom of God becomes the revealer of mysteries. According to Brown, Enoch combines the concept of visionary mystery from Daniel and its source in God's wisdom from Sirach.

> Comparing [the mysteries in Enoch] to the mysteries encountered in the OT, we find that the evil mysteries revealed by the fallen angels are a new facet, yet one quite consonant with the notion of the heavenly assembly... As for cosmic phenomena, they were mysteries in Sirach too (43:32; 16:21); but the idea is more fully treated in Enoch.... Whereas Sirach stressed that secrets could be learned from the law, the wisdom books, and the prophets, Enoch...purports to be a collection of mysteries handed down by a mysterious personage to his descendents.[85]

Book I, then, contains at least two valuations of wisdom that reflect an ambivalence reminiscent of Qoheleth. On the one hand, one may discern God's consistency and faithfulness in the works of creation. The exhortations to observe God's handiwork and behave in a similarly consistent fashion recall the attitude familiar from traditional wisdom literature that proper social order reflects cosmic order. On the other hand, revelation of saving wisdom to the elect —particularly in the form of correct Torah interpretation—is a peculiar property of the end time, and there is no indication Enoch expects the world to be transformed in any way by the wise. The gift of wisdom is God's alone to give, and its function is to enable the elect to survive judgment and enter paradise. The wisdom language and ideas present in the Book of the Watchers function to differentiate the righteous from the ungodly, just as in the wisdom corpus. But because for Enoch wisdom is revealed rather than discerned, the implicit exhortation is not to study the law and be faithful in traditional ways but to espouse the author's particular perspectives on the imminent eschaton and preparation for judgment.[86] Much as for Daniel, to whom wisdom is

---

[85]*Ibid.*, 18.

[86]Cf. 2 En 1a1, which calls Enoch "a wise man...whom the Lord took away," although the rest of the apocalypse makes no further use of sapiential traditions. Coughenour traces the wide-ranging traditions about the character Enoch that call him a sage ("Enoch and Wisdom, " 5-10). 2 Enoch is notoriously difficult to locate as to date and provenance. See the introductory discussion and select bibliography provided by F. I. Anderson

granted that he might understand his apocalyptic visions (Dan 9:22-23), so for Enoch revealed wisdom is the means whereby one responds appropriately to revelation (cf. 1 En 14:3).[87]

Book II (1 Enoch 37-71)

The superscript to the Similitudes makes even more explicit that revealed wisdom is a characteristic of the end time, naming Enoch's vision "the vision of wisdom" (37:1; cf. 92:1).

> This is the beginning of the words of wisdom which I commenced to propound, saying to those who dwell in the earth, "Listen, you first ones, and look, you last ones, the words of the Holy One, which I teach before the Lord of Spirits. It is good to declare these words to those of former times, but one should not withhold the beginning of wisdom from those of latter days. Until now such wisdom, which I have received as I recited (it) in accordance with the will of the Lord of Spirits, had not been bestowed upon me before the face of the Lord of Spirits... " (37:2-4).

There follow Enoch's three parables, the first of which (chapters 38-44) is a picture of the great assize—the righteous and wicked receive destinies appropriate to them—and a cataloguing of heavenly secrets ("I saw all the secrets in heaven, " [41:1]) which testify to the rightness of God's judgment:

> Surely the many changes of the sun have (both) a blessing and a curse, and the course of the moon's path is light to the righteous (on the one hand) and darkness to the sinners (on the other) (41:8).

There is a sense in which for Enoch sin consists in the disruption of God's intended order, for in the midst of these cosmic secrets is related the

---

with his recent translation in *The Old Testament Pseudepigrapha*, vol. 1, 91-100.

[87] As was noted above (p. 72, n. 53), "wisdom " in Daniel is in no way limited or defined as it is here in 1 Enoch. Given Enoch's heavy dependence on the OT, however, and on Daniel in particular, it is likely the seer's conviction that wisdom is required to understand heavenly mysteries is at its foundation drawn from Daniel.

myth of "vanished wisdom"[88] in chapter 42.[89] Lady Wisdom, familiar from Proverbs 8, Sirach 24, and Wisdom 9, seeks in vain for a home, finds a dwelling in the heavens, but then goes looking again, this time among "the children of the people" (42:2). Finding no lodging, she returns to the heavens to settle "permanently among the angels" (42:2), and her absence creates a vacancy which Iniquity fills (42:3). This picture of the earth as devoid of wisdom accords well with the apocalyptic view of the sentence of doom under which the creation labors, awaiting its redemption from beyond, and is probably reflected in the prediction in the Apocalypse of Weeks that "in the sixth week...the hearts of them all shall forget wisdom" (93:8).

Bracketed as it is by descriptions of God's impartial judgment of human beings and the created order (41:8-9; 43:1-2), the myth functions in its context to explain the sinners' lack of righteousness—Wisdom has been removed from the earth—and the righteous people's ability to survive judgment, for God has "strengthened the spirits of the righteous in the name of his righteousness" (41:8). As in Job, wisdom is God's alone to dispense (28:23-28) and is anything but a property of human nature (28:12-13). Only those granted the revelation of saving wisdom (cf. 1 En. 5:8) are counted righteous.[90]

---

[88]So named by H. Conzelmann to distinguish it from what he calls the myths of "wisdom close at hand" (e.g., Prov 8:22ff) and "wisdom concealed" (Job 28, Bar 3:9) ("Paulus und die Weisheit," *NTS* 12 [1965] 231-244; idem, "Wisdom in the New Testament" in *IDBS* [1976] 956-969). Conzelmann's three categories have been explored in detail by his student B. L. Mack in *Logos und Sophia: Untersuchungen zur Weisheitstheologie im hellenistischen Judentum* (Göttingen: Vandenhoeck and Ruprecht, 1973). On the "myth of vanished wisdom," see particularly 32-33.

[89]Stone, following R. H. Charles (*Apocrypha and Pseudepigrapha of the Old Testament* [Oxford: Clarendon, 1913] vol. 2, 213) calls the myth a "small fragment" which is "out of context in 1 Enoch and not typical of it or of the other apocalypses" ("Apocalyptic Literature," 389), but Coughenour correctly sees that "the poem need not be considered as misplaced" ("Enoch and Wisdom," 68). There is no MS evidence to support such a conclusion, and if the context concerns the nature of heavenly secrets, why should their source (i.e., Wisdom) not be a logical topic for speculation, too? The suspicion that chapter 42 is somehow "out of place" in the parable appears more to reflect a prior decision that wisdom and apocalyptic traditions have no relation to one another than specific exegetical decisions.

[90]This "myth of vanished wisdom" apparently enjoyed some currency, since it is referred to in at least two other apocalyptic works from roughly

While the Similitudes relates this myth of "vanished wisdom," and the Apocalypse of Weeks seems to allude to it, the Book of the Heavenly Luminaries (1 Enoch 77-82) contains an apparent reference to the older myth of "wisdom close at hand," although it too has been reinterpreted in apocalyptic terms. Wisdom is still revealed rather than discerned, but rather than being revealed only near the end of history, it has been (at least theoretically) available since antedeluvian times. At 82:2-3 Enoch reminds his son Methuselah:

I have revealed to you and given you the book concerning all these things [i.e., the visions]. Preserve, my son, the book from your father's hands in order that you may pass it on to the generations of the world. I have given wisdom to you, to your children, and to those who shall become your children in order that they may pass it (in turn) to their children and to the generations that are discerning. All the wise ones shall give praise, and wisdom shall dwell upon your consciousness; they shall not slumber but be thinking; they shall cause their ears to listen in order that they may learn this wisdom; and it shall please those who feast on it more than good food.

———

the same time period. In 4 Ez 5:9-10, one of the signs of the approaching eschaton is the fact that "reason shall hide itself, and wisdom shall withdraw into her chamber, and she shall be sought by many but shall not be found, and unrighteousness and unrestraint shall increase on earth." So also, 2 Bar 48:36 promises that "many will say to many in that time, 'Where did the multitude of intelligence hide itself and where did the multitude of wisdom depart?" Interestingly, the full-blown myth in 1 Enoch 42 seems to speak of a primeval withdrawal of Wisdom from the earth—the story is told as one of the many revelations of secrets of the cosmos—but the references to it in 4 Ezra and 2 Baruch indicate an eschatological time frame. Mack concludes, however: "Die Frage nach dem Zietpunkt des Aufenthalts auf die Erden spielt kaum eine Rolle [in the myth itself]. Der Anlass zum Verschwinden ist die Angabe syr.Bar.62,3f. interessant, dass zur Zeit Davids und Salomos die Weisheit da war. Jetzt entschwunden weilt die Weisheit bei Gott (1 Hen.84,3) oder dem Erwälten (1 Hen.46,3)" (Logos und Sophia, 33). Mack takes the righteousness of the elect Son of Man in 1 En 46:3 to be a reference to his wisdom, in light of 48:1-8 (ibid., n. 66).

Although the content of Enoch's wisdom is his visions of the end (in which time his readers consider themselves to be), the literary fiction is that such wisdom has been available to all the (discerning) generations since Methuselah, available to any and all who search for it in Enoch's book.[91]

Whereas in the earlier Book of the Watchers God is the one who reveals his wisdom to the elect, in the second parable vision (chapters 38-44), the revealer is the Son of Man (48:1-49:4) who possesses the wisdom of God from before creation and dispenses it to the righteous (48:7). As in the Book of the Watchers, wisdom is functionally equivalent to righteousness (48:2, 7; 49:2-3). The fountain of righteousness is "surrounded completely by numerous fountains of wisdom" (48:1) which quench the thirst of those who have "hated and despised this world of oppression (together with) all its ways of life and its habits" (48:7). This wisdom that "flows like water" (49:1) from the Son of Man is "the spirit which gives thoughtfulness, the spirit of knowledge and strength, and the spirit of those who have fallen asleep in righteousness" (49:4). Although there appears to be a clear reference here to the description of the Righteous Branch in Isaiah 11 ("the spirit of wisdom and understanding, the spirit of counsel and might, the spirit of knowledge and the fear of the Lord," v.2),[92] it probably also reflects the tradition found in Wisdom (1:4-5, 6-10; 7:21-28) that identified wisdom with the Spirit.[93]

Book III (1 Enoch 72-82)

Following the third parable (chapters 58-71) is yet another of the many long lists of heavenly secrets common in 1 Enoch (60:11-25; cf. 6:7-8; 18:1-16; 69:1-14; 77:1-79:6), similar in some respects to the onomastica of

---

[91] A similar, though more traditional assumption that wisdom is present in the world, and has been since creation, is implicit in the question asked at 101:8: "Did [God] not make the heaven and earth and all that is in them? Who gave the knowledge of wisdom to all those who move upon the earth and in the sea?"

[92] See Knibb, "The Dating of the Parables," 351-352 for discussion of the sources of the Son of Man imagery in the second parable. Cf. D. W. Suter, *Tradition and Composition in the Parables of Enoch* SBLDS 47 (Missoula: Scholars, 1979).

[93] See J. A. Davis, *Wisdom and Spirit: An Investigation of I Corinthians 1.18-3.20 Against the Background of Jewish Sapiential Traditions in the Greco-Roman Period* (Lanham, New York, London: University Press of America, 1984) 7-26.

Egyptian wisdom.[94] Intense curiosity about the universe is common to all five books,[95] but is most characteristic of the Heavenly Luminaries (72-82). The issue at stake for the author is apparently a dispute over proper calendrical observance. Enoch supports an intricately divined 364-day calendar (72:33, 74:10, 12; 82:6; cf. Jub 4:17; 1QapGen 19:25) which his opponents do not. By their inaccurate calculation of time, these evil-doers worship inappropriately "on the four days which are not counted in the reckoning of the year" (75:1; cf. 82:5). The precise descriptions of heavenly and earthly geography and physics are revealed by Uriel to ensure that Enoch and his descendents stay on the straight and narrow, not altering their course as the sinners have by adopting calendrical innovations. Indeed miscalculation of times and seasons is taken to be the very root of all evil, from agricultural failure to idolatry.

> In respect to their days, the sinners and the winter are cut short. Their seed(s) shall lag behind in their lands and in their fertile fields.... They (the stars) shall err against them (the sinners); and modify all their courses. Then they (the sinners) shall err and take

---

[94]M. E. Stone ("Lists of Revealed Things in the Apocalyptic Literature" in *Magnalia Dei*, 414-452) investigates a number of similar lists in great detail, and discovers that they share generally common forms, functions, and contents. The lists summarize the revelations of the seers, "what the writers of the apocalypses thought to lie at the heart of apocalyptic revelation itself" (418), and usually focus on cosmological, astronomical, and speculative mysteries. Stone concludes: "It seems most probable that *part* of this speculative concern of the apocalyptic lists derived from Wisdom sources [particularly Job 28 and 38; Sirach 43; the emphasis in Sirach and Wisdom on the inaccessibility of God's wisdom apart from revelation; and so on], although the lines of connection may prove difficult to trace. It is impossible, however, to see the Wisdom tradition as the *only* source from which the interest in these subjects sprang" (438; emphasis added).

[95]The introductory visions to the Book of the Watchers extol the regularity of nature; the heavenly furniture is catalogued in 14:8-25, and that of the underworld in 18:1-16; Enoch smells the fragrance of dozens of different (named) trees on his journey to the east in 28-32; and he counts the gates of heaven "according to their numbers, their names, their ranks, their seats, their periods, their months" (33:3). In the Similitudes there are lists of angels' names (40:9-10), the mechanics of the weather (60:11-23), and the names of fallen angels and their sins (69:1-15). Again in the Epistle of Enoch, nature proclaims the Creator's power (101:1-9).

them (the stars) to be gods. And evil things shall be multiplied upon them; and plagues shall come upon them, so as to destroy all (80:2, 7-8).[96]

The underlying conviction is that human work and worship, to be authentic, must reflect the angelic and cosmic orders. And it is clear that Enoch considers only those like himself to be so engaged.

Summary

The various consituent apocalypses of 1 Enoch employ a surprising amount of wisdom language and thought, but almost always in ways very different from the classical wisdom corpus. There are repeated references throughout all five books to the wise,[97] God's wisdom,[98] and the granting of salvific wisdom;[99] the Book of the Similitudes is labeled Enoch's "vision of wisdom" (37:1), and the conclusion to the Book of the Heavenly Luminaries similarly calls that revelation "wisdom" (82:2-3). The familiar wisdom motif of cosmic order is central to the Books of the Watchers and the Heavenly Luminaries, and the Book of the Similitudes ascribes to the messiah his traditional attribute of wisdom. But for all these traces of sapiential material, 1 Enoch's outlook is far more characteristic of apocalypses than of wisdom literature, and the function of wisdom traditions is anything but traditional. On our scale of "ideal" types, 1 Enoch stands farthest away from the Wisdom of Solomon.

For 1 Enoch, wisdom is located primarily in heavenly mysteries, so 1 Enoch ranks very near the transcendence pole on our scale of meaning. The most explicit definitions of God's wisdom link it with revelations of heavenly reality. To a much lesser extent, wisdom is also connected with Torah, but only insofar as Torah is understood from Enoch's interpretive perspective. Because wisdom is to be had by means of revelation almost exclusively, only Enoch who speaks with angels—and by extension, those who read Enoch's book(s)—have access to it. Wisdom's content is not guidance for the good life but cosmic secrets: the future of the universe,

---

[96]Cf. also the conviction of the writer of Jubilees that "the land will be corrupted on account of all their deeds, and there will be no seed of the vine...because [the sinners] have forgotten the commandments and covenant and festivals and months and sabbaths and jubilees and all of the judgments" (23:18-19).

[97]Cf. 61:7; 98:1, 9; 100:6; 104:12.

[98]Cf. 48:1, 7; 63:2; 84:3.

[99]Cf. 5:7-10; 37:4; 48:7; 49:1-3; 51:3; 92:1; 101:8; 105:1.

cultic and calendrical specifications, and a particular slant on Torah interpretation. Although God's wisdom is intended to order and balance the creation, human and angelic sin and even the disobedience of heavenly bodies have irreparably disrupted that order. Only those possessed of Enoch's revelation are able to conform to God's intention, and thus the potential for meaningful human life before the end is slight in the extreme. Because the eschaton seems so very imminent in 1 Enoch, the present has greatly reduced value: the purpose of human life is to respond to Enoch's revealed warnings and prepare oneself for the end.

C. 4 Ezra [100]

Michael A. Knibb's study of the wisdom traits in the late first-century C.E. 4 Ezra[101] begins with the several characterizations of "Ezra" in chapter 14. At the beginning of his seventh and final vision,[102] the seer is addressed first as a lawgiver, a new Moses (vv 1-36). Then, as an inspired prophet, he is instructed to dictate all the revelations he has received from God to five speedy stenographers until there are ninety-four books written (vv 37-44). Finally, God instructs Ezra as a wise man[103] to make public (to the

---

[100]See the discussions of introductory matters in Sanders, *Paul*, 409-418; E. Breech, "These Fragments Have I Shored Against My Ruins: The Form and Function of 4 Ezra," *JBL* 92 (1973) 267-274; W. Harnisch, *Verhängnis und Verheissung der Geschichte: Untersuchungen zum Zeit- und Geschichtsverständnis im 4. Buch Esra und in der syr. Baruchapokalypse* FRLANT 97 (Göttingen: Vandenhoeck and Ruprecht, 1969); Nickelsburg, *Jewish Literature*, 287-294; and Charlesworth, *The Pseudepigrapha*, 111-113; idem, "The Triumphant Majority as Seen by a Dwindled Minority: The Outsider According to the Insider of Jewish Apocalypses, 70-130" in *To See Ourselves As Others See Us: Christians, Jews, "Others" in Late Antiquity*, ed. J. Neusner and E. S. Frerichs (Chico: Scholars, 1985) 294-300.

[101]"Apocalyptic and Wisdom in 4 Ezra" *JSJ* 13 (1981) 56-74. See also idem, "Prophecy and the Emergence of the Jewish Apocalypses" in *Israel's Prophetic Heritage: Essays in Honor of Peter J. Ackroyd*, ed. R. J. Coggins, A. Phillips, M. A. Knibb (Cambridge: University, 1982) 155-180.

[102]The earlier vision in 2:42-48 belongs to the Christian framework of the book (chapters 1-2, 15-16), and thus is not part of the original Ezra Apocalypse. See the introductions by B. M. Metzger in *The Old Testament Pseudepigrapha*, vol. 1, 517-523; Nickelsburg, *Jewish Literature*, 287-294; and Stone, "Apocalyptic Literature," 412-414.

[103]As Nickelsburg observes, this portrait of the seer as a sage connects the main character of the apocalypse with the historical Ezra who brought

"worthy and the unworthy," v 46) twenty-four of the books (that is, the Hebrew canon), and to reserve the "seventy that were written last" (v 47, presumably the apocalyptic writings) for the wise. Just as Moses was shown "secrets of the times and...the end times" to "publish openly" and "keep secret" respectively (14:5-6), so Ezra's revelations are accessible only to those able to understand.

> Make public the twenty-four books that you wrote first and let the worthy and the unworthy read them; but keep the seventy that were written last, in order to give them to the wise among your people. For in them is the spring of understanding, the fountain of wisdom, and the river of knowledge (14:45-47).

Such designation of apocalyptic literature as for the wise leads Knibb to conclude that the author considers his own work a wisdom book intended for a learned circle.[104]

Taking his lead from this model of Ezra as a wise man writing for a community of sages, Knibb proceeds to examine the entire book for wisdom characteristics. He notes the familiar parallels between 4 Ezra and the book of Job,[105] and concludes that "4 Ezra has to some extent been intentionally modelled on the Book of Job."[106] There are very real differences between the two works, of course, but they suggest only that the writer of 4 Ezra "was not slavishly trying to imitate this model."[107] Such reliance on Job

---

the Torah to Jerusalem and interpreted it for the people (*Jewish Literature*, 293).

[104] "Apocalyptic and Wisdom in 4 Ezra," 62-64. Although Knibb makes no reference to it, 12:35-38 argues precisely the same point, without the distinction between the Torah and the esoteric writings: "This is the dream that you saw, and this is its interpretation. And you alone were worthy to learn this secret of the Most High. Therefore write all these things that you have seen in a book, and put it in a hidden place; and you shall teach them to the wise among your people, whose hearts you know are able to comprehend and keep these secrets."

[105] I.e., concern with theodicy, use of dialogue to respond (if only vaguely) to the problem of evil, and divine revelation as the final answer to the question; and literary parallels between 4 Ezra 4:7-8 and Job 28:16-18, 4 Ezra 5:36-37 and Job 36:26-27 (ibid., 65-66).

[106] "Apocalyptic and Wisdom in 4 Ezra," 66.

[107] *Ibid.*

supports the picture from chapter 14 of 4 Ezra's having strong links with
the older wisdom tradition.

Job is by no means the only canonical book important for 4 Ezra,
though. Daniel 9-12 seem also to have "been in the mind of the author"[108]
as he composed the dialogue sections. In 4:33-5:13, 5:50-6:28, 7:[75]-[115],
and 8:6-9:13, Ezra asks questions and receives answers much as Daniel does
in Dan 12:5-13. But even more clearly, the fact that the angel orders Ezra to
fast in preparation for visions (5:20, 6:35) seems dependent on Dan 9:3 and
10:2-3.[109]

Beyond clear allusions, 4 Ezra's use of the rest of scripture tends to be
less a matter of citation than reminiscence, or "the fairly obvious use of the
thought and terminology of particular passages."[110] This ostensibly loose
relationship to the biblical text suggests to some that 4 Ezra has "for the
most part...lost its close association with the Old Testament, but is
nonetheless 'sometimes overlaid with layers of new material derived from
the OT'."[111] Knibb challenges this conclusion with several illustrations of
what he considers fairly direct connections between 4 Ezra and the canonical
books.[112] 4 Ezra 6:1-6, he suggests, has a recognizable relationship to Prov
8:22-31, and although he considers the passage in 4 Ezra "relatively
incidental,"[113] it nevertheless appears to be yet another reference to the
myth of wisdom "close at hand." Here, as in Proverbs 8, the creation is born
through the agency of God's wisdom. In answer to Ezra's request of God to
know "through whom you are going to visit your creation" (5:56), God
answers:

> At the beginning of the circle of the earth, before the portals of the
> world were in place, and before the assembled winds blew, and
> before the rumblings of thunder sounded, ...then I planned these
> things [i.e., the creation's aging and passing away (5:55)] and they
> were made through me and not through another, just as the end
> shall come through me and not through another (6:1-2, 6).

---

[108]*Ibid.*, 67.

[109]*Ibid.*, 66-67.

[110]*Ibid.*, 67.

[111]*Ibid.* (citing L. Hartman, *Prophecy Interpreted: The Formation of
Some Jewish Apocalyptic Texts and of the Eschatological Discourse Mark
13 Par*, tr. N. Tomkinson [Lund: Gleerup, 1966] 136-137).

[112]*Ibid.*, 68-69.

[113]*Ibid.*

Knibb's final conclusions about the "sapiential" character of 4 Ezra are most specific and cautious. Although on the basis of chapter 14 it is clear that the book was intended by its author for a wisdom audience of some sort, there is no indication that those sages are identical to the circle responsible for the OT wisdom corpus.[114] Secondly, while Ezra's use of scripture, often from wisdom writings, is much more direct than is that of other apocalyptic writings, the very diversity of texts interpreted—from Torah, prophets, and writings alike—precludes identifying it exclusively with any single OT tradition.[115] And finally, the distinctiveness of 4 Ezra among contemporary documents limits the extent to which conclusions about its possible wisdom background may be applied to other apocalyptic literature.[116]

Knibb stops short of noting one further traditional wisdom motif in 4 Ezra, though, one so familiar that it is easily overlooked. Like Sirach, 4 Ezra considers God's wisdom to be contained in Torah. Although the Torah can be read by the "worthy" and the "unworthy" alike (14:46), it is clear that Ezra considers only the "worthy" to profit from their reading, and it is these who are the "wise" eligible to read the secret books of wisdom. Ezra himself is considered wise because of his study of Torah:

This is the interpretation of the dream which you saw. And you alone have been enlightened about this, because you have forsaken your own ways and have applied yourself to mine, and have searched out my law; for you have devoted your life to wisdom, and called understanding your mother (13:53-55).

So also, the few others in the world who are righteous like Ezra—and their righteousness is clearly a function of legal obedience—are the only ones to survive judgment and thus receive wisdom.[117]

For many miseries will affect those who inhabit the world in the last times, because they have walked in great pride. But think of your own case [Ezra], and inquire concerning the glory of those who are like yourself, because it is for you that Paradise is opened,

---

[114]*Ibid.*, 72.

[115]*Ibid.*, 73.

[116]Ibid., 74. Cf. also Sanders, *Paul* 427, for whom 4 Ezra's distinctiveness among contemporary documents makes it "not a particularly good representative of [first-century] Judaism."

[117]The distinction between the few and the many run throughout 4 Ezra, but see particularly 3:36; 7:[50-51, 60-61]; 8:1-3, 41, 61-62.

the tree of life is planted, the age to come is prepared,...wisdom perfected beforehand.... Therefore do not ask any more questions about the multitude of those who perish. For they...were contemptuous of his Law, and forsook his ways (8:50-52, 56).

Only those who possess the wisdom of Torah are wise enough to qualify for Ezra's secret wisdom about the end times. Whereas in 1 Enoch the elect are those who are given the seer's revelations, Ezra further limits the saved to those who are *first* obedient to the law.[118]

Summary

The author of 4 Ezra uses wisdom language and themes to identify both his own apocalyptic visions (and others like them) and God's law. Although God's wisdom is therefore revealed rather than discerned, the presence of Torah among the people and their equal access to it moves 4 Ezra one stage away from 1 Enoch and the "ideal" transcendence pole. To be sure, as in 1 Enoch, revealed salvific wisdom—here located in revelations *and* Torah— provides the answer to Ezra's question why some are saved and some not: those who are wise, who are faithful to Torah, are granted revelations of the future redemption. But unlike 1 Enoch, 4 Ezra places a great deal more confidence in the efficacy of traditional educational wisdom.[119] The (very) few who are counted righteous have remained faithful against great odds, and Ezra exhorts his readers to remain similarly vigilant that they, too, might become wise—and receive wisdom. Because of his bleak picture of human nature and expectation of an imminent eschaton, Ezra does not seem to be waiting for the transformation or renewal of social order. In fact, not even the cosmic order is still intact, because the creation itself is decaying as rapidly as hope for human righteousness. The challenge of the present,

---

[118]See Nickelsburg, "Revealed Wisdom," 81-82.

[119]The dark side of Ezra's conviction of human freedom and responsibility (3:8; 7:[72, 105]; 8:58-59; 9:7-8, 32-33) is his teaching about the "evil heart" or "evil root" (3:20-27; 4:30; 7:[48]) which infects humanity like a disease (3:22) since the time of Adam and makes human righteousness next to impossible. The result is a very pessimistic but not fatalistic anthropology. "Since the Judge holds people responsible for their deeds," observes Nickelsburg, "obedience to the Torah is a possibility, and to that end Ezra published the Scriptures" (*Jewish Literature*, 294). Sanders's even more radical conclusion is that "in IV Ezra... covenantal nomism has collapsed. All that is left is legalistic perfectionism" (*Paul*, 409). Similarly Harnisch, *Verhängnis und Verheissung*, 42-58.

therefore, lies in urging faithfulness to Torah—although only a few will respond—and consequent preparedness for the end.

D. Qumran

Although there is only scant evidence that the Qumran covenanters themselves composed apocalypses,[120] they certainly valued several—particularly the Enochic corpus. But like the writers of apocalypses, the people of Qumran considered themselves the community of the last days soon to be vindicated by God, and their library reflects the same imminent expectation; the stark distinctions between the present and future ages, earth and heaven, evil and good; and concern with revelations of divine mysteries.[121] Much of the language characteristic of the sapiential tradition is used throughout the nonbiblical documents found at Qumran, particularly words for wisdom and insight.[122] One primary conviction expressed in

---

[120]A few Qumran fragments have been classified as apocalypses, particularly 4Q Visions de 'Amram (J. T. Milik, "4Q Visions de 'Amram et une citation d' Origène," *RB* 79 [1972] 77-97); 4Q Ps Daniel (idem, "Prière de Nabonide et autres écrits araméens de Qumrân 4," *RB* 63 [1956] 407-415); the fragmentary Vision of the New Jerusalem located in 1Q 32, 2Q 24, and 5Q 15; the Angelic Liturgy; the Enochic Book of Giants; and a so-called Apocalypse of Ten Jubilees in 4Q 384-389 (idem, *The Books of Enoch*, 254). With regard to such designations, Collins determines that these texts are either not truly apocalypses (e.g., 4Q Ps Daniel and the Angelic Liturgy) or that they are too fragmentary to permit certain identification (4Q Visions de 'Amram, Vision of the New Jerusalem, the Book of Giants, and the Apocalypse of Ten Jubilees) ("Jewish Apocalypses," 48-49).

[121]Collins correctly notes that "the distinction between apocalypticism and apocalyptic eschatology on the one hand and the literary genre 'apocalypse' on the other has its greatest significance in the case of the Qumran scrolls" (*ibid.*, 48). Although no Qumran document can be labelled an apocalypse with absolute certainty, the community's theology, life style, and self-perception are clearly close enough to the criteria listed above to merit its consideration here.

[122]The presence of wisdom vocabulary and themes at Qumran has been examined by several scholars. See, e.g., W. L. Lipscomb and J. A. Sanders, "Wisdom at Qumran" in *Israelite Wisdom*, 277-285; Nickelsburg, "Revealed Wisdom," 79-81; C. Romaniuk, "Le Thème de la Sagesse dans les Documents de Qumrân," *RevQ* 9 (1977-1978) 429-435; J. A. Sanders, "Two Non-Canonical Psalms in 11QPsᵃ," *ZAW* 76 (1964) 57-75; Küchler,

those contexts appears to be what one might expect from Jews who read 1 Enoch: wisdom is both God's gift in the form of the Torah rightly interpreted, and the mysteries of the imminent eschaton.[123] Both aspects are available only in the covenant community, mediated most often by the Teacher of Righteousness.[124]

> He [that is, the Master] shall conceal the teaching of the Law from men of falsehood, but shall impart true knowledge and righteous judgement to those who have chosen the Way. He shall guide them in all knowledge according to the spirit of each and according to the rule of the age, and shall thus instruct them in the mysteries of marvelous truth that in the midst of the men of the Community they may walk perfectly together in all that has been revealed to them (1QS 9:17-19a).

> From the source of [God's] righteousness is my justification, and from his marvellous mysteries is the light of my heart. My eyes have gazed on that which is eternal, on wisdom concealed from men, on knowledge and wise design (hidden) from the sons of men; on a fountain of righteousness and on a storehouse of power, on a spring of glory (hidden) from the assembly of flesh. God has given them to His chosen ones as an everlasting possession, and has caused them to inherit the lot of the Holy Ones (1QS 11:5-8).

Frühjüdische Weisheitstraditionen, 89-113; Worrell, "Concepts of Wisdom in the Dead Sea Scrolls;" R. Lehmann, "Ben Sira and the Qumran Literature," *RevQ* 3 (1961) 103-116; H. Ringgren, *The Faith of Qumran* (Philadelphia: Fortress, 1963) 115; Hengel, *Judaism and Hellenism*, vol. 1, 218-224; J. C. Lebram, "Die Theologie der späten Chokma und häretisches Judentum," *ZAW* 77 (1965) 202-211.

[123]Brown demonstrates that actually a great deal of Qumran teaching is called a mystery: God's election of the community and imminent judgment of the ungodly, the sect's interpretation of the law, and cosmic and evil mysteries like those in 1 Enoch (*The Term "Mystery"*, 22-30).

[124]In CD 1:8-15, "revelation and knowledge have two aspects familiar to us from 1 Enoch. The Teacher of Righteousness makes known both God's Law and God's eschatological judgment. His opposite number, the Scoffer, teaches falsehood" (Nickelsburg, "Revealed Wisdom," 79).

Who is like Thy people Israel which Thou hast chosen for Thyself from all the peoples of the lands; the people of the saints of the Covenant, instructed in the laws and learned in wisdom...who have learned the voice of Majesty and have seen the Angels of Holiness, whose ear has been unstopped, and who have heard profound things? (1QM 10:9b-11a).

For Thou hast established their ways for ever and ever, [and hast ordained from eternity] their visitation for reward and chastisements;... In the wisdom of Thy knowledge Thou didst establish their destiny before ever they were (1QH 1:19-20).

A new element in the identification of God's wisdom with the Torah is the additional prominence of the prophetic writings at Qumran. Wisdom is necessary not only for correct halakic interpretation, but also for reading the prophets to understand the eschatological future of the community and the world.

...and God told Habakkuk to write down that which would happen to the final generation, but He did not make known to him when time would come to an end. And as for that which He said, "That he who reads may read it speedily" [Hab 2:2], interpreted this concerns the Teacher of Righteousness, to whom God made known all the mysteries of the words of His servants the Prophets (1QpHab 7:1-5).

Not surprisingly, much of the traditional sapiential language occurs in the Hymns of Qumran,[125] where God's wisdom, knowledge, and mysteries are praised (e.g., "For Thou hast given me knowledge through Thy marvellous mysteries" [1QH 4:27b-28a], "there is no [bound] to Thy glory, and to Thy wisdom, no measure..." [9:16b-17]). And as in Proverbs, Sirach, and Wisdom, creation is often connected with God's wisdom:

By Thy wisdom [all things exist from] eternity, and before creating them Thou knewest their works for ever and ever... Thou hast fashioned [all] their [inhabi]tants according to Thy wisdom, and has

---

[125]Of 59 uses of *škl*, 30 are in 1QH; of 178 occurrences of *dᶜh* and related forms, 95 are in 1QH; 10 of the 18 instances of *ḥkmh* and *ḥkm* occur in the Hymns Scroll (see the table in Küchler, *Frühjüdische Weisheitstraditionen*, 89).

appointed all that is in them according to Thy will (1QH 1:7, 14-15).

Although there does not seem to be any interest among the sectarians in the mythical hypostatization of Wisdom, a poetic personification reminiscent of Prov 1:20-33 occurs in what James Sanders calls "a sapiential hymn" that "at Qumran was clearly considered a portion of the Davidic psalter."[126] The psalm attributes to Wisdom the traditional roles of enlightenment about God and guidance in daily living.

For to make known the glory of the Lord
　　Is Wisdom given,
And for recounting his many deeds
　　She is revealed to man:
To make known to simple folk his might
　　And to explain to senseless folk his greatness,
Those far from her gates,
　　Those remote from her portals.
　　. . . . .
From the gates of (the) righteous is heard her voice
　　And from the assembly of saints her song.
When they eat with satiety she is cited,
　　And when they drink in community together,
Their meditation is on the law of the Most High
　　And their words on making known his might.
How far from (the) wicked is her word
　　From all haughty men to know her!
　　　　　　(11QPsᵃ 18:5-8, 12-15)[127]

Similarly, in the poetic homily on Proverbs 7, "The Wiles of the Wicked Woman" (4Q Wiles), Sin or Folly is personified as a harlot who

---

[126]Sanders, "Two Non-Canonical Psalms," 63, 67. "Wisdom's gates, her voice and her song (vv 8, 12) strongly suggest a doctrine of Wisdom heretofore silent in Qumran literature save for Qumran MSS of the sapiential literature already well known before the discoveries at Qumran. Although our psalm does not go beyond a poetizing personification of Wisdom it exceeds in that direction not only the Qumran literature published to date but also the canonical psalter" (*ibid.*, 65).

[127]The translation is Sanders's (*ibid.*, 59-60). For questions of date and provenance see J. H. Charlesworth, "Jewish Hymns, Odes, and Prayers (ca. 167 B.C.E.-135 C.E.)," *JJS* 33 (1982) 414-415.

tempts people away from Wisdom,[128] and the early version of Sir 51:13-19 found in 11QPs^a 21:11-22:1 preserves the erotic *double entendre* of the righteous man's wooing of Lady Wisdom.[129] These texts, too, speak of the older function of wisdom as the teacher of right living rather than the heavenly revealer of divine mysteries.[130]

There seem, therefore, to be two distinct though related appropriations of sapiential language and thought at Qumran: wisdom is both God's guidance of human life in terms of behavior and ethics, and God's heavenly plan for the eschatological future of individuals and the community. The Qumran sectarians consider themselves wise on both counts. By their faithful study and obedience of Torah, their lives are in harmony with God's intentions for the creation; and by their receipt of the revealed wisdom concerning the end times, they are appropriately prepared.

---

[128] See Küchler, *Frühjüdische Weisheitstraditionen*, 102.

[129] For brief introductions to both texts, see T. H. Gaster, *The Dead Sea Scriptures With Introduction and Notes* (Garden City: Anchor-Doubleday, 1976³) 481-485, 495-496.

[130] The same traditional picture of wisdom's role can be seen in the Manual of Discipline. Lipscomb and Sanders point to the conclusion of B. Sharvit ("The Virtue of the Image of the Righteous Man in 1QS," *Beth Mikra* 19 [1974] 526-530 [in Hebrew]) that "the outstanding characteristic of the righteous man or ideal sectarian in 1QS 4:2-14 is wisdom. This emphasis is a product of neither Greek nor gnostic influence, but is to be read in the light of biblical wisdom (Prov) and postbiblical texts (Enoch, Jubilees, T. Levi, Wisdom, and Ben Sira) which characterize the righteous man as one who possesses wisdom" ("Wisdom at Qumran," 282, n. 5). C. Romaniuk also notes the essentially *practical* nature of wisdom at Qumran: whether it is understanding of correct Torah interpretation or of eschatological mysteries, the goal of wisdom is right living ("Le Thème de la Sagesse," 433).

J. Strugnell remarks of the *Mahnrede* fragment in 4Q 185, "[il] est sapientiel dans sa langue et dans ses themes, et...il appartient au genre 'instruction' ou peut-être même 'testament', d'un sage (ou d'un personnage historique) adressé à 'mes fils' ou 'mes peuple'" ("Notes en marge du volume V des *Discoveries in the Judean Desert of Jordan*," *RevQ* 7 [1970] 269). But Küchler, aside from attempting to isolate a few sapiential forms and ideas and offering a new translation, refrains from drawing weighty conclusions about the text's wisdom origins or character, and concludes only that it "stammt aus vorqumranischer Zeit..., wurde aber in Qumran kopiert (späthasmonäische Schrift)" (*Frühjüdische Weisheitstraditionen*, 103, n.22a).

A good deal of the discussion surrounding wisdom at Qumran has focused on whether or not the sectarians were a recognizably "sapiential" community or considered themselves more or less descendants of the traditional sages.[131] That surely seems unduly one-sided, and ignores the overwhelmingly apocalyptic tone of their thought. Consequently, Lipscomb and Sanders separate the psalms from Cave 11, the Qumran version of Sirach's hymn to Wisdom, and "The Wiles of the Wicked Woman" from documents of undisputed Qumran authorship in their discussion, concluding:

> (i) While the Essene texts contain wisdom vocabulary and expressions, a concern for knowledge and instruction, and an ethical dualism characteristic of the wisdom literature,[132] these elements are external to and superimposed upon the basically apocalyptic fabric of Qumran thought. While the Essenes understood themselves to possess wisdom and cast that wisdom into a dualistic framework, the content of wisdom at Qumran is a sectarian apocalyptic vision of truth.[133]

> (ii) It is only among the texts of unknown authorship that we encounter wisdom compositions. These compositions contribute to our understanding of Jewish wisdom in Hellenistic-Roman times, but say nothing definitive about wisdom thinking at Qumran.[134]

Two responses are in order here, though. First, the presence of documents of unknown authorship in the Qumran library raises a methodological issue akin to the use of traditional materials by NT authors.

---

[131]E.g., Worrell, "Concepts of Wisdom," and Küchler, *Frühjüdische Weisheitstraditionen.*

[132]Cf. the essay of Gammie, "Spatial and Ethical Dualism," described above (n. 12).

[133]One comment by Lipscomb and Sanders in a footnote reveals that another dispute hiding behind the debate is the on-going response to von Rad's theory of the origins of apocalypticism: "We do not wish to imply that wisdom and apocalyptic are mutually exclusive systems of thought; on the contrary, it is clear that wisdom was one of the many factors which contributed to the origin and development of apocalyptic thought. The fact that wisdom ideas play no integral role in the apocalyptic thought of the Dead Sea Scrolls suggests, however, that the scrolls do not provide an exemplary or fruitful locus in which to pursue the discussion of the wisdom origins of apocalyptic" ("Wisdom at Qumran," n.7).

[134]*Ibid.,* 280-281.

If Luke takes over whole passages from Mark without altering them or Paul cites traditional confessional affirmations, it can scarcely be maintained that such passages do not reflect those authors' thoughts. So also, unless it can be demonstrated that Qumran writers expressly refute the positions of other documents found with their own, it is illegitimate to say that such other writings "say nothing definitive" about Qumran theology. There is, moreover, sufficient reference to wisdom's classical guiding role in the Hodayot alone to suspect that the sapiential thought of the wisdom psalm in 11QPs^a was at least acceptable to, if not singularly definitive of Qumran theology.[135]

Secondly, if indeed wisdom language and thought are "external to and superimposed upon the basically apocalyptic fabric of Qumran thought,"[136] then what is the *function* of such imposition? What ends does the wealth of wisdom vocabulary and images serve in this otherwise clearly apocalyptic community's literature? Why does this group of people that constitutes itself on the basis of hope in God's imminent apocalyptic salvation employ so many sapiential themes in its worship and devotional life?

The answer appears to be similar to some of what we concluded about 1 Enoch and 4 Ezra: God's wisdom is still the source of cosmic and social order, the guide to the meaning of life and human happiness and well-being, and the solution to the problem of evil as it was in the wisdom corpus. But in contexts where appearance and reality are at severe odds, where the order and balance and harmony of the universe seem overlaid with empirical contradictions—contexts such as Qumran—God's wisdom becomes hidden, first in the Torah and its correct interpretation as that is promulgated in the community, and secondly in visions of heavenly reality that reconfirm wisdom's traditional affirmations of order.[137] That the most traditional

---

[135]Sanders himself notes that 11QPs^a 24:3-17 "was seemingly as 'canonical' as Ps 144 which precedes it or Ps 142 which follows it in 11QPs^a" ("Two Non-Canonical Psalms," 74). P. H. Davids correctly sees that "while this psalm is obviously a wisdom psalm, it must have been congruent with the covenanters' theology" (*The Epistle of James*, 53, n. 148).

[136]Lipscomb and Sanders, "Wisdom at Qumran," 280.

[137]Cf. Küchler's assessment: "Die Ausweitung des Weisheitsbegriffes war von der geschichtlichen Situation gefordert, wollte die Weisheit nicht in geschichtsenthobenen Kollektionen erstarren. Die frühjüdischen Weisen *mussten* die neuen Erfahrungen und die unbekannten Geisteswelten der persischen Zeit und des Hellenismus einbeziehen und ihren eigenen, adäquaten, sie alle *übersteigenden Beitrag leisten*, wollten sie nicht von der

sapiential themes at Qumran appear in liturgical contexts suggests that wisdom language functions first to help define community membership (wisdom as apocalyptic mystery), and second to sustain community life (wisdom as guide and source of meaningful life). While God's wisdom is ultimately an apocalyptic reality, within the community of the faithful elect it presently exercises a traditional ordering and educative function.

Summary

The Qumran covenanters stand yet another step removed from 1 Enoch and 4 Ezra on our continuum of transcendent to immanent meaning. 1 Enoch locates wisdom primarily in heavenly mysteries and less clearly in his unique interpretation of Torah. 4 Ezra finds wisdom first in the Torah and secondly in revelations. At Qumran, however, wisdom is to be sought in God's law and the community's interpretation of it, in heavenly secrets concerning the end times, and also within the elect community. Although the world is polluted by sinners who bring God's wrath on themselves and the earth, and the end is obviously near, the order, balance, and harmony of creation are yet accessible among the faithful wise who set themselves apart. The priestly welcome into the covenant blesses the new member, "May [God] bless you with all good and preserve you from all evil! May He lighten your heart with life-giving insight (*śēkel*) and grant you eternal knowledge! May he raise His merciful face towards you for everlasting bliss" (1QS 2:3). Although there is no potential for social and moral order outside the community, it does exist among the elect, for whom the present is full of possibility for righteous living, proper worship, and preparation for the coming eschatological vindication.[138]

Weisheit der Völker überfahren werden" (*Frühjüdische Weisheitstraditionen*, 111; emphasis his).

[138]If 1QM 2:5-6 refers to the replacement of the Jerusalem establishment by the Qumran hierarchy in an historical rather than purely eschatological time frame (i.e., the first seven years of the war), then the potential for restored social order is even greater.

E. 2 Baruch

The identification of Torah with wisdom seen at Qumran and in 4 Ezra is even more prominent in the roughly contemporary 2 Baruch,[139] but although the book is an apocalypse, there is no description of Baruch's visions as wisdom. At the beginning of Baruch's second conversation with God, which questions the justice of God's treatment of his people,[140] Baruch despairs of understanding God's wisdom:

O Lord, my Lord, who can understand your judgment? Or who can explore the depth of your way? Or who can discern the majesty of your path? Or who can discern your incomprehensible counsel? Or who of those who are born has ever discovered the beginning and end of your wisdom? (14:8-10).

But later it is the wisdom of God's law that makes possible the interpretation of Baruch's vision:

O Lord, my Lord, you are the one who has always enlightened those who conduct themselves with understanding. Your *Law* is life, and your *wisdom* is the right way. Now show me the explanation of this vision. For you know that my soul has always been associated with your Law, and that I did not depart from your wisdom from my earliest days (38:1-4).

---

[139]The possibility of a literary relationship between 4 Ezra and 2 Baruch has been explored a number of times. For a summary of the arguments, see G. B. Sayler, *Have The Promises Failed? A Literary Analysis of 2 Baruch* SBLDS 72 (Chico: Scholars, 1984) 129-134. Both the presence of common terminology and themes, and the use of similar narrative frameworks suggest that more than simply the use of common traditions connects the two documents. See also Nickelsburg, *Jewish Literature*, 288-293; and Sanders, *Paul*, 409; Charlesworth, *The Pseudepigrapha*, 83-85; idem, "The Triumphant Majority," 300-311. The greater likelihood is that 2 Baruch is dependent on 4 Ezra.

[140]Sayler's analysis (*Promises*, 41-118) locates the primary theological issues of 2 Baruch in God's covenant faithfulness, specifically in regard to "the vindication of God as just and powerful" (42-74), and "the survival of the Jewish community" after the crisis of 70 C.E. (74-86). The narrative structure she discerns in the book functions to move Baruch and his community from despair to consolation, from rebellion against God's judgment to faithful obedience to the Torah.

So also, in Baruch's addresses to the people, it is faithfulness to Torah which will ultimately bring about the "consolation of Zion" (44:8). The devastated community will survive the loss of temple, land, and leadership so long as it continues to submit to the law.[141]

> These are they who prepared for themselves treasures of *wisdom*. And stores of insight are found with them. And they have not withdrawn from mercy and they have preserved the truth of the *Law* (44:14).

> Israel will not be in want of a *wise* man, nor the tribe of Jacob, a son of the *Law*. But only prepare your heart so that you obey the *Law*, and be subject to those who are *wise* and understanding with fear (46:4-5).

> For we are all a people of the Name; we, who received the *Law* from the One. And that *Law* that is among us will help us, and that excellent *wisdom* which is in us will support us (48:23-24).[142]

Reference has already been made to the myth of "vanished wisdom" at 48:36,[143] but its literary function is relevant here. In answer to Baruch's prayer giving thanks for God's sovereignty and the law's guidance (48:2-24), God describes to him the judgment day. Baruch "will be taken up" (v 30), but the rest will live for a time in false security, unaware of the impending doom (vv 32-33). The reason for the sinners' deluded tranquility is that "there will not be found many wise men and there will also not be many intelligent ones, but, in addition, they who know will be silent more and more" (v 33).[144] The silence of the righteous, apparently, is the provocation for the question, "Where did the multitude of intelligence hide itself and where did the multitude of wisdom depart?" (v 36). Now it is unclear whether Baruch's being "taken up" (v 30) is simply a metaphor for his escape from destruction (cf. v 29) or is a literal prediction of his removal/death before the judgment day, but there will nevertheless be

---

[141]"By transferring leadership from himself to his successors, Baruch enables the community to take its first step into its future without him. Through his words and actions, he conveys to the people his conviction that God's covenant relationship with them has not been nullified" (*ibid.*, 85).

[142]Cf. also 54:13-14.

[143]See above, p. 85-86, n. 90.

[144]Cf. 70:5, "The wise will be silent, and the foolish will speak."

some—although admittedly "not many"[145]—wise ones remaining who "remember the Law of the Mighty One" (v 39), and who distance themselves in silence from the guilty. So long as there are Torah-faithful Jews, wisdom will not have vanished entirely.

> For the shape of those who now act wickedly will be made more evil than it is (now) so that they shall suffer torment. Also, as for the glory of those who proved to be righteous on account of my *Law*, those who possessed intelligence in their life, and those who planted the root of *wisdom* in their heart—their splendor will then be glorified by transformations.... Therefore, especially they who will then come will be sad, because they despised my *Law*, and stopped their ears lest they hear *wisdom* and receive intelligence (51:2-4).

> Shepherds and lamps and fountains came from the Law and when we [that is, Baruch's generation] go away, the Law will abide. If you, therefore, look upon the *Law* and are intent upon *wisdom*, then the lamp will not be wanting and the shepherd will not give way and the fountain will not dry up (77:15-16).

In contrast to 4 Ezra's extremely pessimistic anthropology, 2 Baruch envisions a real possibility of Torah faithfulness. Indeed such righteousness is the only hope for Israel's survival. Whereas 4 Ezra sees wisdom's ordering function to have left the creation altogether and located itself almost solely in esoteric revelations, 2 Baruch preserves (or regains, if indeed it relies on 4 Ezra) a sense of life's purpose and meaning this side of judgment. Baruch holds out an *historical* future for Israel as well as an *eschatological* one; the potential yet exists for repentance, Torah obedience,

---

[145]Sayler says of the difference between the "not many" in 2 Baruch and the "not many" in 4 Ezra: "In 2 Baruch, the distinction is used to identify as Israel the *few* Jews who have remained loyal to the Mosaic heritage, in contrast to the *many* Jews who have chosen the darkness of Adam. The question of whether the human will is free is not a part of the discussion. In contrast, Uriel [in 4 Ezra] uses the distinction to defend God's decision to let the *many* sinners perish, while the *few* righteous persons obtain salvation.... Here the distinction is part of the argument about theodicy; Uriel is arguing that the structure of creation does not deprive the individual of his ability to attain salvation. Central to Uriel's argument is the assertion, contra Ezra, that the individual is completely free to make his/her decision vis-à-vis God" (*Promises*, 132; emphasis hers).

and its attendant wisdom. Those who remain or become wise testify to God's continuing involvement in and sovereignty over the created order and human history.

Summary

Because 2 Baruch calls only the Torah wisdom, this book stands closer to the immanence pole on our spectrum than any thus far except for the Wisdom of Solomon. Granted, Baruch finds meaning for life in his visions of apocalyptic salvation, but the content of those visions is heavily laden with a traditional exhortation to Torah righteousness. Hope for Baruch's community consists not only in the fact that God will turn the tables on the people's enemies and vindicate their righteous suffering; hope lies also in the possibility of obedience. The nation will survive—that is, social order will be restored and preserved—so long as there are those who pursue the wisdom of God's law. That makes the present more open for 2 Baruch than for any apocalypse we have seen.

III. Conclusions

Although there exists great literary and theological diversity among these early Jewish documents, each of them makes use at some point of both wisdom and apocalyptic traditions to communicate its message. Each of them does so in very different ways, but a certain pattern of usage emerges that makes the various intersections of apocalyptic and wisdom traditions more than random. Put most simply, it appears that the more an author finds meaning accessible in this life, the more he uses traditional wisdom themes in traditional ways. The following chart locates these documents on the spectrum of transcendence to immanence by means of the general questions asked of each.

For all these early Jewish writers, God's wisdom is understood as the principle of order inherent in the universe. That order is perceptible in human experience, however, to lesser and greater degrees. In times of greater discontinuity between religious expectations and concrete reality, God's wisdom is more hidden than manifest, more a matter of apocalyptic hope than present experience. For 1 Enoch and 4 Ezra, God's wisdom is hidden in apocalyptic mysteries and esoteric interpretations of the law. Nature still reveals God's ordering sovereignty to 1 Enoch, but only those specifically enlightened by God are able to recognize the revelation. For 4 Ezra, the order once revealed in nature is itself vanishing as the universe races toward destruction.

	I Enoch	4 Ezra	Qumran	2 Baruch	Wisdom
Location of Wisdom	Mysteries (& Torah)	Torah & Mysteries	Torah & Mysteries & Community	Torah & Community	Creation & God's Spirit
Who has access?	Enoch's readers	Righteous & readers of apoc. books	Community	Righteous	All who seek for it
Means of access	Secret books	Righteousness & secret books	Membership in community	Righteousness	Study of creation & Spirit
Content of Wisdom	God's plan for cosmic future	Torah & God's plan for future	Torah & God's plan for future	Torah	Good life & immortality
Meaningful life before the end?	No	No	Only in the community	Only in the community	Yes

At the other end of the spectrum is the fundamental confidence in God's wisdom expressed by the Wisdom of Solomon. The Sage knows without question that God's ordering of the universe is beyond contradiction: even human history attests that the scales of justice are eventually balanced. But the righteous suffering of individual *persons* is not always similarly avenged in this life. Rather than relinquish his affirmation of divine order, though, Pseudo-Solomon extends the stage of God's active and ordering wisdom beyond this world into the next. Immortality provides the occasion for restoration and justice.

Between the two extremes lie the Qumran covenanters and the writer of 2 Baruch. They, too, affirm that God's wisdom orders, guides, and preserves the creation and human life and society. But the exigencies of contemporary life (estrangement from the Jerusalem establishment for Qumran, and the destruction of the temple for 2 Baruch) sufficiently threaten that affirmation that at least part of its guarantee is pushed into the eschatological future. Presently, order is discernible only in cosmic secrets, the Torah, and the community (the Torah alone for 2 Baruch); eventually, God will make it universally manifest.

Not surprisingly, the extent to which each of these Jews considers God's wisdom immanent or transcendent is correlated with the degree of its accessibility. For 1 Enoch, only those privileged to read Enoch's book(s) can be wise. 4 Ezra says that the (perfectly) righteous may qualify for the secret wisdom of his and other apocalypticists' books. At Qumran, membership in the community—which itself requires ascetic rigor and commitment to Torah righteousness—entitles one to the mysteries of God's wisdom, but those are freely given within the community. 2 Baruch offers wisdom to those who would study and obey Torah, but recognizes that the offer is not widely accepted. The Wisdom of Solomon proclaims that any and all who study the creation, Israel's history, and human nature, who love God and pursue wisdom are called wise.

The most striking variation among these writings is their respective attitudes toward the possibility of meaningful human life before the eschaton. The measure of an author's hope for earthly righteousness and wisdom seems to be in direct proportion to his perception of wisdom's immanence. The writers of 1 Enoch and 4 Ezra, for whom wisdom is most transcendent, have given up hope for the good life among any but the limited number of their own readers, and that only in heaven. The eschaton and God's judgment alone will restore cult and community,[146] and until then one's responsibility is to be righteous before God and discern the signs of the times. The possibility of the sinners' repentance grows slimmer with the passage of time,[147] and although each urges study of the scriptures to those who would survive judgment (1 En 104:10-13; 4 Ez 14:45-48), neither expects a significant response.

Wisdom is less radically transcendent for the Qumran community and 2 Baruch, and they clearly hope for at least some restored social and moral order before the end comes. Wisdom resides partially in the community and creation, and partially in revelations for the people of Qumran. So long as one becomes part of that community, the order established by God's wisdom is available in the pursuit of Torah righteousness and worship. 2 Baruch calls the faithful remnant of Israel to reconstitute itself by means of obedience and regain the social order lost in the judgment of national calamity. The eschaton will ultimately bring final restoration, but until then life can be meaningful and productive within the community of the righteous.

Of all these texts, the Wisdom of Solomon views wisdom as most immanent, and it places the greatest confidence in the possibility of order, balance, and harmony in human experience. The book is directed to both Gentile rulers and faithful Jews under pressure—and it evidences every expectation of accomplishing its aims of exhortation and comfort. Not only does the Sage believe firmly that "a multitude of wise men is the salvation of the world, and a sensible king is the stability of his people" (6:24), he makes use of apocalyptic judgment traditions to ensure that his belief in wisdom's order is not disconfirmed by the present suffering of the righteous.

---

[146]Cf. 1 En 90:28-39; 91:15-19; 4 Ez 7:26-[44]; 10:41-59).

[147]Cf. 1 En 38:6; 60:5-6;63:5-8; 4 Ez 7[72-74, 82, 105, 115]; 8:3, 59-62; 9:11-12.

Although the results of this study cannot be said to sustain Scroggs's claim of a single "apocalyptic-wisdom theology" contemporary with the Apostle Paul,[148] they have shown that the two traditions intersect frequently in Jewish literature. Such intersections are widely diverse in nature and function, but it does seem to be the case that the more a writer relies on traditional apocalyptic traditions, the less traditional is his use of wisdom material, and *vice versa.* The relative balance between the two types of tradition is a measure of an author's hope for earthly happiness and well-being: the more he views God's wisdom as transcendent, the more he anticipates eschatological order; the more immanent is God's wisdom, the greater the possibility for meaningful life in the present.

The next step in our analysis is to examine Romans 9-11 and ask of it the same questions that were asked of these Jewish texts, to see where Paul stands on this continuum of immanence and transcendence, and to discover how his particular use of confluent traditions shapes his argument.

---

[148]Or, for that matter, Küchler's sweeping generalizations about "apokalyptische Weisheit" (above, p. 60, n. 13).

3

Exegesis of Romans
9-11

I. Chapters 9-11 in the Context of the Letter[1]

A. Four Ways to View the Relation of 1-8 to 9-11

The nature of the relationship between Romans 9-11 and the preceding eight chapters has been debated in scholarly circles for over a century. Paul brings to a conclusion his discussion of the reliability of Christian hope with an exalted rhetorical flourish in 8:37-39, only to fall back into a more somber tone with a solemn vow in 9:1. The contrast in tone and the abrupt change in subject it signals have forced interpreters of Romans to explain this apparently rough transition.

---

[1]Cf. also the reviews of scholarship by C. Müller (*Gottes Gerechtigkeit und Gottes Volk: Eine Untersuchung zu Römer 9-11* [Göttingen: Vandenhoeck und Ruprecht, 1964] 5-27); W. S. Campbell, "Some Recent Literature on Paul's Letter to the Romans: A Critical Survey," *Biblical Theology* 25 (1975) 25-34; W. G. Kümmel ("Die Probleme von Römer 9-11 in der gegenwärtigen Forschungslage" in *Die Israelfrage nach Römer 9-11*, ed. L. de Lorenzi [Rome: Abtei von St Paulus vor den Mauern, 1977] 13-33); W. D. Davies ("Paul and the People of Israel," *NTS* 24 [1977] 24-25); J. E. Toews ("The Law in Paul's Letter to the Romans: A Study of Rom. 9.30-10.13" [Ph.D. Dissertation, Northwestern University, 1978] 107-110); P. E. Dinter ("The Remnant of Israel and the Stone of Stumbling According to Paul [Romans 9-11]" [Ph.D. Dissertation, Union Theological Seminary, 1979] 8-9); and most recently by P. Gorday (*Principles of Patristic Exegesis: Romans 9-11 in Origen, John Chrysostom, and Augustine* [New York and Toronto: Edwin Mellon, 1983] 1-10).

The classical view, most popular in the nineteenth century, had its roots in patristic—particularly Augustinian—exegesis of Romans.[2] It holds that the primary argument of the epistle concerning justification concludes with chapter 8, so that Paul's oath of solidarity with Israel in 9:1-5 initiates a new and more or less unrelated discourse on the problem of predestination and free will. This designation of 9-11 as an appendix to the main substance of the letter has contemporary champions in such diverse interpreters as William Sanday and Arthur C. Headlam, C. H. Dodd, and Otto Kuss.[3] Rudolf Bultmann noted what he perceived as a marked inconsistency

[2]See K. H. Schelkle, *Paulus: Lehrer der Väter: Die altkirchliche Auslegung von Römer 1-11* (Düsseldorf: Patmos, 1956); and Gorday, *Principles of Patristic Exegesis.*

[3]"St. Paul has now [with 8:39] finished his main argument" (W. Sanday and A. C. Headlam, *A Critical and Exegetical Commentary on the Epistle to the Romans*, 5th ed. [Edinburgh: T & T Clark, 1902] 225). "The immediate sequel to 8:31-39 is 'well then,...' [12:1ff]" (C. H. Dodd, *The Epistle of Paul to the Romans* [New York: Harper and Row, 1932] 148). "Nach dem hymnischen Abschluss [8:31-39] der ausführlichen Darlegung seiner theologischen Grundgedanken [1:16-8:39] setzt Paulus jetzt ganz neu ein,... Dass die Problematik der Kapitel 9-11 in unmittelbarem engem Zusammenhang mit dem Vorangehenden (1,16-8,39) steht, kann nicht bezweifelt werden; die konsequente und überlegte Durchführung des Themas, die sich keine Abschweifung gestattet, macht es jedoch verständlich, wenn man damit rechnet, dass Paulus hier eine frühere Ausarbeitung einfügt" (O. Kuss, *Der Römerbrief* [Regensburg: Pustet, 1978] vol. 3, 664-665). Cf. also W. Schmithals, *Der Römerbrief als historisches Problem* (Studien zum Neuen Testament 9; Gütersloh: Gütersloher [G. Mohn] 1975) 20-22; F. W. Beare, *St. Paul and His Letters* (Nashville: Abingdon, 1962) 97; K. H. Schelkle, *The Epistle to the Romans: Theological Meditations* (New York: Herder and Herder, 1964) 20.
    Although F. Godet includes chapters 9-11 in the "Doctrinal Treatise" of Romans (1:18-11:36) rather than making them another separate piece alongside the "Practical Treatise" (12:1-15:13), their function is nevertheless subordinate. The doctrine of justification (chapters 1-5) is defended by answers to two potential objections: Can it "produce holiness?" (6-8), and Can it "explain history?" (9-11). "This discussion...may be called the masterpiece of the philosophy of history" (*Commentary on St. Paul's Epistle to the Romans*, tr. A. Cusin [Edinburgh: T & T Clark, 1890[2]] vol. 1, 104).

between Romans 1-8 and 9-11,[4] and virtually ignored 9-11 altogether in his *Theology of the New Testament*.[5] Many scholars have affirmed, wholly or in part, Dodd's thesis that the passage argues a subsidiary point and "represents a somewhat earlier piece of work, incorporated here wholesale to save a busy man's time and trouble in writing on the subject afresh."[6] John A. T. Robinson claims that the passage "reads like an excursus and *could* be detached from the rest without affecting its argument and structure. 12:1 would follow perfectly well on 8:39."[7]

F. C. Baur was the first to challenge the traditional understanding of the main body of Romans as composed of a greater treatise (chapters 1-8) and an unrelated lesser one (9-11). If, he proposed, the letter "is looked on from the reverse direction...a more favourable view may...present itself of the aim and

---

[4]R. Bultmann, "History and Eschatology in the New Testament," *NTS* 1 (1954-55) 5-16.

[5]R. Bultmann, *Theology of the New Testament*, tr. K. Grobel (New York: Charles Scribner's Sons, 1951-55). Bultmann makes only nine passing references to four verses from the passage, and only five of these references are discussed in the chapters on Paul. The μυστήριον of 11:25 Bultmann labels "speculative fantasy" (vol. 2, 132). In his essay on Rom 10:4, Bultmann nowhere considers the three chapters a significant context for the verse, and indeed the essay itself is scarcely an exegetical one ("Christ the End of the Law" in *Essays Philosophical and Theological*, tr. J. C. G. Greig [London: SCM, 1955; original, 1940] 36-66).

[6]Dodd, *Romans*, 150. Cf. also H. Lietzmann, *An die Römer* HNT 3.1 (Tübingen: J. C. B. Mohr [Paul Siebeck], 1928³) 89-107. R. Scroggs ("Paul as Rhetorician: Two Homilies in Romans 1-11" in *Jews, Greeks, and Christians*, ed. R. Hamerton-Kelly and R. Scroggs, [Leiden: Brill, 1976] 271-298) argues that Romans 1-4, 9-11 and Romans 5-8 once existed separately as sermons Paul preached to Jewish and Gentile congregations respectively. This variation on Dodd's speculation begins with the same perception of disjunction at 9:1, but sees 9-11 as more integrally related to 1-4 than does Dodd. J. Kinoshita ("Romans—Two Writings Combined: A New Interpretation of the Body of Romans," *NovT* 7 [1965] 258-277) proposes another suggestion, that a non-Pauline "Manual of Instruction on Jewish Problems" was inserted by a later redactor into the original Apostolic letter at 2:1-5; 2:17-3:20; 3:27-4:24; 5:12-7:25; 9:1-11:36; 14:1-15:3; 15:4-13. Cf. also J. C. O'Neill, *Paul's Letter to the Romans* (Baltimore: Penguin, 1975) 11.

[7]J. A. T. Robinson, *Wrestling With Romans* (Philadelphia: Westminster, 1979) 108; emphasis his.

tendency of the Epistle, as well as of the historical circumstances in which it originated."[8] From Baur's perspective on the growth of the early church as characterized by struggle between Jewish and Gentile factions, Paul's subordination of the claims of historic Israel to the universalism of the gospel moves the church toward its ultimate Catholic synthesis. Romans 9-11 then become "the centre and pith of the whole [letter], to which everything else is only an addition."[9] Baur's comprehensive historical reconstruction was, of course, fraught with major difficulties, not the least being his assumption that the Roman church was composed primarily of *Jewish*-Christians.[10] His perception of the central importance of chapters 9-11 to the entire argument of Romans has nevertheless survived the demise of the Tübingen program, and is now defended with renewed vigor—and for different reasons[11]—by J. Christiaan Beker, Nils A. Dahl, W. G. Kümmel, Johannes Munck, Krister Stendahl, and others.[12] Bent Noack has wide support for his claim that, "We must stop speaking of Romans i-viii and Romans ix-xi as two separate parts of the epistle."[13]

---

[8]F. C. Baur, *Paul the Apostle of Jesus Christ: His Life and Works, His Epistles and Teachings*, tr. A. Menzies (Edinburgh: Williams and Norgate, 1873[2]) 327.

[9]*Ibid.*

[10]See Kümmel, "Die Probleme von Römer 9-11," 16-17, 24.

[11]The diversity among these interpreters is not to be minimized by grouping them together this way. What they share is a fundamental conviction that chapters 9-11 are essential to the full argument of the letter, although they differ greatly about the details of that relationship and the interpretation of the argument itself.

[12]Beker, *Paul*, 63-97; N. A. Dahl, "The Future of Israel" in *Studies in Paul: Theology for the Early Christian Mission* (Minneapolis: Augsburg, 1977) 137-158; W. G. Kümmel, "Die Probleme von Römer 9-11," 13-33; Munck, *Paul*; idem, *Christ and Israel: An Interpretation of Romans 9-11*, tr. I. Nixon (Philadelphia: Fortress, 1967); K. Stendahl, *Paul Among Jews and Gentiles* (Philadelphia: Fortress, 1976); S. Neill, *The Interpretation of the New Testament: 1861-1961* (Oxford: University, 1964) 184; F.-W. Marquardt, *Die Juden in Römerbrief* (Theologische Studien 10 [Zürich: Theologischer, 1971]) 3; Sanders, *Paul*, 488-490; R. E. Brown and J. P. Meier, *Antioch and Rome: New Testament Cradles of Catholic Christianity* (New York: Paulist, 1983) 122; R. Jewett, "Romans as an Ambassadorial Letter," *Int* 36 (1982) 5-20.

[13]B. Noack, "Current and Backwater in the Epistle to the Romans," *ST* 19 (1965) 157.

114   *Function of Apocalyptic and Wisdom Traditions*

Karl Barth's commentary on Romans and his exegesis of 9-11 in his *Church Dogmatics* introduced the possibility of a middle stance between Baur's assertion of the centrality of Romans 9-11 and the conventional 'postscript' view. In this traditionally Lutheran outline, chapters 9-11 simply recapitulate the argument of 1-8 and explore the implications of the doctrine of justification in a specific context, the role of Israel in salvation history. The Jew in Romans is thus allegorized as the prototypical *homo religiosus*.[14] The problem of Israel's unbelief in Romans 9-11 then becomes the story of the church's unbelief.[15] The influence of Barth's Lutheran position has been widespread. For Ernst Käsemann, Israel is the primary example, but nonetheless only an example of God's justification of the ungodly: "In and with Israel [Paul] strikes at the hidden Jew in all of us,"[16] "the archetype of the religious [person] in general."[17] Thus the argument of Romans 9-11, like a sermon illustration, "repeats the argument of the whole letter."[18] Although in his *Commentary on Romans* Käsemann moderates his position somewhat ('Israel' is no longer simply a cipher for 'the religious person'), the issue in chapters 9-11 is nevertheless "an

[14]K. Barth, *The Epistle to the Romans*, tr. E. C. Hoskyns (London: Oxford, 1933 6) 55-76, 330-423; *Church Dogmatics*, ed. G. W. Bromiley and T. F. Torrance (Edinburgh: T & T Clark, 1957) II/2, 215-336. As Stendahl points out, a component of Barth's strategy stands in a long tradition of Lutheran exegesis that ignores the historical context of Paul's struggle to bring Jews and Gentiles together in the church and instead reads in his letters the individual's struggle with a guilty conscience (*Paul Among Jews and Gentiles*, 78-96).

[15]See Beker, *Paul*, 64 for discussion of the exegetical implications of Barth's method. For a more sympathetic appraisal, see C. E. B. Cranfield, *A Critical and Exegetical Commentary on the Epistle to the Romans* (Edinburgh: T & T Clark, 1979) 448-450.

[16]E. Käsemann, "Paul and Israel" in *New Testament Questions of Today*, tr. W. J. Montague (London: SCM, 1969) 184. Cf. also idem, "Justification and Salvation History in the Epistle to the Romans" in *Perspectives on Paul*, tr. M. Kohl (Philadelphia: Fortress, 1971) 60-78.

[17]E. Käsemann, "The Righteousness of God in Paul" in *New Testament Questions of Today*, 179. Cf. also Bultmann's characterization: "A specifically human striving has merely taken on its culturally, and in point of time, individually distinct form in Judaism. For it is, in fact a striving common to all [people] to gain recognition of one's achievement; and this generates pride" ("Christ the End of the Law," 43).

[18]Käsemann, "Paul and Israel," 186.

example of God's faithfulness and [human] unfaithfulness in conflict,"[19] and "the justification of the ungodly is here again the secret theme of the problem raised."[20] Others who similarly see Romans 9-11 as an illustration of Paul's basic doctrine of justification or else a special problem arising from it are C. E. B. Cranfield, Günther Bornkamm, C. K. Barrett, and Anders Nygren.[21]

A fourth alternative is adopted by those who think Romans 9-11 provide a delayed conclusion to the unfinished argument of 3:1-9. These

---

[19]E. Käsemann, *Commentary on Romans*, tr. G. W. Bromiley (Grand Rapids: Eerdmans, 1980[4]) 256. Cf. also his assessment of Rom 1:18-3:20, where "the total emphasis increasingly involves criticism of religious humanity, specifically *represented* by Judaism" (33; emphasis added).

[20]*Ibid.*, 260.

[21]G. Bornkamm, *Paul*, tr. D. M. G. Stalker (New York: Harper and Row, 1971) 149-151; Cranfield, *Romans*, 446. Cf. A. Nygren, *Commentary on Romans*, tr. C. Rasmussen (Philadelphia: Fortress, 1949) 353-408. Noack observes that Nygren in his first edition (*Pauli brev till Romarna* [Stockholm: Svenska Kyrkans Diakonistyrekes, 1944] 360) also considered Romans 9-11 to have "a clearly circumscribed and absolutely necessary function" ("Current and Backwater," 156). C. K. Barrett (*A Commentary on the Epistle to the Romans* [New York: Harper and Row, 1957]) finds the continuity between Romans 1-8 and 9-11 in the fact that both are concerned with "the character and deeds of God who is the source of salvation [1-8] ...and...the character and deeds of God who elected the Jews and now calls the Gentiles [9-11]" (175). Similarly R. C. H. Lenski, *The Interpretation of St. Paul's Epistle to the Romans* (Columbus, OH: Book Concern, 1936) 583-584; R. A. Harrisville, *Romans* (Augsburg Commentary on the New Testament; Minneapolis: Augsburg, 1980) 142; G. Eichholz, *Die Theologie des Paulus im Umriss* (Neukirchen-Vluyn: Neukirchener, 1972) 284-289.

Still other interpreters understand the three chapters to answer hypothetical objections to the argument of 1-8 rather than simply to illustrate it. For H. C. G. Moule (*The Epistle of Paul the Apostle to the Romans* [Cambridge: University, 1952] 40), "St. Paul now turns from the abstract explanation of the ways of Divine Grace, to the discussion of one great and anxious concrete phenomenon. There is a subtle connexion of thought in the transition: the freedom of the Christian's justification, the security of his standing, and the splendour of his hopes, bring up by way of contrast the dark fact of the unbelief of Israel." Somewhat similar is Godet's description of the "masterpiece of the philosophy of history" (*Romans*, 104; see above, n. 3, p. 111).

interpreters claim neither that chapters 9-11 are the climax of the letter nor that they are merely an expansion of the main point. Robinson, for example, goes to great lengths to demonstrate continuity between 3:1-9 and 9:1-11:36,[22] but sees no substantial correlation with the logic of the rest of the letter. Romans 9-11 are not an unimportant appendix to 1-8 (the traditional interpretation); 1-8 are not a relatively unimportant prelude to 9-11 (Baur's interpretation); nor do 9-11 repeat the argument of 1-8 (Barth's interpretation). According to Robinson, Romans 9-11 develop one point raised earlier in the letter (3:1-9).[23]

B. Romans 9-11 as Integral to the Letter

When judging the appropriateness of these four basic options for locating chapters 9-11 in the logic of the letter, several factors support a qualified endorsement of Baur's position, that is, the reading of 9-11 as central rather than peripheral or merely illustrative. Although Baur underestimated the function of chapters 1-8 and therefore overstated the place of 9-11, his perception that the issue of God's dealings with Jew and Gentile is crucial to the whole of Romans was on target. This can be seen by looking at four factors.

First of all, there is the matter of the letter's contingent purpose. In the growing scholarly concern to take seriously the historically contingent origins of the letter, Baur's legacy is rightly claimed by those who argue

---

[22]Robinson, *Romans*, 108-109. H. L. Ellison puts this position most colorfully when he calls 3:1-9 "footnotes" that refer the reader to chapters 9-11 for a fuller explanation of what is meant (*The Mystery of Israel* [Grand Rapids: Eerdmans, 1966] 25).

[23]Cf. also P. J. Achtemeier, *Romans* (Atlanta: John Knox, 1985) 153, for whom the "glimpse of the future [in 8:31-39]...puts into sharp relief a question that has been in the *background* of Paul's whole discussion.... That problem is the persistent unbelief of God's chosen people" (emphasis added). P. Benoit ("Conclusion par mode de synthese" in *Die Israelfrage*, 217-218) claims there are some thematic relationships between 1-8 and 9-11, although the passage's unity nevertheless sets it somewhat apart from the preceding discussion of justification. H. Ridderbos (*Paul: An Outline of His Theology*, tr. J. R. de Witt [Grand Rapids: Eerdmans, 1975; original 1966] 355) remarks that at Romans 9 Paul "returns once more—and now in a much more concentrated and detailed manner—to this acknowledgement [in 3:1-9] of Israel's privileges." Cf. idem, *Aan de Romeinen* (Kampen: J. H. Kok, 1959) 203-204.

against the older view of Romans as "a compendium of Pauline dogma in the form of an apostolic letter."[24] A number of occasions for Paul's writing have been suggested,[25] but it seems best to concede with Beker a "convergence of motivations,"[26] among which the fate of Paul's collection for Jerusalem and the relationship between Jews and Gentiles in the Roman church rank highest on the list.[27] The fact that Paul writes to a mixed congregation of Jews and Gentiles (Romans 14-15) on the eve of his delivery of the collection to Jerusalem (15:30) suggests that Ἰουδαίῳ τέ

---

[24]Baur, *Paul*, 323-324.

[25]See, for example, the options presented in *The Romans Debate*, ed. K. P. Donfried (Minneapolis: Augsburg, 1977).

[26]Beker, *Paul*, 71-74; similarly H. Y. Gamble, *The Textual History of the Letter to the Romans: A Study in Textual and Literary Criticism* SD 42 (Grand Rapids: Eerdmans, 1977) 137.

[27]J. Jervell argues that "the essential and primary content of Romans...is a reflection upon...the defense which Paul plans to give before the church in Jerusalem" ("The Letter to Jerusalem" in *The Romans Debate*, 64). Alternatively, W. Wiefel claims Romans "was written to assist the Gentile Christian majority, who are the primary addressees of the letter, to live together with the Jewish Christians [recently returned from Claudian exile] in one congregation, thereby putting an end to their quarrels about status" ("The Jewish Community in Rome and the Origins of Roman Christianity" in *The Romans Debate*, 113; similarly P. S. Minear, *The Obedience of Faith* [London: SCM, 1971] 1-36; and W. Marxsen, *Introduction to the New Testament*, tr. G. Buswell [Philadelphia: Fortress, 1968] 95-104). Beker's point is that the epistolary context cannot be limited either to Paul's situation or that of the Roman church alone, but that both bear on the occasion of the letter. Given the profoundly theological—rather than ecclesiological—focus of the entire letter (it is the righteousness of *God* that is under discussion), surely anticipation of Paul's defense of his ministry has exercised considerable influence on the development of his argument. Romans is nonetheless a letter rather than simply a "brief" or "dress rehearsal" for his impending Jerusalem encounter. The Roman Christians are addressees not only because of their supposed influence in ecclesiastical diplomacy, but also because their contingent circumstances— including apparent friction between Jews and Gentiles—appropriately merit apostolic reflection and response. The integrity, constancy, and righteousness of God demand the oneness of the church, demonstrated both by Paul's presentation in Jerusalem and the unity of the Roman congregation.

πρῶτον καὶ Ἕλληνι (1:16; 2:9-10) is not merely another rhetorical cliché parallel to those in 1:14.[28] The repeated mentions of Jew and Gentile in the same breath[29]—as well as references to each ethnic group alone[30]—are surely more than incidental to a letter that devotes three long chapters to the subject of the relationship between Jews and Gentile Christians and their respective situations before God.

The issue of Jew and Gentile is central to the entire letter, announced at 1:16 where the gospel is described as "the power of God for salvation to everyone who believes [that is, to Jew and Gentile alike], to the Jew first and also to the Greek." Throughout the first four chapters, although God judges Jews and Gentiles alike to be under the power of sin, and all are similarly justified by faith (1:16; 2:11; 3:9; 3:22; etc.), Paul three times reiterates Jewish priority and advantage (1:16; 2:9-10; 3:1-2). Moreover, even when Paul is most careful to place Jews and Gentiles on the same footing before God, he still maintains their different identities. At 3:30, where the very oneness of God demonstrates God's impartial judgment, the circumcised are judged ἐκ πίστεως and the uncircumcised διὰ τῆς πίστεως. There is no substantial difference between the prepositions here, and the two phrases are clearly parallel.[31] Paul retains the relative uniqueness of Israel and the Gentiles, even as he disallows ethnic or religious claims to preferred status before God. So also, at 4:11-12, Abraham is the father of all those who follow in his faithful footsteps, both circumcised and uncircumcised believers.[32]

The subject of Jew and Gentile is not mentioned explicitly in chapters 5-8, although the question of the role of God's law in the economy of salvation, an issue at the very heart of Jewish-Gentile relations in the church, is dealt with several times (5:12-21, 6:15, 7:1ff, 8:2-4).[33] As

---

[28]"Greeks and barbarians, wise and foolish" (1:14) are common designations for "everyone"; cf. *tôb wera* , i.e., "everything" in Gen 2:17.

[29]1:16; 2:9-10; 3:9, 29; 9:24, 30-31; 10:12; 11:25; 15:10

[30]Gentiles alone—1:5, 13; 2:14, 24; 4:17; 11:11, 13; 15:9-12, 16, 18, 27; 16:4, 26. Jews alone—2:17, 28-29; 3:1, 29.

[31]A broad consensus reflected by Käsemann, *Romans*, 104; N. A. Dahl, "The One God of Jews and Gentiles (Romans 3:29-30)" in *Studies in Paul*, 189.

[32]I am grateful to Professor P. W. Meyer for this observation.

[33]This is the most troubling weakness in Scroggs's often intriguing argument ("Paul as Rhetorician," see above, n.6). If Romans 5-8 is a sermon designed for Gentile audiences (Scroggs does not even identify them

Hendrikus Boers has noticed,[34] every one of the rhetorical questions asked in Romans 1-11[35] serves to mark a transition in the argument, and each one concerns the problem of the Jews and the law. Although the correspondence is greatest between the questions of 3:1-9 and those in 9:1-11:32,[36] the consistency with which Paul advances his case by reference to Israel and the law throughout the letter is impressive. The topic is taken up explicitly yet once again in 15:7-10 with a summary statement of the points scored in 11:13-27. Christ's servanthood to Israel functions to establish both the promises to the patriarchs and the Gentiles' glorifying of God (15:8-9).[37] The string of Bible verses invoked at 15:9-12 to prove that Christ establishes both Israel's salvation and the inclusion of the Gentiles also sets

---

as godfearing Gentiles who might have some investment in the law), then why does Paul make such labored and repeated attempts to justify the place of the law in salvation history? The first person plural of 7:6 alone is enough to raise doubts about an exclusively Gentile audience.

[34]"The Problem of Jews and Gentiles in the Macro-Structure of Romans," *Neotestamentica* 15 (1981) 1-11.

[35]3:1; 3:3b; 3:5c; 3:9; 3:27a; 3:31; 4:1; 4:9; 6:1; 6:15; 7:7; 7:13; 8:31; 9:14; 9:19; 9:30; 11:1; 11:7; 11:11; 11:19. Boers neglects to mention 10:18 and 19, although they too support his thesis. On the rhetorical questions in 9-11, see further below, pp. 144-145.

[36]"Note also that the issues raised in the first two questions in 3:1 and 3 are taken up again in the last four in 11:1, 7, 11, 19. The question concerning the untrustworthiness of some in Israel, raised in 3:3, is taken up again in 11:1, and answered conclusively by what Paul remembers about Elijah in 11:2-5. The question concerning the extra of the Jew and the value of circumcision which he raised in 3:1, and confirmed and answered in only a very preliminary way in verse 2, before he was side-tracked by the question of verse 3, is answered conclusively by the reference to the wild branches that were grafted in on the cultured olive tree, and 11:17-32, after the side-tracking question of 3:3 was answered by the reference to Elijah in 11:2-5. The answer is given in a nutshell in the provocative exclamation of 11:18. 'It is not you who bear the roots, but the roots you!' Once all this has been achieved, Paul has no difficulty in concluding the entire argument with the doxology of 11:33-36" (Boers, "The Problem of Jews and Gentiles," 3-4).

[37]On the relation of 15:7-12 to chapters 9-11, see J. T. Koenig, "The Jewishness of the Gospel: Reflections By A Lutheran," *Journal of Ecumenical Studies* 19 (1982) 64-67.

the two groups side by side (cf. particularly v 10: ἔθνη μετὰ τοῦ λαοῦ αὐτοῦ).

Thus the theme of God's dealings with Jew and Gentile runs throughout the letter so consistently that the specific discussion of Israel *coram deo* in 9-11 can hardly be less than essential to the whole argument. The extended discussion of Israel's place in the economy of salvation is the final resolution of a tension inherent in the letter from the very statement of its theme (1:16): God is absolutely impartial in judgment and salvation, but Israel nevertheless has salvation-historical advantage. This tension in Paul's argument between God's impartiality and faithfulness to Israel provides the conceptual framework for the whole letter. God's impartial treatment of all can never be seen as abandonment of God's elect, but neither can God's faithfulness to Israel be construed as partiality. Everything Paul has to say about justification and life in the Spirit depends on these twin aspects of God's consistent righteousness.

The second reason 9-11 must be seen as integral to the letter is that two themes, those of "boasting" and "works", present in the earlier parts of the letter reappear and are resolved in Romans 9-11. The entire letter is composed of interlocking arguments (σύγχυσις) whose conclusions are often delayed until succeeding sections are introduced or even completed (e.g., 3:1-9, 4:15-16, 5:20a, etc.).[38] Chapters 2-5 deal with contrasts between true and false boasting,[39] excluding Jewish boasting in the law and describing the believer's rightful boasting in Christ.[40] The corresponding warning against Gentile boasting appears in 11:18. So also, the argument of chapters 9-11 appears to be structured, at least in part, by repeated contrasts with ἔργα, another theme that is prominent earlier in the letter:[41]

---

[38]See S. K. Stowers, *The Diatribe and Paul's Letter to the Romans* SBLDS 57 (Chico: Scholars, 1981); Dahl, "Israel," 139ff; W. A. Meeks, *The Writings of St. Paul* (New York: W. W. Norton, 1972) 68; E. Gaugler, *Der Brief an die Römer* (Zurich: Zwingli, 1945-1952) vol. 1, 71, for brief discussions of this stylistic feature of Romans, and G. Kennedy, *New Testament Interpretation Through Rhetorical Criticism* (Chapel Hill: University of North Carolina, 1984) 89, for a similar analysis of 2 Cor 2:14-6:13.

[39]2:17, 23; 3:27; 4:2; 5:2, 3, 11.

[40]Cf. also 15:17, rightful apostolic boasting.

[41]2:6, 15; 3:20, 27, 28; 4:2, 6. This phenomenon provides the strongest evidence for Barth's case that chapters 9-11 recapitulate 1-8 (see above, pp. 114-115). But rather than really substantiating such a claim, this

9:6-29	Election is based not on works but on God who calls—cf. 9:12 ἐξ ἔργων. . .τοῦ καλοῦντος
9:30-10:21	Israel's hardening is evident in its understanding of righteousness as from works, not faith—cf. 9:32 ἐκ πίστεως. . .ἐξ ἔργων
11:1-32	God's salvation of both Jew and Gentile is a function not of works, but of grace—cf. 11:6 χάριτι. . .ἐξ ἔργων. . .χάρις

A third reason for seeing chapters 9-11 as essential to the full argument of Romans is, as Dahl points out, that elements of epistolary style are more prevalent in 9-11 than in 1:16-8:39. He concludes on this basis that "in Romans 9-11 Paul not only unfolds the theological theme of the letter as a whole, but also addresses the epistolary situation more directly than in most parts of Romans 1-8."[42] For that reason, Dahl regards the doxology of 11:33-36 as the conclusion not only to chapters 9-11, but to the entire argument of the letter to that point.[43]

Finally, the consistent theological theme of the letter requires that chapters 9-11 be seen as integral to its full argument. Barth's claim that 9-11 recapitulate the argument of 1-8 correctly identifies the essential continuity of the letter's argument, but ignores the fact that Israel's status is by no means left unmentioned until 9:1. If 9-11 were no more than an illustration of the principle of justification, the subject of Israel and the Gentiles would not figure so prominently prior to those chapters. Nowhere in the letter is this specific problem of Jew and Gentile in clearer or more extended focus than in chapters 9-11, but it is present from the beginning as the starting point of the argument. The God who raised Jesus from the dead is the God of Israel revealed in scripture (1:3-4). But the redemption God is

---

prominence of the contrast between ἔργα and call/faith/grace in 9-11 simply demonstrates the fact that Paul's doctrine of justification is a product of his argument that Jew and Gentile fare alike before God.

[42]E.g., expressions of personal feeling (9:1-5; 10:1-2), use of ἀδελφοί (10:1; 11:25), the conventional introductory formula οὐ γὰρ θέλω ὑμᾶς ἀγνοεῖν (11:25), and so on (Dahl, "Israel," 140-141).

[43]*Ibid.*, 157; cf. Ellison, *Mystery,* 27.

effecting in Jesus is for Gentiles as well as for Jews (1:13). Both
affirmations—God's faithfulness and consistency toward Israel, and God's
impartial treatment of all—together provoke Paul's understanding of
justification. It is his refusal to relax the tension between the two that
results in his doctrine of justification. The universality of the gospel as Paul
preaches it in Romans is a function of his wrestling with the relationship
between Jew and Gentile in the plan of salvation; his doctrine of *iustificatio
impii* is not an abstract notion from which he draws various concrete object
lessons.

> We could say that Romans 9-11 illustrates Paul's doctrine of
> justification by faith. However, we express ourselves more
> correctly when we say that from the beginning Paul's view of the
> relation of Israel to the Gentiles profoundly shaped his doctrine of
> justification. Only later, especially in the thought of Augustine and
> of Luther, did the doctrine of justification become fundamentally
> important apart from the problem of Israel and the Gentiles.[44]

Rather than providing concrete illustration of the doctrine of justification,
the standings before God of historic Israel and Gentile Christianity are for
Paul what occasion his particular formulation of the doctrine in Romans.
Because God is both completely impartial—judging and redeeming Jew and
Gentile on the same terms—and completely faithful to Israel, Paul's
argument about the righteousness of God in Romans is not complete
without chapters 9-11.

These factors—the contingent purpose of Romans, its literary structure,
its epistolary style, and its consistent theological theme—demonstrate that
the argument begun in 1:16 continues, despite the transition between
chapters 8 and 9, to its conclusion at 11:28-32. Rather than being a
postscript to the main body or its recapitulation, Romans 9-11 are instead
central to the argument of the whole letter. Baur correctly saw the centrality
of 9-11, but for the wrong reasons: it is not the historical problem of the
relationship between Jews and Gentiles in the church, but the theological

---

[44]Dahl, "Israel," 156. Cf. also Stendahl: "This problem [Jews and
Gentiles] was, however, not a live one after the end of the first century,
when Christianity for all practical purposes had a non-Jewish constituency.
Yet it was not until Augustine that the Pauline thought about the Law and
Justification was applied in a consistent and grand style to a more general
and timeless human problem" ("The Apostle Paul and the Introspective
Conscience of the West" in *Paul Among Jews and Gentiles*, 85).

problem of the righteousness of God who deals with both Israel and the church which prompts Paul's argument in Romans. That argument must of necessity address the issues raised in 9-11—witness their mention early in the letter (3:1-9)--before it can conclude that "God has consigned all to disobedience in order that he might have mercy on all" (11:32).

Having determined the place in the letter of Romans 9-11, we now move on to ask in what ways confluent apocalyptic and wisdom traditions contribute to the argumentation of the three chapters, and in this way to understand their structure and function in the letter. We do so in three stages: by locating the apocalyptic and wisdom traditions present in 9:1-11:32, by tracing the functions of those intersecting traditions in the argument of the three chapters, and by examining the role of the concluding wisdom hymn in 11:33-36.

II. The Confluence of Apocalyptic and Wisdom Traditions

Romans 9-11 are part of neither an apocalypse nor a wisdom book, but a letter. The chapters are marked by a style of argumentation more common among philosophical teachers[45] than among sages or visionaries. Paul nevertheless employs a number of motifs from both apocalyptic and wisdom literature, and it is to those motifs—and the function of their intersection in the argument—that we now turn.

Since this passage is from neither of the literary genres examined in Chapter Two, but from a letter that is one of several from the same hand, it may be necessary to add further comparative criteria to the search for confluent traditions. Paul's own vocabulary, style, use of traditional material, and so on, are as revealing of his theological background and purposes as are any individual similarities his letters might bear to other kinds of literature. Although the Apostle does not write apocalypses, he does refer to "the abundance of revelations" he has received (2 Cor 12:1-7), and heavenly mysteries to which he is privy (1 Cor 2:7; 15:51; Rom 11:25), all of which concern the eschatological plan of salvation. The claim that a given motif is sapiential or apocalyptic in character may therefore on occasion be documented not only by reference to wisdom books and apocalypses, but also by parallels within the Pauline corpus.

---

[45]"In the letter Paul presents himself to the Romans as a teacher. The dialogical style of the diatribe is central to this self-presentation.... In Romans...Paul uses the style of indictment and protreptic and presents himself to the Roman Christians not as a spiritual father and guide, but as a 'philosophical' or religious-ethical teacher" (Stowers, *The Diatribe and Paul's Letter to the Romans*, 179).

A. Apocalyptic Traditions

Apocalyptic material in Romans 9-11 can be discerned in three ways: thematically, linguistically, and stylistically.

(1) Thematic evidence. To begin with, Paul's wrestling with the nature and destiny of Israel is itself the central theme of two apocalypses we have already examined. 4 Ezra and 2 Baruch both respond to a threat to historic Israel's integrity and future as the people of God by promising an eschatological solution they have discerned by revelation. So too Paul reveals a heavenly μυστήριον concerning Israel's fate (11:25). While the perceived danger is different—Paul reacts not to the destruction of Jerusalem, but to the possibility that God has shifted loyalty from Israel to the Gentiles—the dynamics of response are the same. Ezra asks, "Why has Israel been given over to the Gentiles?" (4 Ez 4:23); Baruch asks, "If you destroy your city and deliver up your country to those who hate us, how will the name of Israel be remembered again?" (2 Bar 3:5); and Paul asks, "Has God rejected his people?" (Rom 11:1). Jeopardized national survival calls into question God's faithfulness to his elect, and each of these authors responds ultimately by pointing to revelation:

It shall be that whoever remains after all that I have foretold to you shall be saved and shall see my salvation and the end of my world (4 Ez 6:25).

The Most High...revealed to me a word that I might be comforted, and showed me visions that I might not be again sorrowful (2 Bar 81:4).

Lest you be wise in your own conceits, I want you to understand this mystery,[46] brethren: a hardening has come upon part of Israel until the full number of the Gentiles come in, and so all Israel will be saved (Rom 11:25-26).

Both 4 Ezra and 2 Baruch speak of the 'full number' of the elect as a prelude to the eschaton, even as Paul discusses the πλήρωμα of Israel (11:12) and of the Gentiles (11:25):[47]

---

[46]See futher below, p. 129, on the revelatory nature of μυστήριον for Paul.

[47]Cf. also Rev 6:11; 7:4; 14:1. See Käsemann, *Romans*, 313; Michel, *Römer*, 241. See also 1 En 10:20-22, in which the righteousness of Israel is

Did not the souls of the righteous in their chambers ask about these matters, saying, 'How long are we to remain here? And when will come the harvest of our reward?' And Jeremiel the archangel answered them and said, 'When the number of those like yourselves is completed; for he [God] has weighed the age in the balance, and measured the times by measure, and numbered the times by number; and he will not move or arouse them until that measure is fulfilled' (4 Ez 4:35-37).

For when Adam sinned and death was decreed against those who were to be born, the multitude of those who would be born was numbered. And for that number a place was prepared where the living ones might live and where the dead might be preserved. No creature will live again unless the number that has been appointed is completed (2 Bar 23:4-5).

Furthermore, the belief that the eschaton will follow 'all' Israel's repentance was apparently widespread in early Judaism, particularly apocalyptic texts.[48] For example, T.Dan. 6:4 warns that "the enemy is eager to trip up all who call on the Lord, because he knows that on the day in which Israel trusts, the enemy's kingdom will be brought to an end."[49] And a similar tradition probably stands behind Acts 3:19-20—"therefore repent and turn back in order that your sins might be wiped out, so that times of refreshment might come from the presence of the Lord and he

---

a prelude to Gentile faith, even if a precise causal relationship between the two is not outlined:
> And you cleanse the earth from all injustice, and from all defilement, and from all oppression, and from all sin, and from all iniquity which is being done on earth; remove them from the earth. And all the children of the people will become righteous, and all the nations shall worship and bless me; and they will all prostrate themselves to me.

[48]D. C. Allison, "The Background of Romans 11:11-15 in Apocalyptic and Rabbinic Literature," *Studia Biblica et Theologica* 10 (1980) 229-234.

[49]Cf. also T.Sim. 6:2-7; T.Jud. 23:5; As.Mos. 1:18; 2 Bar 78:6-7; Apoc.Abr. 23:5; contrast 4 Ez 4:38-43.

might send you the appointed Christ"[50] (cf. 2 Pet 3:11-12, σπεύδοντας τὴν παρουσίαν τῆς τοῦ θεοῦ ἡμέρας). Dale Allison notes that the traditional pattern of thought among these and later rabbinic texts[51] contains three elements:

(1) Contemporary Israel has missed the mark and must repent.
(2) Before the end comes, [Israel] will repent.
(3) When [it] does, the end will come.[52]

Although Paul more or less reproduces the traditional sequence, he refuses to highlight Israel's repentance, and emphasizes instead God's mercy.

> Paul by-passes the notion of repentance and places God's gracious activity at center stage.... [I]t is God who guarantees salvation, not any human work. Nevertheless, the eschatological sequence of Rom. 11:11-15 has antecedents in Jewish literature.[53]

One further theme familiar from some apocalypses is Paul's claim that God bears the vessels of wrath with much long-suffering (9:22; cf. 3:25-26), that he patiently withholds his wrath until an appointed time.[54] 2 Bar 59:6 lists among the warnings of the end time "the suppression of wrath [and] the abundance of long-suffering," and Ezra marvels "For how long the time is that the Most High has been patient with those who inhabit the world, and not for their sake, but because of the times which he has foreordained" (4 Ez 7:[74]).

These themes—the eschatological salvation of Israel, the notion of the "full number" of the elect, the anticipation of "all" Israel's salvation, and God's patient suppression of wrath—are standard apocalyptic themes that play a significant role in Paul's argument in Romans 9-11.[55]

---

[50]See P. F. Feiler, "Jesus the Prophet: The Lukan Portrayal of Jesus as the Prophet Like Moses" (Ph.D. Dissertation, Princeton Theological Seminary, 1986) 57-59.

[51]E.g., B.Sanh.97b; b.Sabb.118b; Sifre Deut.41 (Allison, "Background," 230).

[52]*Ibid.*, 231.

[53]*Ibid.*, 232.

[54]Käsemann, *Romans*, 270.

[55]Because these traditions are so widespread, it is hardly necessary to postulate Paul's literary dependence on any particular Jewish documents. Although it is of course possible he was familiar with 1 Enoch, he could

(2) Linguistic evidence. Paul employs a good bit of vocabulary in Romans 9-11 that not only reflects attitudes common in apocalyptic contexts generally, but ideas in his own letters which customarily carry apocalyptic weight.

a. ὀργή. In 9:22, God bears with much long suffering the σκεύη ὀργῆς in order ἐνδείξασθαι τὴν ὀργήν. The notion of God's wrath is central to the letter. It is revealed (ἀποκαλύπτειν) from heaven against human godlessness and injustice (1:18), executed by God's servants in positions of civil authority (13:4, 5), and promised repeatedly for the last judgment (2:5, 8; 3:5; 5:9; 12:19). That God's wrath has both historical and eschatological manifestations is of course common in Judaism and Christianity,[56] and as Paul's characterization of the vessels of wrath as κατηρτισμένα εἰς ἀπώλειαν clearly indicates, he considers ὀργή part and parcel of the apocalyptic scenario.[57]

b. δόξα. Similarly, the glory for which the vessels of mercy are prepared (9:23; cf. 9:4) is that eschatological δόξα θεοῦ (5:2) in which Christian hope consists (cf. 8:18, 21) and which defines the character and power of God (cf. 1:23; 3:7, 23; 4:20; 6:4; 11:36; 15:7). God's glory is that final apocalyptic vindication of God's sovereignty which will be shared with the elect. Koch notes the almost "catch-word" nature of glory in Jewish apocalyptic literature,[58] and Paul's use of προητοίμασεν εἰς confirms that meaning in the Romans 9 context as well,[59] parallel as it is to ἀπώλειαν (v 22).

c. καταισχύνω. Just as ὀργή and δόξα are properties of the end time, so is Paul's use of καταισχύνω in the Isa 28:16 citation at Rom 9:33 and 10:11, significantly in the future passive. Of the twelve other instances

---

hardly have read 4 Ezra or 2 Baruch. The point remains that these apocalyptic ideas are sufficiently prominent in Paul's religious environment as to constitute part of the standard theological resources available to him.

[56]G. Stählin, "ὀργή, κ.τ.λ.," 430-447; cf. Beker, *Paul*, 192-194; Käsemann, *Romans*, 269-272.

[57]Cf. particularly Rom 2:5; 5:9; 1 Thess 1:10; 5:9.

[58]*Rediscovery*, 28-32. Cf. Chapter Two above, p. 68, n. 45.

[59]Beker, *Paul*, 362-393; cf. G. Kittel, "δοκέω, κ.τ.λ." in *TDNT* (1964) vol. 2, 249-251.

of αἰσχύνομαι and related words in the Pauline corpus,[60] six refer to eschatological shame—either the possible failure of the apostolic mission (2 Cor 9:4; 10:8; Phil 1:20),[61] or of Christian hope in general (Rom 1:16; 5:5; 1 Cor 1:27). Rom 5:5 provides the clearest parallel to the Isaiah citation in 9:33,[62] and since 'not being put to shame' and 'being saved' are clearly parallel in 10:11-12 (cf. also 1:16), it appears certain Paul considers Isa 28:16 to promise protection from shame at the last judgment to those who believe in the rock of stumbling.

d. σῴζω. The complex of salvation language (σῴζω, σωτηρία, ῥύομαι) in Romans 9-11 further witnesses to Paul's apocalyptic world view (9:27; 10:1, 9, 10, 13; 11:11, 14, 26). Salvation is exclusively a future reality for Paul,[63] grounded in the death and resurrection of Jesus, but to be fully accomplished only at his parousia.[64] The ῥυόμενος of Isa 59:20 in Paul's oracular mystery at Rom 11:26 is most likely Ἰησοῦς ὁ ῥυόμενος ἡμᾶς ἐκ τῆς ὀργῆς τῆς ἐρχομένης (1 Thess 1:10), since he is the agent of the God who raises the dead, who delivers from danger, and may be trusted again to deliver (2 Cor 1:10).[65]

e. ζωή. That Paul considers the phenomena of Gentile faith and Israel's hardening and ultimate salvation to be marks of the end time is attested by his use of ζωὴ ἐκ νεκρῶν at 11:15. Israel's temporary rejection has meant the reconciliation of the world, but Israel's full reception will mean nothing less than life from the dead. This life is what Paul commonly calls ζωὴν αἰώνιον (Rom 2:7; 5:21; 6:22, 23; Gal 6:8), life which is granted by the God who raises the dead/makes the dead alive (Rom 4:17, 24; 8:11; 2 Cor 1:9; etc.). All this is derived from the widespread Jewish apocalyptic notion that the resurrection attends the eschaton.[66]

---

[60]Rom 1:16; 5:5; 6:21; 1 Cor 1:27 (x 2); 11:4, 5, 22; 2 Cor 7:14; 9:4; 10:8; Phil 1:20.

[61]Cf. 2 Cor 7:14, where the averted disappointment is present rather than eschatological.

[62]Käsemann, *Romans*, 279.

[63]Note particularly Rom 5:9-10; 13:11; Phil 3:20.

[64]Cf. Ridderbos, *Paul*, 487-488; W. Foerster, "σῴζω, κ.τ.λ." in *TDNT* (1971) vol. 7, 992; Barrett, *Romans*, 27-29.

[65]Cf. W. Kasch, "ῥύομαι" in *TDNT* (1968) vol. 6, 998-1003.

[66]E.g., Ez 37:1-14; Isa 53:10; Job 19:25; Psalm 73; Isa 26:19 (ἀναστήσονται οἱ νεκροί, LXX); Dan 12:12 (A. Oepke, "ἀνίστημι, κ.τ.λ." in *TDNT* [1964] vol. 1, 368-372). See also Str-B IV, 1166-1198.

f. πλοῦτος. When Paul speaks of the wealth of the world and of the Gentiles in 11:12, it is the wealth of God's salvation as in 10:12, the wealth of God's glory as in 9:23, and the wealth of God's kindness as in 2:4, "the fulness of eschatological blesssing,"[67] whose depth Paul praises in the concluding hymn (11:33). "Riches is for [Paul] a term to denote the being of Christ [as in 2 Cor 8:9], the work of God in Christ, and the eschatological situation of Christ's community"[68] (cf. 1 Cor 1:5; 2 Cor 6:10; 9:11).

g. μυστήριον. As David Aune observes, "The term 'mystery' is virtually a technical term in early Jewish and early Christian apocalyptic and prophetic texts."[69] That mysteries belong to God's apocalyptic plan of salvation has been amply documented from Jewish literature as well as Christian.[70] That the μυστήριον of 1 Cor 15:51 is apocalyptic in content is commonly agreed,[71] and the context at the end of Romans 11 confirms its similar meaning there.[72] The closest parallels to Paul's use are in 1 Enoch, each of which introduces a revelation of future events:

> For I know this mystery; I have read the tablets of heaven and have seen the holy writings, and I have understood the writing in them; and they are engraved concerning you (103:2).

> And now I know this mystery: For...they will speak evil words and lie, and they will invent fictitious stories and write out my Scriptures on the basis of their own words (104:10).

> Again know another mystery: that to the righteous and the wise shall be given the Scriptures of joy, for truth and great wisdom (104:12).

---

[67]Käsemann, *Romans*, 305.

[68]F. Hauck and W. Kasch, "πλοῦτος, κ. τ. λ." in *TDNT* (1968) vol. 6, 328-329.

[69]Aune, *Prophecy*, 333.

[70]Brown, *Semitic Background*, 40-52; see above, Chapter Two. Käsemann disputes Brown's claim and counters that the mystery is "the salvation event as such, which is concealed and awaits its disclosure" (*Romans*, 312). Even this understanding of the content of the mystery, however, is purely apocalyptic. See also G. Bornkamm, "μυστήριον" in *TDNT* (1967) vol. 4, 815-817; 822-823.

[71]Aune, *Prophecy*, 250, and the literature cited there.

[72]Käsemann, *Romans*, 311-316; Beker, *Paul*, 334-335.

(3) Stylistic evidence. Several elements of Paul's exegetical technique and writing style in Romans 9-11 convey his apocalyptic conviction:

a. His pesher interpretations of Gen 21:12 and Deut 30:12-14 with the characteristic phrase τοῦτ᾽ ἔστιν (9:8; 10:6-8) so familiar from Qumran biblical interpretation;[73]

b. His prophetic freedom with scripture generally throughout the three chapters;[74] and

c. His specific phraseology in the last half of 11:25—ἄχρι οὗ τὸ πλήρωμα τῶν ἐθνῶν εἰσέλθῃ. As Joachim Jeremias observes of 1 Cor 11:26 (τὸν θάνατον τοῦ κυρίου καταγγέλλετε ἄχρι οὗ ἔλθῃ), the use of ἄχρι οὗ with the subjunctive and without ἄν "introduces a reference to reaching the eschatological goal."[75] At 1 Cor 11:26 the goal is the Lord's parousia; at 1 Cor 15:25—which speaks explicitly about τὸ τέλος (v 24)—

---

[73]Ellis, *Paul's Use*, 43-45; J. A. Fitzmyer, "The Use of Explicit Old Testament Quotations in Qumran Literature and in the New Testament," *NTS* 7 (1960-1961) 297-333; P. Vielhauer, "Paulus und das Alte Testament" in *Oikodome* (Munich: Chr. Kaiser, 1979; original 1969) 196-228. See further below, pp. 225-229.

[74]The greatest concentration of OT texts in the Pauline corpus is in Romans 9-11, and the chapters demonstrate nearly every interpretive technique the Apostle employs. Of 89 citations of scripture, 28—or 31%—are in these three chapters of Romans. Yet the chapters constitute only 6% of the pages devoted to the undisputed letters in the Nestle text. This profound dependence on biblical interpretation together with Paul's frequent personification of scripture (9:17, 25, 27, 29; 10:5-8, 11, 19-21; 11:4 [ὁ χρηματισμός], 9) suggest that he understands his argument to be resting on revelation. Aune discusses the character of Paul's "charismatic exegesis" as marked by three essential features: "it is *commentary*, it is *eschatological*, and it is *inspired*" (*Prophecy*, 339-346; emphasis his). On the variety of interpretive techniques used in 9-11, see Ellis, *Paul's Use*, 121-124.

[75]*The Eucharistic Words of Jesus*, tr. N. Perrin (New York: Charles Scribners' Sons, 1966²; original, 1935) 253. Although the essay deals with μέχρι rather than ἄχρι, cf. also W. G. Kümmel, "'Das Gesetz und die Propheten gehen bis Johannes'—Lukas 16,16 in Zusammenhang der heilsgeschichtlichen Theologie der Lukasschriften" in *Verborum Veritas: Festschrift für Gustav Stählin zum 70. Geburtstag*, ed. O. Böcher and K. Haacker (Wuppertal: R. Brockhaus, 1970) 89-102.

it is Christ's subjection of all his enemies; at Gal 3:19 it is the arrival of the promised σπερμα, Christ; and in Luke 21:24, a curiously similar text to Rom 11:25, it is the "fulfilling of the times of the Gentiles."[76] The phrase in Rom 11:25 points to the arrival of the πλήρωμα τῶν ἐθνῶν which precedes Israel's salvation, an event itself apocalyptic in nature.

These thematic, linguistic, and stylistic features of Romans 9-11 demonstrate that the chapters are profoundly shaped by apocalyptic convictions. Paul views the present situation from the perspective of the revelation he has received concerning God's eschatological salvation of all. In content, language, and tone, Romans 9-11 resemble passage after passage in Jewish apocalypses, and evoke reminiscences of other Pauline texts that speak in apocalyptic terms of the end time. It is scarcely remarkable, therefore, that the majority of modern commentators notes the apocalyptic nature of at least the conclusion to the argument.[77]

B. Wisdom Traditions

The wisdom traditions in Romans 9-11 are not nearly so prominent as the apocalyptic. Two passages, however, seem to be influenced by wisdom texts and traditions—9:20-23 and 10:6-8; reflection on the underlying occasion of the argument bears similarity to a wisdom concern for balance and order; and as we shall see, the three chapters conclude with a traditional wisdom hymn.

---

[76]Whether the "times of the Gentiles" refers to the period of the Gentile mission as reflected in Mark 13:10 (so R. Geiger, *Die Lukanische Endzeitreden* [Bern: Herbert Lang, 1973] 207; H. Farrell, "The Eschatological Perspective of Luke-Acts" [Ph.D. Dissertation, Boston University, 1973] 178) or to the period of Gentile domination of Jerusalem (so J. A. Fitzmyer, *The Gospel According to Luke X-XXIV* AB 28A [Garden City: Doubleday, 1983] 1346-1347; J. T. Carroll, "Eschatology and Situation in Luke-Acts" [Ph.D. Dissertation, Princeton Theological Seminary, 1986]), the goal is still an eschatological one.

[77]E.g., Beker, *Paul*, 331-337; Käsemann, *Romans*, 257-321; Cranfield, *Romans*, 573-588.

(1) 9:20-23.[78] Although the opening clause of the question in v 20 (μὴ ἐρεῖ τὸ πλάσμα τῷ πλάσαντι) clearly comes from Isa 29:16, the second half (τί με ἐποίησας οὕτως) does not. In Isaiah, the πλάσμα does not ask a question at all, but makes two arrogant accusations: οὐ σύ με ἔπλασας and οὐ συνετῶς με ἐποίησας. In a similar Isaianic context (45:9), a πηλός asks τί ποιεῖς; (cf. Job 9:12; Wis 12:12), and the passage's broader context concerns a hypothetical challenge to God's sovereign mercy (Isa 45:9-13, where Cyrus is the vessel spoken of). Jeremiah, too, employs the image of a potter and clay (18:1-11) to describe God's freedom to mold and remold Israel (vv 4, 7). But in neither Isaiah 29 nor Jeremiah 18 are there *two* sorts of vessels as there are in Romans 9, vessels created for such different purposes that one of them should argue with its maker. In Sir 33:12-13 and Wis 15:7, however, this familiar OT image is used in such a way as to distinguish between σκευή made for "clean" and "contrary" purposes (Wis 15:7), and between ἄνθρωποι (Sir 33:13) whom God either "blessed and lifted up" or "cursed and brought low" (v 12).

To return for a moment to the prophetic use of the potter and clay, we see that it addresses God's freedom to judge Israel, as Jeremiah's subsequent picture of the broken vessel illustrates so graphically (19:1-15). In both Isa 29:16 and Jer 18:6 there is one pot over which the potter is sovereign, a pot whose defiance is mocked as ludicrous. In the two wisdom contexts, though, the prophetic image has been employed to address another issue altogether: a distinction between two kinds of people or things. Even though Wis 15:7 introduces a description of foolish idolatry (15:8-17) rather than God's sovereignty, the allusion to the potter is evocative of the prophetic image of God. The one who himself is taken from clay and will return to it (v 8) usurps God's rightful place as creator by fashioning objects of clay which he worships. Ironically, the idolatrous κεραμευς who forms (πλάσσει, v 7) his vessels is the one who ἠγνόησεν τὸν πλάσαντα αὐτόν (v 11), that is, the legitimate κεραμεύς God.[79]

It would appear, therefore, that Paul's putting of Isa 29:16 into the mouth of his interlocutor at Rom 9:20 reflects the development of that

---

[78]On this passage see the early insights of E. Grafe, "Das Verhältnis der paulinischen Schriften zur Sapientia Salomonis" in *Theologische Abhandlungen: Carl von Weizsäcker zu seinem siebzigsten Geburtstag 11 December 1892*, ed. A. Harnack, *et al.* (Freiburg: J. C. B. Mohr [Paul Siebeck] 1892) 253-286, particularly 264-270; and Ellis, *Paul's Use*, 77-80.

[79]See also Reese, *The Book of Wisdom*, 158-160.

tradition in the sapiential contexts of Wis 15:7[80] and Sir 33:13.[81] At stake in his argument is not simply God's judgment—on Israel or on anyone else—but God's freedom to elect some and not others. The question τι...εποιησας in Rom 9:20, though possibly echoing a similar one that occurs in a number of places in scripture (Isa 45:9; Job 9:12; Wis 12:12), is most likely to have come from Wisdom 12 alone, given its similar function there in the service of a discussion of God's impartial judgment and mercy.

> For who will say, "What hast thou done?"
> Or who will resist thy judgment?
> Who will accuse thee for the destruction of nations which thou didst make?
> Or who will come before thee to plead as an advocate for the unrighteous?
> For neither is there any god besides thee, whose care is for all people,
> to whom thou shouldst prove that thou hast not judged unjustly;...
> For thy strength is the source of righteousness,
> and thy sovereignty over all causes thee to spare all (Wis 12:12-13, 16).

(2) 10:6-8. Although Hans Windisch was the first to identify a literary relationship between Paul's exegesis of Deut 30:12-14 and a similar one in Bar 3:29-30,[82] the argument has been made again more recently by Jack Suggs[83] and supported by a number of commentators on Romans 10.[84] The three passages—from Deuteronomy 30, Baruch 3, and Romans 10—are set in parallel columns to demonstrate the similarities.

Deut 30:12-14	Bar 3:29-30	Rom 10:6-8
[12] τίς ἀναβήσεται ἡμῖν	[29] τίς ἀνέβη	[6] τίς ἀναβήσεται
εἰς τὸν οὐρανὸν	εἰς τὸν οὐρανὸν	εἰς τὸν οὐρανὸν
καὶ	καὶ	τοῦτ᾽ ἔστιν
		χριστὸν

---

[80]Cf. Cranfield, *Romans*, 491-492.

[81]Cf. Käsemann, *Romans*, 272.

[82]"Die göttliche Weisheit der Juden und die paulinische Christologie," 224.

[83]"'The Word Is Near You': Romans 10:6-10 Within the Purpose of the Letter;" see above, p. 40, n. 175.

[84]E.g., Käsemann, *Romans*, 289; Lietzmann, *Römer*, 52-53; Lagrange, *Romains*, 257; Barrett, *Romans*, 199.

λήμψεται αὐτὴν ἡμῖν καὶ
ἀκούσαντες αὐτὴν ποιή-
σομεν. 13 οὐδὲ πέραν τῆς
θαλάσσης ἐστιν λέγων
Τίς διαπεράσει ἡμῖν εἰς
τὸ πέραν τῆς θαλάσσης
καὶ

λήμψεται ἡμῖν αὐτὴν καὶ
ἀκουστὴν ἡμῖν ποιήσει
αὐτὴν καὶ ποιήσομεν.

14 ἔστιν σου ἐγγὺς τὸ
ῥῆμα σφόδρα ἐν τῷ
στόματί σου καὶ
ἐν τῇ καρδίᾳ σου
καὶ ἐν ταῖς χερσίν σου
αὐτὸ ποιεῖν.

ἔλαβεν αὐτὴν καὶ
κατεβίβασεν αὐτὴν ἐκ
τῶν νεφελῶν;

30 τίς διέβη
πέραν τῆς θαλάσσης
καὶ

εὗρεν αὐτὴν καὶ οἴσει

αὐτὴν χρυσίου
ἐκλεκτοῦ ;

καταγαγεῖν

7 ἢ
τίς καταβήσεται
εἰς τὴν ἄβυσσον

τοῦτ᾽ ἔστιν χρισ-
τὸν ἐκ νεκρῶν
ἀναγαγεῖν;

8 ἀλλὰ τί λέγει;
ἐγγύς σου τὸ
ῥῆμα ἐστιν ἐν τῷ
στόματί σου καὶ
ἐν τῇ καρδίᾳ σου

τοῦτ᾽ ἔστιν τὸ
ῥῆμα τῆς πίστεως
ὃ κηρύσσομεν.

Baruch's hymn to wisdom (3:9-4:4), similar in many ways to Job
28:12-28, says that Israel alone of the nations has been graced by God with
Wisdom in the form of the Torah.[85] The partial quotation of Deut 30:12-14
in Bar 3:29-30 functions to contrast human inability to attain wisdom (v
31) with the Creator's omniscience (vv 32-35) and granting of Torah
wisdom to Jacob (v 36). Whereas the point in Deuteronomy is admonitory,
that Israel hear and do the law, the point in Baruch is polemical, that Israel
enjoys a privileged status vis-à-vis the nations in having access to the
law.[86] Paul's interpretation of the same passage serves to demonstrate that

[85]On the equation of Torah with Wisdom, see above, Chapter Two.
[86]Suggs, "'The Word is Near You'," 309.

the gospel is equally near to the whole world (Rom 10:6-8), and further functions to interpret Lev 18:5, ὁ ποιήσας αὐτά... ζήσεται (10:5).[87]

Both Baruch and Paul quote Deut 30:12a almost *verbatim*: Paul removes ἡμῖν and eliminates the phrase καὶ λήμψεται αὐτὴν ἡμῖν, Baruch changes the tense of ἀναβαίνω and λαμβάνω to aorist. Baruch alters Deut 30:12b rather markedly, though, by substituting καὶ κατεβίβασεν αὐτὴν ἐκ τῶν νεφελῶν for καὶ ἀκούσαντες αὐτὴν ποιήσομεν, thus extending the metaphor. Paul does not cite that half of the verse at all, but his interpretation (χριστὸν καταγαγεῖν) appears to have been influenced by Baruch's alteration, since καταβιβάζω and κατάγω are synonymous.

Neither Baruch nor Paul cites Deut 30:13a, but both pick up with the second rhetorical question in v 13b beginning with τίς. Here again, Baruch's reading seems to have influenced Paul's, since Baruch prefers διαβαίνω to διαπεράζω, presumably to preserve the parallelism with ἀναβαίνω in the preceding verse, and Paul too uses a form of βαίνω. Because he has changed the image from going *across* the sea to descending *into* the abyss,[88] the prefix is κατά- rather than διά-.

Baruch does not cite Deut 30:14 at all, although as Suggs points out its intent is not far from Baruch's.[89] Paul, on the other hand, quotes it directly, leaving out only the adverb σφόδρα, and rearranging the order of the first five words to emphasize ἐγγύς and σου. It is its nearness *to you* that Paul stresses about the word of faith, since its availability to all is the focus of his argument. The ἐν ταῖς χέρσιν of Deut 30:14, itself an addition to the MT by the LXX, is not useful to him, since there is no similar third element of the traditional formulation about confessing and believing, (10:9-10) so he does not include it.

There is one final reason to suspect Paul's exegesis of Deut 30:12-14 has been filtered through Baruch's. At the end of Baruch's poem about

---

[87]See below, pp. 155-158.

[88]The connection between θάλασσα and ἄβυσσος in scripture is frequent, particularly in wisdom contexts. Paul's substitution clearly stands in the service of his own image—Christ came down from heaven and was brought up from the dead—but his particular vocabulary may have been suggested by any number of texts, perhaps Ps 106:26—ἀναβαίνουσιν ἕως τῶν οὐρανῶν...καταβαίνουσιν ἕως τῶν ἀβύσσων (Käsemann, *Romans*, 300; cf. also Sir 24:5; 51:26; Deut 33:13; Ps 106:26; 134:6).

[89]Suggs, "'The Word Is Near You'," 309.

Wisdom is the traditional promise that ζωή awaits those who take hold of wisdom (4:1; cf. Prov 3:18; 4:22-23; 8:35; 9:11; etc.). So too Paul's setting of Lev 18:5 beside Deut 30:12-14 interprets the ζήσεται of the former by means of the latter. The wisdom of God which is immanent by means of Christian proclamation is the true interpretation of the law's righteousness, and the one who confesses and believes what God has done will indeed live. In Suggs's words, "To obey Christ in faith is to obey the law in truth."[90]

Ever since Windisch first noticed the connection between Paul's and Baruch's readings of Deut 30:12-14, everyone who has shared his conclusion has assumed with him that some kind of traditional wisdom christology stands behind Romans 10.[91] In every case, these commentators have pointed to 1 Cor 1:24 and 30 to say that Paul has previously made such a move to equate Christ with Wisdom, so his apparent christianized equation of Torah with Wisdom in Romans 10 must mean, as Suggs puts it, that "Christ = Wisdom = Torah."[92] As we saw in Chapter One, however, the assumption that 1 Corinthians 1-2 witness to a wisdom christology is itself based on a prior assumption that the christological hymn in Col 1:15-20 is authentically Pauline.[93] Furthermore, the utter lack of development in Romans 10 of any christological themes, and the continuing emphasis in the chapter on the preaching of the word of faith suggest that when Paul

---

[90]*Ibid.*, 311.

[91]E.g., Suggs, "'The Word Is Near You'," 308-312; Käsemann, *Romans*, 290; Barrett, *Romans*, 199.

[92]"'The Word Is Near You'," 304; cf. W. D. Davies, *Paul and Rabbinic Judaism* (above, p. 26, n. 106) to whom Suggs acknowledges "heavy indebtedness" (304, n. 2). Curiously, as strongly as Davies argues for wisdom christology in Paul, he *disputes* Windisch's—and therefore Suggs's—interpretation of Rom 10:6-8, and dismisses the possibility that Paul knows the Baruch passage in less than a paragraph: "The words in Baruch refer to the undiscoverability of Wisdom whilst Paul uses them in Rom 10.6ff to describe the essential accessibility or nearness of Christ in order to prove that the Jews who reject Him are without excuse. In any case the mere fact that Baruch uses a passage in the description of Wisdom cannot be regarded as proof that Paul could only have used it in the same connection" (*Paul and Rabbinic Judaism*, 154). Davies apparently misses the point of Baruch's sermon by hearing only vv 29-31 of it. The description of wisdom's proverbial inaccessibility is a rhetorical foil to highlight wisdom's nearness to Israel in the God-given Torah.

[93]Above, pp. 24-25.

identifies wisdom as the word that is near, he refers not to the person of Christ but to the gospel.

It is tempting to merge the two too quickly—as though the extent of the gospel were circumscribed by the Christ event—particularly when Paul himself sometimes uses the word χριστός as a short-hand reference to the whole gospel.[94] But although Käsemann is correct to say, "The exalted Christ is present only in Christian proclamation,"[95] the obverse is not quite true. The gospel which proclaims the power of God (Rom 1:16; 1 Cor 1:18, 24) is indeed the word of the cross (1 Cor 1:18). But it includes not only the cross but also the remaining work of redemption yet to be accomplished before the parousia, the subjection of Christ's enemies (1 Cor 15:24-28), the resurrection (15:51-55; 1 Thess 4:13-18), the judgment (Rom 2:5-11), the deliverance of believers from God's wrath (1 Thess 1:10), the sharing of God's glory (Rom 5:2), and all the things God has prepared that human eye has not seen, ear heard, nor heart conceived (1 Cor 2:9)—including the fulness of the Gentiles and Israel's eventual salvation (Rom 11:25-26). The gospel is itself the wisdom of God, near to all, able to save all, and in Christian terms equivalent to Torah, since, as we shall see, the righteousness of God for all is the goal of Torah.[96]

Suggs observes that "Baruch affirms of the Torah what Paul affirms of Christ: that by this instrument 'the word is near you'."[97] If Suggs were to allow that "Christ" stands for a great deal more than simply the person of Jesus, crucified and raised, he would be correct. But to call Jesus himself "incarnate wisdom"[98] limits Paul's understanding of the gospel and misses the point of his biblical interpretation in Rom 10:6-8.

(3) Not only have these individual passages in Romans 9-11 been influenced by wisdom traditions, but there is also a sense in which the argument itself responds to a general concern of sapiential writers: a concern for balance and order. And the μυστήριον which supplies the conclusion is, like the heavenly secrets of the apocalypses, part of God's wisdom.

In the oldest traditional Israelite wisdom of Proverbs, social order is seen to be grounded in natural order.[99] In much later wisdom literature, the focus shifts from human experience that discerns order to a putative cosmic force that "holds all things together" (Wis 1:7), "know[s] the structure of the

---

[94]E.g., Rom 10:4, 17; 1 Cor 1:24, 30.
[95]*Romans*, 290.
[96]See below, pp. 151-154.
[97]"'The Word Is Near You'," 309.
[98]*Ibid.*, 311.
[99]Cf. von Rad, *Wisdom In Israel*, 74-96.

world and the activity of the elements" (7:17), and "orders all things well" (8:1).[100] The wisdom traditions picked up by the apocalyptic writers also frequently concern this cosmic order and balance and harmony.[101] But sometimes, as in Pseudo-Solomon's review of Israel's history (Wisdom 10-12) and the life of the righteous individual (chapters 1-5), the order affirmed is the balancing of the moral scale: righteousness is rewarded and wickedness punished.

Paul's wrestling with God's relationship to Israel and the Gentiles in Romans 9-11 similarly concerns a question of balance, balance that is at once cosmic, historical, and moral. In Romans he affirms repeatedly that both Jew and Gentile share the same status before God: sinners to be justified by faith alone. The fact is, however, that Gentiles are responding to the gospel and Jews are staying away in droves. The careful tension Paul has sought to maintain between God's impartiality and faithfulness to Israel threatens to collapse if this apparent imbalance is not addressed. The argument of chapters 9-11 responds to this threat both by explaining the reason for the imbalance—God has purposely ordered events so that both the Jewish and Gentile missions have important roles in salvation history—and by promising in a heavenly mystery ultimate restoration of order.

Paul's concern is not simply with demographic asymmetry. The πλήρωμα of both Israel and the Gentiles is *theologically* necessary if he is to maintain what he does about God. The parallel clauses of 11:28-32—and particularly the πάντας...πάντας of v 32—reflect not simply a concern for the church's balanced membership, although that is also true. Georgi's study of the purpose of the collection in 2 Cor 8:13-15 and the cosmic and social value of ἰσότης[102] shows that balance within the community is an important incentive for Paul's relief effort. But far more significantly, Romans 9-11 are driven by a concern for the integrity and consistency of God. The God who in Christ redeems the whole world is the God who elects Israel to be a peculiar people. And neither Gentile presumption nor Jewish disobedience will be permitted finally to thwart God's purpose. That purpose is "salvation for everyone who believes, for the Jew first and also for the Greek" (1:16), and the πᾶς and the πρῶτον of that purpose are in dynamic

---

[100]Cf. Sir 16:27, "[God] arranged his works in an eternal order;" 43:10, "at the command of the Holy One [the stars] stand as ordered;" 33:15, "Look upon all the works of the Most High; they...are in pairs, one the opposite of the other;" 42:24, "All things are twofold, one the opposite of the other, and he has made nothing incomplete."

[101]Particularly 1 Enoch; see above, pp. 79-90.

[102]*Die Geschichte der Kollekte*, 62-67.

tension until the last day when both are finally brought to completion. The wisdom of God's mysterious purpose is for Paul not so much the ordering wisdom that "holds all things together" (Wis 1:7) as it is the wisdom that *corrects* imbalance and *restores* order. And it is such saving wisdom that is praised in the hymn he quotes in 11:33-36.

III. The Argument of Romans 9-11

The apparent shifts in Paul's definition of Israel within the three chapters pose the first of the many questions facing the interpreter of Romans 9-11. Under just how many rubrics does Paul discuss Israel? On the one hand, he calls Israelites his συγγενείς...κατὰ σάρκα (9:3; cf. 11:1), clearly referring to the ethnic totality of Israel (cf. the benefits in 9:4-5). So also, from 11:11 to the end of his argument, Israel is without question the historical people of God (πλήρωμα αὐτῶν, 11:12; πᾶς Ἰσραήλ, 11:26). He begins his argument at 9:6, however, with what appears to be a distinction within Israel between those who are Ἰσραηλ and those who are merely ἐξ Ἰσραήλ (9:6),[103] between Abraham's σπέρμα and his τέκνα, between the children of σάρξ and of ἐπαγγελία (9:8). The distinction is reminiscent of 2:28-29 (the difference between authentic faithfulness to the law and outward compliance) and 4:11-12 (Abraham's true descendants, cf. also Gal 4:21-31). The τέκνα τῆς ἐπαγγελίας have done nothing to merit their status (9:11), and their call depends solely on God who is merciful (9:16). If, as the parallelism indicates, the τέκνα τῆς ἐπαγγελίας discussed in 9:6-13 are to be identified with ὃν θέλει ἐλεεῖ in 9:18, then the same people seem also to be described as the σκεύη ἐλέους of 9:23. That means that the children of promise, the vessels of mercy, are called "not from the Jews only but also from the Gentiles" (9:24). In some sense, then, "Israel" can include Gentiles as well as Jews, because God's continuing election of Israel has always taken the same approach as it has now with Gentiles. Israel is God's elect, and God elects because of who God is, not because of who people are.

---

[103]L. Gaston's peculiar understanding of ἐξ Ἰσραήλ as referring to apostate Jews or Gentiles—i.e., those "outside Israel" ("Israel's Enemies in Pauline Theology," *NTS* 28 [1982] 413)—not only misunderstands the direction of Paul's argument, but forces his grammar as well. Used with expressions having to do with begetting and birth, ἐκ clearly denotes origin (cf. BAG, 234 [3.b]) rather than separation. Gaston's interpretation would require ἔξω. Further on Gaston's exegesis of Romans 9-11, see Excursus below, pp. 176-205.

Furthermore, "Israel" also describes unbelieving Jews, those who unsuccessfully pursue the law (9:31; cf. 11:7), who are ignorant of God's righteousness, seeking instead to establish their own (10:3), who hear the gospel (10:18) yet are still disobedient and contrary (10:20-21)—that is, hardened by God (11:7-8, 11, 25). In addition to these, however, are called the λεῖμμα, the Jews like Paul whom God has elected according to grace just as he spared the 7,000 who did not fall prey to idolatry in Elijah's day (11:4). But not even those hardened are permanently excluded, since their fulness will further enrich the world (11:12), even as their being cast off has meant the reconciliation of the world, and their final reception will mean nothing less than life from the dead (11:15; cf. 11:25).

Are there then one, two, or three definitions of Israel in Romans 9-11? Is Israel (1) the whole historical people descended from the patriarchs, (2) the children of the promise—both Jew and Gentile, or (3) the faithful remnant of Israel, that is, Jewish Christians? Many scholars like Peter Richardson harmonize them all under the third option: "It is impossible to stress too much that over all of Romans 9-11 stands 9:6b: 'not all descendants of Israel belong to Israel'."[104] By this they mean that "Israel" in Romans 9-11 always signifies Jewish Christians. The futuristic context of 11:11-32, though, and especially the universal tone of 11:28-32 (πάντας... πάντας, v 32) seem to resist such a reading. Most of all, the πλήρωμα of Israel (11:12) is clearly contrasted with the λεῖμμα of 11:5, and the Jews whom Paul hopes to make jealous by his ministry to the Gentiles are those who have stumbled but are *not* destined to fall (11:11).

Are there then two ways of describing Israel: the remnant and the whole people? It is commonly assumed that the children of the promise in 9:8 are Jewish Christians,[105] so that the reference to the remnant in 9:27 is neither new nor unexpected. That interpretation ignores the fact that all three double illustrations in chapter 9 are functionally parallel and illustrate the same phenomenon: God's merciful creation of a people. With the impartial election of the patriarchs (9:6-13), the raising up of Moses and hardening of Pharaoh (9:14-18), and the potter's vessels of wrath and mercy (9:19-23), Paul repeatedly emphasizes that God's gracious call is independent of human worth or identity. The inclusiveness of 9:24 ("not only...but also") speaks unambiguously of a mixed community. This means that the first mention

[104]*Israel in the Apostolic Church* (Cambridge: University, 1969) 130.

[105]E.g., Käsemann, for whom they represent "a true Israel within Judaism" (*Romans*, 263); or Cranfield, for whom they are "members of the Israel within Israel" (*Romans* 474).

of the remnant in 9:27, referring to Jews and Gentiles, is not equivalent to the second one in 11:5 that speaks specifically of Jews like Paul.[106]

Hence Paul has a single understanding of Israel in Romans 9-11 that is drawn not from ethnic or historical characteristics, but theological ones. Because Paul's definition of Ἰσραήλ depends on his understanding of God who is at once ὁ καλῶν (9:12, 24), ὁ ἀγαπῶν, ὁ μισῶν (9:13), ὁ ἐλεῶν, ὁ οἰκτιρῶν (9:15-16), ὁ σκληρύνων (9:18), and ὁ ποιῶν (9:21), that definition must be fluid enough to encompass the dynamic of God's free and creative election. Ἰσραήλ is thus discussed in Romans 9-11 from three perspectives, although none ever totally leaves behind the others: (1) all of ethnic Israel (9:1-5, 31; 10:1-3; 11:11-36), (2) the remnant of Israel (11:1-6) composed of faithful Jews of whom the Apostle is an example, and (3) the children of the promise (9:8, 24; cf. 4:9, 12, 16) who are Abraham's spiritual descendents, including those of both Jewish and Gentile heritage.[107] Israel continues for Paul to be a single reality created by God's consistent merciful acts of election; its composition is therefore by definition not to be limited by ethnicity.

This fluid definition of Ἰσραήλ in Romans 9-11 adds to the confusion surrounding a second major problem with Romans 9-11, the coherence of the argument itself. The passage is clearly a literary unity, bracketed by the opening oath and concluding hymn. But beyond that, how does the argument hold together, if indeed it does? Most interpreters see three distinct points: God is free to call whom he chooses (9:6-29), Israel deserves its own fate (9:30-10:21), God will nevertheless save all Israel (11:1-32).[108] The problem then arises from trying to ascertain the coherence among these points. Noack is so impressed by the apparent inconsistencies among the arguments of Romans 9-11 that he attributes to Paul a sort of spiritualist

---

[106]Commentators almost universally assume that the ὑπόλειμμα of Isa 10:22 makes the verse useful for Paul's argument, because they think it foreshadows the λεῖμμα of Rom 11:5 and therefore also refers to Jewish Christians (e.g., Käsemann, *Romans*, 275). As the exegesis of Rom 9:6-29 below indicates, however, it is not ὑπόλειμμα but λόγον...ποιήσει κύριος that more likely suggested the citation (see below, p. 150).

[107]Beker, *Paul*, 333-334.

[108]See, for example, Sanday and Headlam, *Romans*, 278, and the respective outlines of the chapters in Käsemann, *Romans*, 260-321; Nygren, *Romans*, 361-408; and U. Wilckens, *Der Brief an die Römer* (Zürich: Neukirchener, 1980) vol. 2, 1.

'automatic writing' experience: when the Apostle launches into his oath of solidarity at 9:1 he has no idea of the conclusion he will reach at 11:11-27.

> The solution is granted Paul during his wrestling with the problem, the mystery is revealed to him at the very moment of his dictating the second part of ch. xi, vv. 13-36. It is completely inconceivable that Paul should have known right from the beginning, that is from ix.1, that he would end by revealing to the Romans the mystery of God's salvation.... Romans ix-xi...are Paul's vexed monologue written down immediately, with questions and answers, complaint and comfort, objections and assertions, prayers and thanksgiving. As a matter of fact, the paragraphs from ix.1 to xi.10 do not contain the slightest hint at the final solution, simply because that solution does not yet exist.[109]

This position is admittedly somewhat extreme, but Noack gives voice to the frustration many feel at trying to follow the Apostle's train of thought. Perhaps the difficulty lies not in understanding the answer(s) Paul provides, but in articulating his question(s). Paul Meyer diagnoses the source of the difficulty as stemming from an *a priori* decision about the 'problem' to which Paul responds.

> On the assumption that what primarily troubles Paul in these chapters is his own Jewish people's rejection of the proclamation of Jesus as the Messiah, the three chapters are read as three different and rather unrelated, not to say logically incompatible, attempts to explain and understand this *contemporary* turn of events, this "disobedience of Israel": in 9, by attributing it to God's absolute sovereignty and freedom to elect and to reject (divine determinism); in 10, by attributing it to the Jews' own responsible refusal of the Christ (human freedom); and in 11, by describing it as a temporary expedient that makes possible the inclusion of the Gentiles in God's redemptive purpose and that therefore, frustrating God's sovereignty in appearance only, actually contributes to the

---

[109]Noack, "Current and Backwater," 165-166. Similarly N. Hyldahl ("Jesus og jøderne ifolge I Tess 2,14-16," *SEA* 27-28 [1972-1973] 238-254), who also sees in the μυστήριον of 11:25 a prophecy revealed to Paul spontaneously in the course of writing. See the discussion in D. Aune, *Prophecy in Early Christianity and the Ancient Mediterranean World* (Grand Rapids: Eerdmans, 1983) 252-253, and further below, pp. 162-163.

salvation of "all Israel" (11:26) and the ultimate victory of God's
purpose (not so much in spite of human resistance as through it,
not wiping it out so much as using it).[110]

Just what is it that evokes Paul's discussion in Romans 9-11? If the
problem stems only from Israel's current unbelief, the three chapters take on
the disconnected character just described.[111] If, on the other hand, we assume
that the three chapters argue a single sustained case, then what emerge are
two occasions for the argument: Jewish unbelief and Gentile faith,[112] and

---

[110]P. W. Meyer, "Romans 10:4 and the 'End' of the Law" in *The
Divine Helmsman*, ed. J. L. Crenshaw and S. Sandmel(New York: KTAV,
1980) 70; emphasis his.

[111]A variation on this traditional schema is one which views the three
chapters as salvation historical perspectives on Israel's past (9:6-29), present
(9:30-10:21), and future (11:1-32) (M. A. Getty, "An Apocalyptic
Perspective on Rom. 10:4," *Horizons in Biblical Theology* 4-5 [1982-1983]
79-131; cf. the modified form of the proposal in U. Luz, *Das
Geschichtsverständnis des Paulus* BEvT 49 [Munich: Chr. Kaiser, 1968]).
This admittedly tidy way of organizing the chapters fails to recognize (a)
that Israel is not the only subject under discussion, and (b) that the
chronological arrangement breaks down at 9:24 with the *present* election of
Gentiles, and at 10:18 with the *accomplished* spread of the gospel.
Moreover, such an argument ultimately rests on the overstated distinction
between "justification" and "salvation history" given prominence in the
debate between K. Stendahl ("The Apostle Paul and the Introspective
Conscience of the West" and "Sources and Critiques" in *Paul Among Jews
and Gentiles*, 78-96 and 125-133) and E. Käsemann ("Justification and
Salvation History in the Epistle to the Romans" in *Perspectives on Paul*,
60-78).

[112]L. Gaston correctly challenges the assumption that the problem of
Jewish unbelief alone prompts chapter 9 when he asks, "How is it that
people can say that chapter 9 deals with the unbelief of Israel when it is
never mentioned, and all human activity, whether doing or believing,
whether Jewish or Gentile, is expressly excluded from consideration?"
("Israel's Enemies," 411). But by denying that Jewish unbelief is at stake *at
all* in the three chapters, Gaston totally ignores 11:23 (ἐὰν μὴ ἐπιμένωσιν
τῇ ἀπιστίᾳ; cf. 3:3) and consequently overstates his case. The πίστις
vocabulary so central to Romans (πιστεύειν, ἀπιστεύειν, πίστις, ἀπιστία
are used 59 times in the letter) is totally absent from 9:6-29, but is used
twelve times in 9:30-10:21, and three more times in 11:1-27, including the

from those occasions the single problem of God's consistency. What Paul said with regard to God's dealings with the world through Christ in chapters 1-8—that God is both impartial and faithful—he now says in chapters 9-11 with regard to God's dealings with Israel.

There are a number of substantive issues raised in the text itself, all but the first put as questions. The three that structure the passage (9:6, 9:30, 11:1) ask about (1) the possible failure of God's word,[113] (2) the phenomenon of Gentile righteousness and Jewish unrighteousness, and (3) the possible rejection of God's people. The other questions develop those themes or meet potential objections:

(1) 9:6   God's word has not failed [has it?]
    9:14   There is no injustice with God, is there?
    9:19   Why then does God still find fault?
(2) 9:30-32 Why did the Gentiles who did not pursue righteousness receive it while Jews who pursued the law did not attain it?
    10:14-15 How are they to call upon one whom they have not believed? (believe...heard? hear...preached? preach...sent?)
    10:18   They have heard, have they not?
    10:19   Israel has understood, has it not?
(3) 11:1   God has not rejected his people, has he?
    11:11   Israel has not stumbled so as to fall, has it?

It is customary to understand that what is at stake for Paul in Romans 9-11 is the ἀλήθεια θεοῦ (15:8; cf. ἀληθής, 3:4, which is parallel to πίστις θεοῦ, 3:3). That faithfulness has been challenged by Israel's unbelief and must be demonstrated for Israel if it is to be trustworthy for the church.[114] Cranfield exemplifies this assumption:

———————————————

crucial 11:21 just noted. Clearly faith and unbelief are very much at stake in at least part of Romans 9-11, even if they do not figure in the first third of the argument.

[113]Although 9:6 is not put in the grammatical form of a question, οὐχ οἷον δὲ ὅτι is surely a denial of one possible answer to a question much like that posed in 3:3 (εἰ ἠπίστησαν τινες, μὴ ἡ ἀπιστία αὐτῶν τὴν πίστιν τοῦ θεοῦ καταργήσει;). On such a reading, τὴν πίστιν τοῦ θεοῦ καταργηθῆναι is functionally equivalent to τὸν λόγον τοῦ θεοῦ ἐκπεπτωκέναι.

[114]E.g., Beker, *Paul*, 331; Käsemann, *Romans*, 257-260.

[T]he very reliability of God's purpose as the ground of Christian hope is called in question by the exclusion of the majority of Jews. If the truth is that God's purpose with Israel has been frustrated, then what sort of a basis for Christian hope is God's purpose? And, if God's love for Israel...has ceased, what reliance can be placed on Paul's conviction that nothing can separate us from God's love in Christ ([8:]38ff)?[115]

If Jewish unbelief jeopardizes only God's faithfulness, though, why is the OT concept of the remnant employed at 11:5 not sufficient to answer the question? Is not the existence of some faithful Jews enough to demonstrate that God's continuing faithfulness to Israel is not compromised by the Christian mission? Rom 11:1-10 would seem to indicate that it is. Paul totally rejects the possibility that God has abandoned his people (μὴ γένοιτο) and offers himself (καὶ γὰρ ἐγώ, 11:1) in demonstration of the fact of continuity. The rest of the argument in 11:11-27, however, suggests that the remnant alone does not answer Paul's question. It suggests further that the question concerns more than Israel's unbelief. Jouette Bassler observes:

> Because [Paul] continues and argues further, and in some tension with what he has just said, that not merely a remnant but the *whole* of Israel will be saved, the suspicion is raised that perhaps the argument of Chapters 9-11 is not totally comprehended under the idea of a defense of God's faithfulness.[116]

The assumption that defense of the faithfulness of God provokes the argument of Romans 9-11 is based on a prior assumption that all three issues raised in 9:6, 9:30-32, and 11:1 are basically synonymous, that each is a different way of viewing the current situation of Jewish unbelief. To be sure, the issues of the reliability of God's word in 9:6 and the rejection of God's people in 11:1 could be seen to be asking the same thing—although, as we shall see, 9:6-29 deals with more than the status of Israel alone. But the middle question, in 9:30-32, introduces the additional element of Gentile faith.[117] Not only does Israel's election seem to be endangered, but the

---

[115]Cranfield, *Romans*, 447. Similarly, F. F. Bruce, *Romans* (Tyndale New Testament Commentaries; Grand Rapids: Eerdmans, 1985²) 173.

[116]Bassler, *Divine Impartiality*, 161; emphasis hers.

[117]As Toews observes in his history of research, "the exegetical center of the discussion [of Romans 9-11] has been chaps 9 and 11.... [It] has been possible for studies of Rom. 9-11 to neglect the whole central section of

Gentiles appear to have taken it over. Not only did Israel fail to attain to the law of righteousness in spite of its pursuit of it, the Gentiles who did *not* pursue righteousness *have* attained it. This highlights another aspect of the problem, and casts doubt on the conclusion that it is only God's faithfulness to Israel that is at stake for Paul in Romans 9-11, or that it is Jewish unbelief alone that provokes the question in the first place.

Paul addresses *two* problems in Romans 9-11: Jewish unbelief and Gentile belief. These twin realities threaten not only a conviction of God's faithfulness to Israel, but also the certainty of God's impartiality. Gentile faith and Jewish unbelief could be interpreted to mean either (a) God is impartial but has ceased to be faithful to Israel, or (b) God has elected only the Gentiles and is therefore neither impartial nor faithful. But Paul repeatedly affirms both God's impartiality and faithfulness.[118] In the carefully balanced rhetorical conclusion at 11:28-32,[119] he maintains the tension that has run through the letter from the beginning:

κατὰ μὲν τὸ εὐαγγέλιον ἐχθροὶ δι' ὑμᾶς,
κατὰ δὲ τὴν ἐκλογὴν ἀγαπητοὶ διὰ τοὺς πατέρας
      ἀμεταμέλητα γὰρ τὰ χαρίσματα καὶ ἡ κλῆσις τοῦ θεοῦ.
ὥσπερ γὰρ ὑμεῖς ποτε ἠπειθήσατε τῷ θεῷ, νῦν δὲ ἠλεήθητε
      τῇ τούτων ἀπειθείᾳ,
οὕτως καὶ οὗτοι νῦν ἠπείθησαν τῷ ὑμετέρῳ ἐλέει ἵνα καὶ
      αὐτοὶ νῦν ἐλεηθῶσιν.
συνέκλεισεν γὰρ ὁ θεὸς τοὺς πάντας εἰς ἀπείθειαν
      ἵνα τοὺς πάντας ἐλεήσῃ.

The parallel γάρ clauses set God's irrevocable election of Israel directly beside his impartial judgment and redemption of all, without resolving the tension. The same has been true in Romans ever since 1:16, where Paul calls the gospel "the power of God for salvation to *everyone* who believes, to the Jew *first* and also to the Greek." What is at stake in Romans 9-11 is not merely God's faithfulness to Israel, but God's trustworthiness as the God who elects and redeems impartially.

Paul's argument in 9.30-10.21" ("The Law in Paul's Letter to the Romans," 111-112).
    [118]See above, pp. 118-120.
    [119]See Barrett, *Romans*, 224.

Paul's question, then, arises not simply from the contemporary historical situation of his own successful Gentile mission, nor only from the salvation-historical problem of God's faithfulness to Israel, but from the intersection of the two. Paul's preaching of the gospel that is for all on equal terms rests on the dependability of God who elected for himself a peculiar people. For God to be the God who creates out of nothing, who is merciful apart from human deserving, and with whom there is no partiality, faithfulness can never be construed as favoritism. That is precisely the danger posed by Gentile faith and Jewish unbelief, that God's faithfulness could be thought of somehow as loyalty which has been transferred from Israel to the church—a not uncommon notion, as witnessed by the first and fourth evangelists. Far from negating Paul's preaching, the Christian mission to Gentiles and attendant Jewish resistance bear witness to God's consistent and faithful calling into being of a people. Just as Paul has previously shown that God uses even the power of sin to accomplish his purpose with the law (5:12-21, 7:13-25), so 9-11 demonstrate that God uses even Jewish opposition to the gospel to make known his merciful sovereignty.[120]

Romans 9-11 argue not three separate points but one sustained case in three stages. First, Paul demonstrates that God has always elected Israel just as he has now called the Gentiles, without regard for human worthiness (9:6-29). Second, he explains that the current imbalance of Gentile faithfulness and Jewish unbelief is a function of God's impartiality—Israel is hardened in order that the Gentiles might hear the gospel (9:30-10:21). And third, he says that the contemporary hardening of part of Israel will be ended by the imminent fulness of Gentile faith (11:1-32). The following detailed analysis of Romans 9-11 supports this contention and demonstrates the way confluent apocalyptic and wisdom traditions have shaped the argument.

A. 9:1-29

After the opening oath and benediction of 9:1-5, chapter 9 is structured by three sets of parallel assertions:

(1) Ancestry is by God's promise rather than birth (6-9)
    Election is by God's call rather than human works (10-13)
(2) God's sovereignty is not arbitrary, but serves his purposes of wrath and mercy—e.g., Pharaoh (14-18)

---

[120]Meyer, "Romans 10:4," 66-67; cf. also Stuhlmacher, *Gerechtigkeit Gottes*, 91-99.

God's sovereignty is not arbitrary, but serves his purposes of wrath
and mercy—e.g., a potter's vessels (19-23)
(3) Both Jews and Gentiles have been called in the same way (24):
God mercifully calls Gentiles (25-26)
God mercifully calls Jews (27-29)

The first two statements argue two aspects of the same point: God's
promise and call are unrelated to human descent or activity. Ishmael was
also Abraham's son, but Isaac was his heir; Jacob's election over his elder
brother preceded their birth and respective (righteous or unrighteous) lives.
The next two statements make a second point in two ways, one with an
illustration from history, the other with an illustration from experience.
Pharaoh's hardening, far from being an act of divine caprice, served to
demonstrate God's power and make known God's name; the potter creates
vessels for specific purposes, the vessels of dishonor/wrath for the sake of
the vessels of honor/mercy—again that God's wrath and power might be
demonstrated and made known.

Thus far in the argument, Paul has said nothing to which a non-
Christian Jew might take exception. Not even 9:6 is beyond the realm of
traditional Jewish understanding: even Jews know that not all Abraham's
descendents are his heirs.[121] Any Jew would affirm Paul's claim that God
has elected Isaac and not Ishmael, Jacob rather than Esau. It is common
knowledge that Pharaoh's hardening was for God's glory and Israel's
ultimate good. The vessels of wrath and mercy function as illustrations of
the same point—God suffers Israel's enemies for Israel's sake. From a
traditional Jewish perspective, the argument to this point offers nothing
remarkable.

At 9:24, however, when Paul identifies the vessels of mercy as a *mixed*
group—οὐ μόνον ἐξ᾿Ιουδαίων ἀλλὰ καὶ ἐξ ἐθνῶν—he makes the first
distinctively Christian claim of the argument.[122] It is scarcely unexpected,

---

[121]That Ishmael's and Esau's children are commonly viewed either as
Israel's enemies or non-Israelites is clear from Ps 83:6; Jub 15:28-32;
20:11-13; Mekilta, Bahodesh 5; and the Targum of Pseudo-Jonathan on
Genesis 22, among other texts (see Gaston, "Israel's Enemies," 405-406).

[122]Because 9:6-13 and 14-23 are intended to outline standard Jewish
claims about divine election, rather than Christian ones, 9:6—οὐ...πάντες
οἱ ἐξ᾿Ισραὴλ οὗτοι ᾿Ισραήλ—should not be read to exclude unbelieving
Jews from the start (*contra* the vast majority of commentators). What is new
in Paul's argument is not that "not all Israel is Israel." In the biblical terms
he is using, Jews already know that. What is new is what comes at 9:24—

of course. The same οὐ μόνον...ἀλλὰ καί has referred to Jew and Gentile already at 3:29 and 4:12, 16 (cf. 4:23-24), and Paul affirms the equal standing of Jew and Gentile at 1:16, 2:11, and 3:9, 22. But the notion that God's call is not only for Jews but also for Gentiles applies standard Jewish election theology to non-Jews. God's merciful election of Gentiles is in no way different from God's merciful call of Israel.[123] The wisdom tradition of the potter's vessels in 9:20-23 serves to recast the question of Israel's abiding election into an affirmation of God's impartiality.[124]

---

the inclusion of Gentiles. The question of Israel's potential exclusion does not arise in the argument itself until 9:30, and is not asked explicitly until 11:1, although it may be in the front of commentators' minds at 9:6. What this means is that the alleged contradiction between 9:6 and 11:25—on the one hand, only Christians are true Israelites, and on the other hand, all Israel will be saved—is perceived rather than real. Although in 9:24-29 Paul certainly redefines Israel, he does so by *in*cluding believing Gentiles rather than *ex*cluding unbelieving Israel. Ultimately, only 11:20 (τῇ ἀπιστίᾳ ἐξεκλάσθησαν) and 11:23 (ἐὰν μὴ ἐπιμένωσιν τῇ ἀπιστίᾳ) suggest the possibility of the rejection of unbelieving Jews, and even those stand under the shadow of 11:25 (πᾶς Ἰσραήλ).

[123]Although Cranfield fails to see the emphasis in chapter 9 on the creation of an ethnically diverse people, he correctly emphasizes the importance of the concept of mercy (*Romans*, 448). Cf. also Barrett, *Romans*, 185.

[124]It is important here to recognize that the σκεύη ὀργῆς and σκεύη ἐλέους do not function consistently as allegorical symbols for "Israel" and "the Gentiles." Gentiles are not even mentioned until the next sentence, and the argument to this point has focused solely on God's manner of electing Israel. The vessels of wrath and mercy do not "stand for" specific groups of people so much as the entire image "stands for" the principle of God's impartial and purposeful election. God hardens whom he will and elects whom he will to the end that his glory might be made known and his people created out of no people. The assumption that the vessels of wrath and mercy refer to unbelieving Jews and Christian Gentiles rests on a backward reading of the letter: to understand the vessels of wrath "destined for destruction" as unbelieving Israel necessitates knowledge of 11:17-24 prior to 9:22. This simple methodological error of interpreting one passage by a later one is nearly universal in exegesis of Romans 9-11.

This astounding claim demands biblical proof, which is supplied in vv 25-29, again in parallel fashion. Paul appears to wrench Hos 2:25 and 2:1 from their historical contexts to apply them to Gentiles rather than to Israel, but the distinction is in truth not that great: God always calls τὸν λαόν into being from τὸν οὐ λαόν. Paul then does precisely the same thing with Isa 10:22 and 1:9 which describe God's saving election of Israel, again despite Israel's deserving. Those Gentiles who were οὐ λαὸς μου...οὐκ ἠγαπημένη...οὐ λαὸς μου have become μου λαός....ἠγαπημένη...υἱοὶ θεοῦ ζῶντος (vv 25-26), not because of their ethnic or moral claims, but because God has called them (καλέσω, v 25; κληθήσονται, v 26). Although Israel's sons are ὡς ἡ ἄμμος τῆς θαλάσσης (v 27), they would have been ὡς Σόδομα...καὶ ὡς Γομόρρα (v 29) had God not mercifully saved a remnant (v 27) and left behind a seed (v 29). The σπέρμα of Isa 1:9 (Rom 9:29) recalls Abraham's σπέρμα in 9:7, showing that although God has extended a merciful call to Gentiles, his prior call of Israel has in no way been abrogated.

At the center of these proofs of God's creative mercy—mercy that creates people out of nothing—stands the biblical authority for the claim Paul made at 9:6. God's word has not failed, but will surely and swiftly be accomplished (v 28).[125] God's electing word has not collapsed for two reasons: it is not intended to apply to Israel alone, and the inclusion of the Gentiles has been on precisely the same grounds as Israel's election.

Paul treats the apocalyptic theme of the nature and destiny of Israel in Romans 9 by reference to a wisdom tradition concerning a potter's two kinds of vessels to say something substantially different from what his contemporaries say. In the face of a threat to God's relationship with Israel (the implied question behind 9:6), Paul does not assert God's ultimate vindication of Israel. Instead, he reconceives the threat (and thus disarms it) by showing God's past behavior is consistent with God's present behavior. The apocalyptic promise of faithfulness in v 28—God will surely and swiftly accomplish his word on the earth—is grounded in a wisdom argument that demonstrates God's present impartiality in electing all on the same terms.

---

[125]Taking συντέμνων to refer to the shortening of time rather than the cutting short of the people, cf. Dan 5:27 LXX (*contra* Käsemann, *Romans*, 275).

B. 9:30-10:21

The second stage of Paul's argument proceeds from the conclusion just drawn that God's election of Jews and Gentiles alike does not cause his word of election to collapse. If that is true, he asks, then how is it that the contemporary situation—that is, Gentile righteousness and Jewish failure to attain this righteousness (9:30-31)—appears so unbalanced? Jews have not attained the law of righteousness they pursued, but Gentiles have received righteousness they never sought. Why is this if God consistently elects impartially? Paul's answer comes in two parts: 9:32-10:13 and 10:14-21. The first concerns the nature of the gospel; the second, God's relation to Israel through the gospel.

The answer to Paul's question about the imbalance of the present situation in 9:30-31 focuses on the second half of it, the fact that Israel has not attained the law of righteousness, because this fact calls into question the claim just made that God continues to call Israel. By pursuing the law οὐκ ἐκ πίστεως ἀλλ' ὡς ἐξ ἔργων, Israel stumbles over the stumbling stone God has put in Zion (9:33). What that means is that because they are ignorant of the righteousness of God and seek instead to establish their own, they refuse to submit to God's righteousness (10:3). Now in what sense is *stumbling* over the stone equivalent to *not submitting* to God's righteousness? The latter act implies willfulness, the former a lack of such intentionality.[126] The answer is in 10:4, where the γάρ indicates Paul is offering a warrant for his claim of 10:3. The reason Israel is ignorant of God's righteousness, seeks to establish its own, and therefore does not submit to God's righteousness is that τέλος...νόμου χριστὸς εἰς δικαιοσύνην παντὶ τῷ πιστεύοντι.

Perhaps no verse in the entire Pauline corpus is so obscure, admitting of so many diverse and mutually exclusive interpretations as Rom 10:4. Decisions about the force of τελος [127] and the relation of v 4 to 10:1-3 and

---

[126]Meyer, "Romans 10:4," 63.

[127]The majority of commentators claims that τέλος signifies "termination." E.g., P. Althaus, *Der Brief an die Römer* NTD 6.11 (Göttingen: Vandenhoeck and Ruprecht, 1970) 108; Beker, *Paul*, 106-107 and 184-187; G. Bornkamm, *Das Ende des Gesetzes: Paulusstudien: Gesammelte Aüfsatze I* (Munich: Chr. Kaiser, 1963); F. F. Bruce, "Paul and the Law of Moses," *BJRL* 57 (1975) 259-279; Bultmann, "Christ and the End of the Law," 54; J. A. Fitzmyer, "Paul and the Law" in *A Companion to Paul: Readings in Pauline Theology*, ed. M. J. Taylor (New York: Alba, 1975) 75; Getty, "Apocalyptic Perspective," 91-121. F. Hahn, "Das

Gesetzesverständnis im Römer- und Galaterbrief," *ZNW* 67 (1976) 49-51; Käsemann, *Romans*, 279-285; O. Michel, *Römer*, 224; F. Mussner, "'Christus (ist) des Gesetzes Ende zur Gerechtigkeit für jeden, der glaubt' (Röm 10,4)" in *Paulus: Apostat oder Apostel? Jüdische und christliche Antworten* (Regensburg: Pustet, 1977) 31-44; Sanders, *Paul*, 550; Schoeps, *Paul*, 171; H. Schlier, *Der Römerbrief* HTKNT 6 (Freiburg: Herder, 1977) 311; P. Stuhlmacher, "'Das Ende des Gesetzes': Über Ursprung und Ansatz der paulinischen Theologie," *ZTK* 67 (1970) 14-39; D. Zeller, *Juden und Heiden in der Mission des Paulus: Studien zum Römerbrief* (Stuttgart: Katholisches Bibelwerk, 1973) 193.

Others who argue alternatively that τέλος signifies "goal" or "destination" are R. Badenas, "The Meaning of *Telos* in Romans 10:4" (Ph.D. Dissertation, Andrews University, 1983); A. J. Bandstra, *The Law and Elements of the World: An Exegetical Study in Aspects of Paul's Teaching* (Kampen: J. H. Kok, 1964) 101-106; P. Bläser, *Das Gesetz bei Paulus* NTA 19.1-2 (Münster: Aschendorfer, 1941) 173-181; R. Bring, "Paul and the Old Testament: A Study of the Ideas of Election, Faith and the Law in Paul With Special Reference to Rom. 9:30-10:30," *ST* 25 (1971) 20-60; Cranfield, *Romans*, 515-520; idem, "St. Paul and the Law," *SJT* 17 (1964) 43-68; Davies, *Paul and Rabbinic Judaism*, 69; G. E. Howard, "Christ the End of the Law: The Meaning of Romans 10:4ff," *JBL* 88 (1969) 331-337; Meyer, "Romans 10:4," 61, 75-76; C. T. Rhyne, *Faith Establishes the Law* SBLDS 55 (Chico: Scholars, 1981) 103-104; Suggs, "'The Word Is Near You': Romans 10:6-10 Within the Purpose of the Letter;" Toews, "The Law in Paul's Letter to the Romans," 238-245; U. Wilckens, "Was heisst Paulus: 'Aus Werken des Gesetzes wird kein Mensch gerecht'?" in *Evangelisch-Katholischer Kommentar zum Neuen Testament* (Neukirchen: Neukirchener, 1969) 51-77.

A third option is chosen by exegetes who follow Barth (*Romans*, 375) and sit on the fence, claiming τέλος means both "goal" and "termination", e.g., Barrett, *Romans*, 198; Bruce, *Romans*, 203; J. W. Drane, *Paul: Libertine or Legalist?* (London: SPCK, 1975) 133; Kuss, *Römerbrief*, vol. 3, 752-753; F. J. Leenhardt, *Epistle to the Romans: A Commentary*, tr. H. Knight (London: Lutterworth, 1961) 266. R. Jewett rightly dismisses this compromise position as an attempt "to have one's cake and eat it too" ("The

10:5ff are only two of the several major roadblocks to understanding this passage. So it seems well to postpone a final verdict on those thorny matters concerning v 4 until the shape of the entire argument is in clearer focus. Whatever it means that Christ is the τέλος of the law, it is at least clear that this is true because (γάρ, v 5) scripture says so. The apposition of Lev 18:5 to Deut 30:12-14 and the elaborate explanatory pesher on Deuteronomy 30 that follows[128] are designed to prove that the gospel (τὸ ῥῆμα τῆς πίστεως δ' κηρύσσομεν, v 8) is close at hand (vv 5-8) and that the gospel is the righteousness of faith/God (v 6). This exposition of scripture is grounded (ὅτι, v 9) in Christian tradition about confessing and believing (vv 9-10),[129] which is itself buttressed (γάρ, v 11) by an appeal to scripture (v 11).[130]

The argument has come full circle now, since the citation of Isa 28:16 at 10:11 echoes 9:33b—with one significant alteration. By his addition of πας to the verse from Isaiah, Paul makes explicit in v 11 what has been implicit in his interpretation of the verse from 9:33. Faith in the λίθος τοῦ προσκόμματος keeps one from being put to shame regardless of one's ethnic identity or prior religious status. That Paul's interpretation of Isa 28:16 functions to support his argument about divine impartiality can be seen also from his other uses of πᾶς ὁ πιστεύων at 1:16, 3:22, and 4:11, all of which are in the context of discussing Jew and Gentile before God.

Law and the Coexistence of Jews and Gentiles in Romans" [*Int* 39 (1985) 353]).

[128]See further below, pp. 155-158.

[129]For a discussion of the traditional elements, see P.E. Langevin, "Sur la Christologie de Romains 10,1-13," *Laval Theologique et Philosophique* 35 (1979) 35-54.

[130]It is of course possible to force a resumptive γάρ to bear too much causal freight, but in vv 2-5, at least, the argument is clearly building on itself step by step (see Meyer, "Romans 10:4," 65; and Kuss, *Römerbrief*, 748). In vv 11-13 the same logical force of γαρ seems similarly evident. When Paul uses γάρ to introduce a text from scripture, as he does at both 10:11 and 10:13, he does so because he thinks scripture proves his point— "I say so *because* the Bible says so..." (cf. also Rom 2:24; 4:3; 9:15; 10:16; 11:34; 12:19; 13:9; 14:11; 1 Cor 1:19; 2:16; 3:19-20; 6:16; 9:9-10; 10:26; 15:27; 2 Cor 6:2; 9:7; Gal 3:10; 4:27; 5:14).

The final two verses of this section (12-13) repeat the alternation of scripture and tradition evident in vv 5-11. The reason (γάρ, v 12) πᾶς ὁ πιστεύων ἐπ' αὐτῷ οὐ καταισχυνθήσεται (v 11) is that God is impartial. The same God is κύριος πάντων, πλουτῶν εἰς πάντας τοὺς ἐπικαλουμένους αὐτόν (v 12). This traditional affirmation of divine impartiality is then itself grounded (γάρ, v 13) in scripture. The πᾶς ὃς ἂν ἐπικαλέσηται in v 13 is the same as πᾶς ὁ πιστεύων in v 11, and Paul evidently considers the verses from Isaiah 28 and Joel 3 functionally equivalent.[131]

The gospel, then, as Paul describes it in 9:30-10:13, is marked by its nearness and availability to *all* who believe. The gospel which proclaims God's righteousness (10:3; cf. 1:16), the righteousness of faith (9:30; 10:6), is available to all because God is an impartial God (10:12; cf. 3:29). The identity of the stone over which Israel stumbled (9:33; 10:11) is neither Christ nor the law,[132] but the gospel, the "word of faith which we preach" (10:8), the power of God for salvation which overturns any understanding of God's righteousness as for Jews only. The reason Israel failed to attain to the law of righteousness (which is itself equivalent to God's righteousness or the righteousness of faith) is a function of the argument of 9:6-29—Israel was ignorant (10:3) that God's merciful election applies to all, both Jew and Gentile. Consequently, the τέλος of 10:4 must mean "goal" rather than

---

[131]καταισχύνω and σώζω are linked at 9:33-10:1 as well (cf. also 1:16—οὐ...ἐπαισχύνομαι...σωτηρίαν).

[132]Because so many NT writers use "stone" texts such as Isa 28:16 and Ps 118:22 to make christological claims (e.g., 1 Pet 2:4-8; Matt 21:42; Luke 20:17; Acts 4:11), most commentators leap to the assumption that Paul too makes christological use of Isa 28:16 here in Rom 9:33. The great contribution of Meyer's study ("Romans 10:4") and Toews's dissertation ("The Law and Paul's Letter to the Romans") is their independent demonstrations that those other NT citations of Isa 28:16 presuppose a connection with Ps 118:22, to which Paul does not refer. Both Meyer and Toews push their insight one step too far by claiming that the λίθος προσκόμματος is then the law, an untenable possibility given the restatement of the verse in Rom 10:11 after 10:8. But they have rendered valuable service by breaking open the previously unchallenged scholarly assumption that 9:33—and, by extension, 10:4—make christological affirmations.

"termination," since the gospel[133] announces that impartial righteousness of God.

Israel sought God's righteousness unsuccessfully when it pursued the νόμον δικαιοσύνης (9:31). Because Israel expected the νομος to be attained ἐξ ἔργων (9:32), it failed to recognize (οὐ κατ᾽ ἐπίγνωσιν, 10:2) the inclusive righteousness of God that is the law's intended goal. Had Israel pursued the law of righteousness ἐκ πίστεως (9:32)—that is, by faith in the God whose righteousness is for all—it would indeed have attained that νόμον (9:31). Paul has already said at 9:12 (cf. 9:16) that human works have always been excluded by God's call; so also are they now precluded by the gospel that is near. All of which is to say that in large measure the newness of the gospel is also profoundly consistent with God's past dealings with his people. The law's goal—that is, God's righteousness—has been achieved by the gospel that is to the Jew first but also to the Gentile.

To pursue that law ὡς ἐξ ἔργων, as unbelieving Israel has, is to make distinctions where God makes none, and thus to fail to receive God's righteousness. To pursue God's righteousness ὡς ἐξ ἔργων evidences ζῆλος...οὐ κατ᾽ ἐπίγνωσιν (10:2) because such pursuit defines God's righteousness in terms of human rather than divine action. The imagery of the race course that dominates the argument of 9:30-33[134] and was hinted at already in 9:16 (ὁ τρέχων) gets turned on its head at 10:4 when the achieved goal is a divine accomplishment rather than a human one. To pursue God's righteousness by works is to consider that it is accomplished by human πράξαντες (9:11), θέλοντες, or τρέχοντες (9:16) rather than by God who is ὁ καλῶν (9:12), ὁ ἐλεῶν (9:16), [ὃς] θέλει (9:18; cf. 9:22), ὁ πλάσας (9:20), ὁ κεραμεύς (9:21), [ὃς] ἐκάλεσεν ἡμᾶς οὐ μόνον ἐξ Ἰουδαίων ἀλλὰ καὶ ἐξ ἐθνῶν (9:24).

This definition of God's righteousness is itself biblical, Paul says. In 10:5-8 he personifies two voices of the law: Moses, who writes of the δικαιοσύνη ἐκ νόμου in Lev 18:5, and the ἐκ πίστεως δικαιοσύνη who

---

[133]Χριστός stands as a synecdoche for the entire gospel, as it does in 10:17 (ῥῆμα Χριστοῦ), and in 1 Cor 1:24, 30 (see R. G. Hamerton-Kelly, *Pre-Existence, Wisdom, and the Son of Man*, 115). The gospel which is Χριστὸς ἐσταυρωμένος (1 Cor 1:23) is θεοῦ δύναμις (1:24; 2:5; cf. Rom 1:16), and encompasses all that eye has yet to see, ear has yet to hear, and human heart yet to conceive (2:9). Significantly, in the 1 Corinthians context too the gospel is a σκάνδαλον to Jews (1:23).

[134]Meyer, "Romans 10:4," 62.

speaks in Deut 30:12-14. As in Gal 3:12, Lev 18:5 exemplifies the principle of ἐξ ἔργων νόμου,[135] but in Romans 10 the contrasting principle of ἐκ πίστεως is drawn not from a prophetic text (Hab 2:4) but from Torah. Each element of Rom 10:4 is picked up and expanded in Paul's exegesis in 10:5-13:

τέλος νόμου	Μωϋσῆς γὰρ γράφει τὴν δικαιοσύνην τὴν ἐκ νόμου—Lev.18:5 (10:5)
Χριστὸς	ἡ δὲ ἐκ πίστεως δικαιοσύνη—Deut 30:12-14 (10:6-8)
	ὁμολογήσῃς...καὶ πιστεύσῃς (10:9)
εἰς δικαιοσύνην	εἰς δικαιοσύνην...δὲ...εἰς σωτηρίαν (10:10)
παντὶ τῷ πιστεύοντι	πιστεύεται (10:10); πᾶς ὁ πιστεύων (10:11); πᾶς ὁ ἐπικαλουμένος (10:12-13)

---

[135]N. A. Dahl ("Contradictions in Scripture" in *Studies in Paul*, 159-177) examines the function of the contrast between Lev 18:5 and Hab 2:4 in Galatians 3, and determines that Paul explains the conflict between the two by identifying the different contexts and functions of the verses. Hab 2:4 contains the principle of justification "by faith;" Lev 18:5, the principle of "by works of the law." Clearly the two are mutually exclusive, and Hab 2:4 is the correct one. Lev 18:5 does not, however, cease to be an expression of God's will because it opposes Hab 2:4. Paul's exegesis in Gal 3:15-25—the law is not a codicil added to God's covenant with Abraham (vv 15-18) but was given as a provisional measure τῶν παραβάσεων χάριν (v 19) and was itself never "able to make alive" (v 21)—makes clear that Lev 18:5, although an expression of God's will, "was not an *enduringly valid* expression of God's will" (173; emphasis added). Scripture itself demonstrates the custodial purpose of the law: "Rightly understood, the Law is in harmony with the promises. It had a subordinate function which contributed to the realization of the promises" (174). In a later footnote referring to Rom 10:4, Dahl suggests that "Paul would here [in 10:5-6] seem to have made a distinction within the Old Testament concept of the Law" (176). As the following exegesis demonstrates, Paul discerns within the law the two possible responses to God—ἐκ πίστεως and ἐξ ἔργων νόμου—and the correctness of the former.

Lev 18:5 promises that "the person who does these things will live by them."[136] The Jew seeking δικαιοσύνη ἐκ νόμου assumes that "these things" are the ἔργα νόμου, those human endeavors whereby people "seek to establish their own" righteousness (10:3), and zealously pursues the right goal by the wrong means. Even the law points up the futility of human ποιεῖν. The introductory phrase from Deut 9:4—μὴ εἴπῃς ἐν τῇ καρδίᾳ σου (10:6)—implicitly warns against mistaking human righteousness for divine,[137] and foreshadows the ἐν τῇ καρδίᾳ σου of Deut 30:13 to follow (10:8). Just as the law and the prophets bear witness to the righteousness of God that is now manifested χωρὶς νόμου (3:21), so the law itself guards against misunderstanding its divinely intended goal. In fact, "these things" by which a person lives are the bringing Christ down from heaven and raising him from the dead that God alone has accomplished (10:6-7). The reason Deut 30:12-14 witnesses to the δικαιοσύνη ἐκ πίστεως is that it highlights—with no little irony—the foolishness of people's attempts to do what God has already done on their behalf.[138] Those ironic questions beginning with τίς in 10:6-7 recall the similar question asked at 9:20 ("Who are you to answer back to God?") and function much as do the rhetorical questions in 11:34-35 ("Who has known the mind of the Lord? Who has become his counselor? Who has given to him that he might also be repaid

---

[136]Reading with the text of the UBS³ and the Nestle²⁶, which corrects the 25th edition. See the arguments of B. M. Metzger (*A Textual Commentary on the Greek New Testament* [London and New York: United Bible Societies, 1975²] 524-525) in support of reading ὅτι before ὃ ποιήσας, αὐτοῖς rather than αὐτή, and thus retaining αὐτά.

[137]"Do not say in your heart,...'It is because of my righteousness that the Lord has brought me in to possess this land'" (Deut 9:4). This text illustrates why one ought not push too far the notion that Paul alludes to the entire context of a partial verse he quotes, since for Deuteronomy the real reason Israel has been granted the land is not its own righteousness, but "the wickedness of these nations" (9:4-5).

[138]Cranfield applies Lev 18:5 in 10:5 to Christ, "who has done the righteousness which is of the law in His life and, above all, in His death, in the sense of fulfilling the law's requirements perfectly and so earning as His right a righteous status before God" (*Romans*, 521). This interpretation starts from the premise that 10:4 makes a christological affirmation, and further requires that Cranfield understand Christ as somehow the subject as well as the object of καταγαγεῖν and ἀναγαγεῖν in 10:6-7 although God is clearly the actor.

by him?"): to unmask as ultimately foolish the confusion of human and divine action. The righteousness ἐκ νόμου, the righteousness of God's gracious sovereignty, can never be accomplished by human beings because it requires that of which only God is capable (10:6-7) and which God alone dispenses universally (ἐγγύς σου, 10:8; οὐ...διαστολή, 10:12) to those who call upon his name (10:12).

Commentators chide Paul for deliberately truncating Deut 30:14 by deleting the final two words—αὐτὸ ποιεῖν—and thus distorting the original sense of the text,[139] but from the Apostle's perspective, the word which is near has already been accomplished by God. We have already established that Paul's exegesis of Deut 30:12-14 has been filtered through the sapiential tradition that equates God's wisdom and God's law.[140] The function of that wisdom tradition in Paul's argument now becomes clear. Deuteronomy 30 promises to Baruch that God's wisdom is accessible to all, present in God's ubiquitous law. So Paul, for whom God's righteous law reaches its τέλος in the gospel of Christ, employs Deuteronomy 30 to affirm the universal availability of the gospel. Human ἔργα—whether the works of the law, going up to heaven, or descending into the abyss—are precluded by God's self-revelation in the wisdom of the gospel. The only appropriate response to God, then, is faith in God's impartial righteousness, "the word of faith which we preach" (10:8).[141]

Paul answers the διὰ τί; of 9:32, therefore, first in 9:32-10:13 by saying that the gospel God set before Jews and Gentiles has become salvation for Gentiles and a stumbling block for Israel, precisely because of its availability to all.[142] In 10:14-21, then, he goes on to say that even

---

[139]E.g., Schoeps, *Paul*, 213-218; Barrett, *Romans*, 199.

[140]Above, pp. 133-137.

[141]Paul's uses of Χριστός (Rom 10:4), ῥῆμα τῆς πίστεως (10:8), and ῥῆμα Χριστοῦ (10:17) are all ways of referring to the εὐαγγέλιον of God's righteousness (1:16). Similar shorthand reference to the gospel is expressed by ὁ λόγος τοῦ σταυροῦ in 1 Cor 1:18, ὁ λόγος μου which is parallel to τὸ κήρυγμά μου in 1 Cor 2:4 (cf. ὁ λόγος ἡμῶν, 2 Cor 1:18), ὁ λόγος τοῦ θεοῦ (1 Cor 14:36; 2 Cor 2:17; 4:2), ὁ λόγος τῆς καταλλαγῆς (2 Cor 5:19), ὁ λόγος ζωῆς (Phil 2:16), and simply ὁ λόγος (Phil 1:14). Repeatedly, the emphasis is on the word of what God has accomplished in Christ rather than on any particular word(s) spoken.

[142]This dual nature of the gospel—as saving righteousness and stone of stumbling—functions for Paul much as Jesus' parables do for Mark: *in*

Israel's misunderstanding has in part been God's doing. The causal chain in 10:14-15 (calling upon comes from believing, believing from hearing, hearing from preaching, preaching from being sent) is designed to prove essentially what 9:28 claims: God accomplishes his purpose. The preachers have been sent; faith results from the preaching. But, he observes in v 16, not all have obeyed the gospel. Does this mean the gospel has failed? No, this too is prophesied by Isaiah (v 16), who knew that faith (ἐπίστευσεν) comes from the report (ἀκοή) of the gospel (cf. v 17) and that not all obey. Could the problem, then, be that Israel has not heard? No, Ps 18:5 proves that the preaching has been world-wide (cf. ῥῆμα vv 17-18). Furthermore, it is not even a matter of Israel's not knowing (ἔγνω, v 19; cf. ἐπίγνωσιν, v 2). What Deut 32:21 predicts (and therefore what has happened in Israel's encounter with the preaching of the gospel) is that God will make Israel jealous of the Gentiles (v 19), and Isaiah predicts (v 20; Isa 65:1) that the Gentiles will find God without looking for him. The question raised in 9:30-31 is answered in 10:19-20 in reverse order: Israel has not attained righteousness (9:31) because God wants to make Israel jealous of the Gentiles (10:19); the Gentiles have received righteousness (9:30) because God chooses to be revealed to those who do not seek or ask after him (10:20). But the same verse of scripture documents God's continual—and continuing—offer of mercy to Israel: "All day long I have held out my hands to a disobedient and contrary people" (10:21; Isa 65:2). Paul shifts the adverbial phrase ὅλην τὴν ἡμέραν from Isa 65:2 to the front of the citation to emphasize God's abiding relationship with his people.[143] Israel's stubbornness is not minimized, but is embraced by divine sovereignty. God has used the gospel (a) to trip up Israel while the Gentiles believed so as to make Israel jealous, and (b) to reach out in mercy to the people God foreknew.

---

order to keep those outside from understanding τὸ μυστήριον...τῆς βασιλείας that the disciples have been given (Mark 4:11) *until* the appropriate time (see J. Marcus, "Mark 4:10-12 and Marcan Epistemology," *JBL* 103 [1984] 564-565). In Mark's case, the appropriate time is Jesus' death and resurrection; for Paul, it is the πλήρωμα τῶν ἐθνῶν (Rom 11:26).

[143]Correctly Barrett, *Romans*, 205-206; *contra* those who claim the citation functions only to indict Israel (e.g., Nygren, *Romans*, 388).

C. 11:1-32

The third stage of the argument begins (11:1) with a preliminary conclusion to the preceding argument and a question elicited by it: Since God continues to reach out to Israel, "I therefore say, God has not rejected his people, has he?" The answer comes in two parts, 11:1b-6 and 7-10. First of all, the existence of faithful Jews like the Apostle himself proves the psalmist's claim that "God has not rejected his people" (11:2; Ps 94:14). The addition of ὅν προέγνω strengthens the possessive αὐτοῦ of the Psalm verse, even as it adds a certain ironic tone to the ἢ οὐκ οἴδατε that follows. Israel and the Roman church may not be aware that God is in control of Israel's destiny, but God has known all along.

The citations from 1 Kgs 19:10-18 demonstrate not Paul's role as Elijah *redivivus*,[144] but his likeness to the "seven thousand who did not bow the knee to Baal" (11:4). In both cases (οὕτως...καί, 11:5) God has left *for himself* a faithful remnant. Paul adds ἐμαυτῷ to the verse from 1 Kings to insist that the remnant demonstrates God's continuing mercy and faithfulness, rather than the remnant's worthiness. As in chapter 9, so here election is "the election of grace" rather than of works (11:5-6). The second half of the answer to the question of 11:1 focuses on God as much as the first half did. Just as God elects the remnant, so God hardens the unbelieving λοιπούς (11:7). This, too, is demonstrated by scripture (καθάπερ γέγραπται, 11:8). The citation is an amalgamation of Isa 29:10 and Deut 29:3,[145] drawing πνεῦμα κατανύξεως from the former and ἔδωκεν ὁ θεός,

---

[144]*Contra* Käsemann, *Romans*, 301.

[145]On this as Paul's other uses of scripture in Romans 9-11, see J. W. Aageson, "Scripture and Structure in the Development of the Argument in Romans 9-11," *CBQ* 48 (1968) 265-289; E. E. Ellis, *Paul's Use of the Old Testament* (Edinburgh and London: Oliver and Boyd, 1957); Getty, "Apocalyptic Perspective," 102-118; O. Michel, *Paulus und seine Bibel* (Gütersloh: Gütersloher, 1929); D. O. Via, "A Structuralist Approach to Paul's Old Testament Hermeneutic," *Int* 28 (1974) 201-220; A. Maillot, "Essai sur les citations veterotestamentaires contenues dans Romains 9 a 11, ou comment se servir de la Torah pour montrer que le 'Christ est la fin de la Torah'," *Etudes Theologiques et Religieuses* 57 (1982) 55-73; E. Brandenburger, "Paulinische Schriftauslegung in der Kontroverse um das Verheissungswort Gottes (Röm 9)," *ZTK* 82 (1985) 1-47; M. A. Seifrid, "Paul's Approach to the Old Testament in Rom 10:6-8," *Trinity Journal* 6 ns (1985) 3-37; C. A. Evans, "Paul and the Hermeneutics of 'True

βλέπειν, ὦτα, ἀκούειν, and ἕως τῆς ἡμέρας from the latter. What both Isa 29:10 and Deut 29:3 have in common, and what apparently connects the verses for Paul, is ὀφθαλμούς, which is also the catch-word that draws Ps 68:23 into the proof at Rom 11:9-10.[146] What it means that οἱ...λοιποὶ ἐπωρώθησαν (11:7) is that God has stupefied, blinded, and deafened the λοιπούς to the gospel—even though, as Paul has shown in 10:16-21, the proclamation goes out to all. Whether Paul intends the τράπεζα in Ps 68:23 to suggest the law,[147] Jewish table fellowship,[148] Israel's cult,[149] or "in a general way...the divine hardening,"[150] it is more likely that it is not that word but the phrase οἱ ὀφθαλμοί...τοῦ μὴ βλέπειν, repeating part of Deut 29:3, which makes the citation appropriate. The psalmist's use of σκάνδαλον (68:23, Rom 11:9) further recalls the stone of stumbling in 9:33, and reemphasizes the fact that God is responsible for Israel's blindness, even as he has caused its stumbling.

At 11:11, as at 11:1, Paul concludes what has come before with a question that further advances his argument. If God has blinded Israel and continually 'bends their neck' (11:10), is this a permanent condition? Of course not, since Israel's very hardening has meant the Gentiles' salvation, which will itself result in Israel's. The relationship between the Gentiles' salvation and Israel's jealousy and consequent salvation outlined in 11:11-15 and illustrated by the image of the olive tree in 16-24[151] is not unprepared for. It has been hinted at twice already: generally in the dynamic of vessels

---

Prophecy': A Study of Romans 9-11," *Bib* 65 (1984) 560-570; H. Hübner, *Gottes Ich und Israel: Zum Schriftgebrauch des Paulus in Römer 9-11* FRLANT 136 (Göttingen: Vandenhoeck and Ruprecht, 1984).

[146]The addition of καὶ εἰς θήραν to the first line of the psalm represents Paul's replication of a common OT parallelism of πάγις and θήρα (Ps 34:8; 123:6-7; Prov 11:8-9; cf. Am 3:4, 5).

[147]Sanday and Headlam, *Romans*, 315.

[148]Barrett, *Romans*, 211.

[149]Käsemann, *Romans*, 302.

[150]Cranfield, *Romans*, 552.

[151]See K. H. Rengstorf, "Das Ölbaum-Gleichnis in Röm 11,11ff.: Versuch einer weiterführenden Deutung" in *Donum Gentilicium: New Testament Studies in Honour of David Daube*, ed. E. Bammel, C. K. Barrett, W. D. Davies (Oxford: Clarendon, 1978) 126-164 and the literature cited there.

of wrath borne for the sake of vessels of mercy (9:22-23), and specifically in the citation from Deuteronomy 32 in 10:19. The subject of παραζηλόω in that verse changes from God to the Apostle himself in 11:14 as he magnifies his God-given mission to Gentiles on Israel's behalf. Moses said it first (10:19) and now Paul's ministry confirms God's intention to harden Israel so that Gentiles can believe and thus provoke Israel to jealousy and so to faith.

The concrete ramifications of this back-and-forth nature of God's dealings with Israel and the Gentiles[152] are a precluding of boasting (11:18-21) and a warning to both Christian Gentiles and non-Christian Jews to heed the χρηστότητα καὶ ἀποτομίαν θεοῦ (11:22). The former are warned to remain in God's kindness; the latter, not to remain in their unbelief (ἐὰν ἐπιμένῃς...ἐὰν μὴ ἐπιμένωσιν, vv 22-23). The God who hardened Israel on the Gentiles' behalf can also cut off the latter-day branches (v 24). Here as in chapter 9 God's call is sovereign and is independent of human effort. From the very beginning of the argument, God's kindness and severity have been two sides of the same reality: ἠγάπησα...ἐμίσησα (9:13), ἐλεήσω...οἰκτιρήσω (9:15), ἐλεεῖ...σκληρύνει (9:18), τὴν ὀργήν...πλοῦτον τῆς δόξης (9:22-23).[153] And the way those two sides of God's nature[154] are discerned historically is in the way Israel's hardening serves the Gentiles, and Gentile faith serves Israel.

The μυστήριον of vv 25-26 actually reveals nothing new by this point in the argument.[155] Israel's hardening has been explicitly in view since 11:7 and the Gentiles' faith since 11:14, but even more, their interdependence has been central to Paul's thinking ever since 9:24. The combined citation from Isa 59:20-21 and Isa 27:9 which is part and parcel of the oracle[156] lends the weight of scripture to Paul's prophecy. His crucial substitution of ἐκ for

---

[152]Cf. Beker: "the surprising wavelike or undulating dynamic of God's salvation-history, the 'interdependence' of God's dealings with Gentiles and Jews" (*Paul*, 334).

[153]Cf. Sir 5:6, "For both mercy and wrath are with him;" and 16:11-12, "For mercy and wrath are with the Lord; he is mighty to forgive, and he pours out wrath. As great as his mercy, so great is also his reproof."

[154]On Jewish traditions about God's two natures, see Dahl, "Contradictions," 168; G. Stählin, "ὀργή, κ.τ.λ." in *TDNT* (1967) vol. 5, 424; W. Bousset, *Die Religion des Judentums im späthellenistischen Zeitalter* (Tübingen: J. C. B. Mohr, 1926) 350-351.

[155]*Contra* Noack, "Current and Backwater," 165-166.

[156]Aune, *Prophecy*, 252.

ἕνεκεν in Isa 59:20 reaffirms exactly what he says at 9:5, that from Israel κατὰ σάρκα comes the Christ who will turn away godlessness from Jacob, even as he has from the Gentiles.

In the μυστήριον of 11:25-26, more than anywhere in Romans 9-11, apocalyptic and wisdom traditions coalesce to advance—and in this case, conclude—Paul's argument. As with his other uses of the word,[157] this revelation of a divine mystery is the disclosure of God's wise plan for the eschatological future. Followed as it is by the wisdom hymn of 11:33-36, there is no question Paul considers the indirectness of Israel's eschatological salvation a function of the depth of God's wisdom. As so often was the case with Jewish apocalypticists' uses of confluent apocalyptic and wisdom traditions, so Paul's merging of the two perspectives shifts his focus from exclusive dependence on future vindication to the present possibility of meaningful human life before the eschaton. He reveals the mystery at 11:25 for a profoundly paraenetic purpose: ἵνα μὴ ἦτε ἑαυτοῖς φρόνιμοι.

The Gentile mission which Paul magnifies (11:13) receives its present urgency from its role in God's apocalyptic design to save all; the time before the end is full of potential for bringing about the πλήρωμα τῶν ἐθνῶν (11:25). Gentile Christians dare not boast in their position since it is God who has given it to them. Moreover, their unsought-for righteousness (9:30) benefits not only themselves but ultimately πᾶς᾽Ισραήλ whose full acceptance it will provoke.

The concluding summation of the argument in 11:28-32[158] reasserts the interdependence of Jew and Gentile by affirming both God's irrevocable election of Israel (v 29) and God's impartial judgment and redemption of all (v 32). Paul's certainty that Israel will eventually receive mercy is evident in the progression in vv 30-31: Gentiles were once disobedient but now have received mercy; in the same way, Israel is now disobedient in order that they might receive mercy. This restoration of order, this final consequence of God's impartiality and faithfulness elicits from the Apostle praise which is singularly appropriate to the argument just concluded. Paul gives thanks not for God's sovereignty, God's mercy, or God's faithfulness, but for God's wisdom.

---

[157]1 Cor 2:1, 7; 4:1; 13:2; 14:2; 15:51. The clearest parallel is 1 Cor 2:7, where what Paul and his colleagues speak is the θεοῦ σοφίαν ἐν μυστηρίῳ whose content is ἃ ἡτοίμασεν ὁ θεὸς τοῖς ἀγαπῶσιν αὐτόν (2:9).

[158]See above, p. 146.

D. The Wisdom Hymn

The praise of God in Rom 11:33-36 has long been recognized to have traditional elements with parallels in both Jewish and Greco-Roman sources.[159] So too, for some time, the passage's poetic or hymnic structure has been analyzed.[160] More recently, scholars have noted the wisdom character of the hymn and some of the theological implications of that stylistic heritage.[161] This section (1) reviews the hymnic elements of the passage, (2) assesses the evidence regarding its authorship, and (3) examines its meaning and function at the end of Romans 11 to demonstrate that Paul quotes a traditional synagogue hymn because the mystery of God's salvation of Israel and the Gentiles is part and parcel of the wisdom of God.

(1) Rom 11:33-36 exhibits a number of hymnic characteristics. Eduard Norden suggests the following strophic arrangement to highlight the parallel structure of nine lines:[162]

(v 33)   ὦ βάθος πλούτου καὶ σοφίας καὶ γνώσεως θεοῦ
           ὡς ἀνεξεραύνητα τὰ κρίματα αὐτοῦ
           καὶ ἀνεξιχνίαστοι αἱ ὁδοὶ αὐτοῦ.

(v 34)   τίς γὰρ ἔγνω νοῦν κυρίου;
           ἢ τίς σύμβουλος αὐτοῦ ἐγένετο;

(v 35)   ἢ τίς προέδωκεν αὐτῷ,
           καὶ ἀνταποδοθήσεται αὐτῷ;

(v 36)   ὅτι ἐξ αὐτοῦ καὶ δι' αὐτοῦ καὶ εἰς αὐτὸν τὰ πάντα·
           αὐτῷ ἡ δόξα εἰς τοὺς αἰῶνας, ἀμήν.

---

[159]E. Norden, *Agnostos Theos* (Leipzig: Teubner, 1913) 240-250.

[160]G. Bornkamm, "The Praise of God" in *Early Christian Experience*, tr. P. L. Hammer (New York: Harper and Row, 1969), 105-111; R. Deichgräber, *Gotteshymnus und Christus-hymnus in der frühen Christenheit* (Göttingen: Vandenhoeck and Ruprecht, 1967) 60-64; W. H. Gloer, "Homologies and Hymns in the New Testament: Form, Content, and Criteria for Identification," *Perspectives in Religious Studies* 11 (1984) 115-132; V. van Zutphen, "Studies on the Hymn in Romans 11,33-36" (Ph.D. Dissertation, Würzburg, 1973); E. Stauffer, *New Testament Theology* (London: SCM, 1948) 338-339; R. P. Martin, *Worship in the Early Church* (Grand Rapids: Eerdmans, 1974) 36-37, 46; idem, "Aspects of Worship in the New Testament Church," *Vox Evangelica* 2 (1963) 7-9.

[161]Particularly Wilckens, "σοφία, κ.τ.λ.," 518; and A. T. Hanson, *The New Testament Interpretation of Scripture* (London: SPCK, 1980) 21-96.

[162]*Agnostos Theos*, 241.

The first three lines laud divine wisdom, the next four ask three rhetorical questions that highlight the immeasurability of that wisdom, and the final two form a doxology in praise of God's universal and eternal sovereignty.

Reinhardt Deichgräber notes the repeated use of triads: the three genitives dependent on βάθος (v 33a), three parallel rhetorical questions each beginning with τίς (vv 34-35a), and the three prepositions of the τὰ πάντα formula (v 36a).[163] Günther Bornkamm points to the chiastic structure of the relationship between the divine attributes and the rhetorical questions:[164]

πλούτου	(v 33a)
σοφίας	"
γνώσεως	"
ἔγνω	(v 34a)
σύμβουλος	(v 34b)
προέδωκεν	(v 35a)

"Wealth" is that which no one is in a position to give God; divine "wisdom" is that which precludes God's need for a human counselor; and God alone has "knowledge," since no one "has known the mind of the Lord."

There are no fewer than nine references to God using the typical hymnic pronoun αὐτός;[165] the exclamation ὧ in v 33 is familiar from numerous OT and early Jewish hymns;[166] and rhetorical questions are common in hymns from all religious traditions, not only Judaism.[167] Finally, the concluding ascription of praise in v 36b parallels numerous Jewish doxologies, some of them nearly *verbatim*:[168]

---

[163]*Gotteshymnus*, 62.

[164]"The Praise of God," 107.

[165]Deichgräber, *Gotteshymnus*, 61. For some reason, Deichgräber counts only eight. The prevalence in hymnic contexts of pronominal and participial references to God is documented by Norden (*Agnostos Theos*, 201-206), Stauffer (*Theology*, 338-339), and Gloer ("Homologies," 127-128).

[166]Deichgräber, *Gotteshymnus*, 62 (cf. Pss 8:2,10; 65:3; 83:2; 103:24 [LXX]; Sir 17:29).

[167]*Ibid.*, 61.

[168]*Ibid.*, 37-38; cf. Charlesworth, "Prolegomenon," 266-272, 281-283.

παρὰ τοῦ θεοῦ, ᾧ ἡ δόξα εἰς τοὺς αἰῶνας τῶν αἰώνων, ἀμήν.
(4 Maccabees 18:24)

...σου ἔστιν ἡ δόξα εἰς τοὺς αἰῶνας, ἀμήν.
(Prayer of Manasses 15)

These observations are more than sufficient to conclude that Rom 11:33-36 represent a hymn or hymnic composition. Its strophic sructure of nine lines, the repetition of triads, the chiastic relationship among the divine attributes and rhetorical questions, the repeated pronominal references to God, and the doxological conclusion are all indications of hymnic material. Their concentration in so brief a passage gives these four verses a complex and self-sufficient structure characteristic of numerous hymns from antiquity.

(2) Traditional material. The most striking characteristic of this text is the apparent plurality of sources for its various elements. The interweaving of customarily "Jewish" and "Hellenistic" words and ideas makes this passage among the most interesting pieces of traditional material in the Pauline corpus. This intimate combination of such traditionally distinct styles of language and thought, most of which seem to have arrived in Rom 11:33-36 by the route of diaspora Judaism, testifies to the truth of Martin Hengel's observation that stark contrasts between so-called Jewish and Hellenistic thought forms in the first century are illegitimate.[169]

The βάθος of God is a category Paul uses in another wisdom context, 1 Cor 2:10, and there are numerous OT references to the depth of wisdom (e.g. Eccl 7:24, cf. 1 En 63:3) and Greek antecedents for the metaphor βάθος πλούτου in Sophocles, Aeschylus, and Pindar.[170] On the assumption that at 1 Cor 2:10 "[Paulus] sicher von einer Quelle abhängt," Norden suggests that in Rom 11:33, as well, the Apostle makes use of a source from hellenistic Judaism that praises the depth of divine wisdom.[171]

The α-privative verbal adjectives ἀνεξεραύνητα and ἀνεξιχνίαστοι of v 33 are typically Greek speculative notions—the inscrutability and indetectability of the divine—but they are used to describe very biblical words—God's κρίματα and ὁδοί. The root of ἀνεξιχνίαστος, however, 'footprints' (ἴχνος), is a helpful reminder that the word can also be understood as an appropriately 'biblical' idea, and indeed Günther Harder has

---

[169]*Judaism and Hellenism*, vol. 1, 310.
[170]*Agnostos Theos*, 243.
[171]*Ibid.*

shown that the word is frequently found in Jewish prayer language.[172] The uses of ἀνεξιχνίαστος in LXX wisdom contexts (e.g., Job 5:9, 9:10, and 34:24), and in the (probably authentic) Jewish prayers discovered by Wilhelm Bousset in the Apostolic Constitutions VII,35,8-10,[173] fuel the suspicion that the poetic parallelism of v 33 comes to this hymn from diaspora synagogue worship.[174]

The double quotation from scripture in vv 34-35 presents a particular challenge, as the language of Isa 40:13 is clearly from the LXX (τίς ἔγνω νοῦν κυρίου; καὶ τίς αὐτοῦ σύμβουλος ἐγένετο ὃς συμβίβα αὐτόν;), but that of Job 41:3 is like neither the LXX (ἢ τίς ἀντιστήσεταί μοι καὶ ὑπομενεῖ) nor an independent translation of the MT. Hanson argues that the Targum on Job provides the greatest similarity to the rhetorical question in v 35:[175]

> Who has been beforehand with me in the works of creation, that I have to pay him back? Is not everything under the heaven mine?

Moreover, Hanson traces the uses of Isa 40:13 and Job 41:3 in rabbinic interpretation, and discovers that both verses are connected with notions of a pre-existent Torah and are often interpreted together.[176] Although Isa 40:13 could be (and was) quoted by itself, Job 41:3 has little meaning alone, apart from its context. Ultimately, Hanson claims that the dual citation in Rom 11:34-35 functions as a christological proof text referring to Christ as the preexistent Wisdom of God, and on that basis assumes that the association of the two verses in Jewish tradition must predate Paul's.[177] His final conclusion is that

> the combined citation in Romans 11:34-35 is in fact an implicitly Christological statement. Paul has ended his exposition of the whole design of God, and exclaims with admiration at the depth and unexpectedness of that design. But, far from suggesting that God's

---

[172]G. Harder, *Paulus und das Gebet* (Gutersloh: C. Bertelsmann, 1936) 51-55.

[173]E. Peterson, "ἀνεξιχνίαστος" in *TDNT* (1964) vol. 1, 358.

[174]Cf. also Käsemann, *Romans*, 318; Charlesworth, "Prolegomenon," 283.

[175]Hanson, *The New Testament Interpretation*, 85.

[176]E.g., Pesikta Rabbati 25.2; Pesikta de Rab Kahana 9.2 (*ibid.*, 86-88).

[177]*Ibid.*, 93.

intention has always been inscrutable, he implies by his two
citations that it has always been known to God's counsellor, the
pre-existent Christ, or Son, to whom God disclosed his whole
mind and in whom his whole plan for the redemption and
justification of [humanity] has been carried out.[178]

That conclusion must be rejected, not only because it presupposes a
great deal of second-guessing on the part of Paul's readers who would
presumably be expected to detect a most subtle christological reference, but
because it assigns to vv 33-36 a completely different role in their context
and attributes to Paul another agenda than are otherwise evident. Christ has
not been mentioned in the argument since 10:17, and God is clearly the
subject of the preceding discussion, the source of the mystery of salvation
(11:21-32). That the verses from Isaiah 40 and Job 41 are linked in later
Jewish tradition and associated with God's wisdom is helpful for
understanding the hymn, however, and provides yet another indication of its
traditional origins. It seems improbable that Jews of subsequent generations
would have taken the same exegetical step to combine these verses if they
had first been linked in a Christian writing, whether or not that Christian
text made an explicitly christological point. It is more likely, as Hanson
suggests, "that the two verses were already associated in the Jewish
exegetical tradition when Paul used them."[179]
There are numerous precedents for the three rhetorical questions about
God's wisdom,[180] but the closest parallel is in 2 Baruch:

> But who, O Lord my God, understands your judgment, or who
> searches out the depth of your way, or who considers the heavy
> burden of your path, or who can reflect on your incomprehensible
> decree, or who of those ever born has found the beginning and end
> of your wisdom? (14:8-10)

As Käsemann notes, the words may be very similar, but the intention
is quite different from Paul's. Whereas Baruch despairs of understanding
God's ways and therefore resigns himself (at least provisionally) to not
knowing, Paul's doxology expresses joy and thanksgiving for the revelation
of the μυστήριον of God's mercy, however inscrutable it may be.[181] The

---

[178]*Ibid.*, 91
[179]*Ibid.*
[180]Cf. Sir 1:3,6; 16:20; 18:4b-6; etc.
[181]Käsemann, *Romans*, 319.

poetic praise of God's wisdom near the conclusion of 2 Baruch, on the other hand, *follows* the answer to Baruch's questions and the resolution of his despair, and that passage functions very much as Rom 11:33-36 does, even though it lacks verbal similarities.

> Who can equal your goodness, O Lord for it is incomprehensible.
> Or who can fathom your grace which is without end?
> Or who can understand your intelligence?
> Or who can narrate the thoughts of your spirit?
> Or who of those born can hope to arrive at these things,
>   apart from those to whom you are merciful and gracious? (75:1-5)

Baruch praises not only God's goodness and grace, but God's intelligence and the "thoughts of [God's] spirit" (vv 3, 4). What was hidden about God's wisdom in 14:8-10 is now (relatively) known, and Baruch gives thanks. Although no one yet understands God's wisdom (75:3; cf. 14:10), the tone of the later passage—significantly a passage in response to Baruch's revelation—is decidedly laudatory rather than despairing.

So also 1 En 93:11-14, although not poetic in form, follows the revelation of the Apocalypse of Weeks and marvels with numerous rhetorical questions about the depths of God's thought and the enormity of heavenly mysteries.

> For what kind of a human being is there that is able to hear the voice of the Holy One without being shaken? Who is there that is able to ponder his (deep) thoughts? Who is there that can look directly at all the good deeds? What kind of a person or even perhaps a spirit—or, even if he ascended (into the heavens) and saw all (these heavenly beings and) their wings and contemplated them; or even if he can do (what the heavenly beings) do?—and is able to live? What kind of a person is anyone that is able to understand the nature of the breadth and length of the earth? To whom has the extent of all these been shown? Is there perchance any human being that is able to understand the length of heaven, the extent of its altitude, upon what it is founded, the number of the stars, and (the place) where all the luminaries rest?

A still closer parallel may be found in the hymns of the Qumran sectarians. Two in particular express similar thanksgiving for God's revelations of mysteries and insight. Their expressions of wonder at the magnitude of God's wisdom are particularly similar to Paul's.

I thank you, O Lord,
For you gave me insight into your truth,
    And your wonderful secrets [or: mysteries] you made me know,
    And your steadfast love to [sinful] man,
    And your great compassion to the perverted heart.
Who is like you among the gods, O Lord?
    And what is like your truth?
    And who is declared innocent before you when he is judged?
There is no spirit who can answer against your judgment;
    And no one can stand before your wisdom.
But all the sons of your truth you will bring in forgiveness before you,
    To cleanse them from their sins in your great goodness,
    And in the abundance of your compassion to make them
For you are an eternal God,
    And all your ways are established forever and ever;
    There is none but you.
And what is the man of chaos and the master of nothingness,
    That he should understand your wonderful deeds?
                    (1QH 7:26-33)

And what then is man? He is but earth.
          [From clay] he is pinched off, and to dust is his return.
Yet you make him wise in wonderful deeds like these,
    And a council [sic][182] of truth you make him know.
And I am dust and ashes,
    What can I devise unless you desire it?
    And what can I plan without your will?
    What strength have I unless you make me stand?
    And how shall I have insight unless you so intend for me?
    And what shall I say unless you open my mouth?
    And how shall I return answer unless you give me insight?
                    (1QH 10:3-7)[183]

---

[182]Surely the context demands "counsel" rather than "council" at this point to translate *sôd*; E. Lohse translates it "Rat" (*Die Texte aus Qumran: Hebräisch und Deutsch mit masoretischen Punktation* [Munich: Kösel, 1971²] 151). One suspects an undetected typographical error in Kittel's book.

[183]Translations from B. P.Kittel, *The Hymns of Qumran* (Chico: Scholars, 1981), 101, 138-139. For questions of date and authorship, see Charlesworth, "Jewish Hymns, Odes, and Prayers," 413-414.

In each of these cases—2 Bar 75:1-5, 1 En 93:11-14, and 1QH 7:26-33; 10:3-7—rhetorical questions about God's wisdom are asked to offer thanksgiving for a revelation of God's mysterious plan of redemption. The similarity of these questions to those from Isaiah 40 and Job 41 in Rom 11:34-35 plus their identity of function provide another clue to the traditional nature of the hymn in Romans 11.

The τὰ πάντα formula of Rom 11:36 was recognized as early as 1651 to bear striking resemblance to the "Bekenntnisformel der stoischen Theologie" Norden finds in Marcus Aurelius and elsewhere:[184]

All that is harmonious to you, O world, is also harmonious to me. Nothing comes to me too early or too late if it appears timely to you. All that your courses of years bring is fruit to me, O nature: ἐκ σου πάντα, ἐν σοι πάντα, εἰς σε πάντα (Περὶ ἑαυτοῦ, IV, 23).

The formula recurs throughout the NT,[185] and was very likely, as Käsemann contends,[186] drawn from Stoicism by the vehicle of hellenistic Judaism. The use of the phrase in Rom 11:36 makes one significant change, substituting διά for ἐν, which eliminates the pantheism implicit in the Stoic formulation. Since the same substitution is made in 1 Cor 8:6, but not in Eph 4:6 or Col 1:16-17, it may be that this is a distinctive Pauline alteration of the tradition.

Finally, four Pauline hapax legomena (ἀνεξεραύνητα, v 33b; ἀνεξιχνίαστοι, v 33c; σύμβουλος, v 34b; and προέδωκεν, v 35a) isolate at least some vocabulary as unusual or uncharacteristic. Of course the latter two derive from the scripture quotations, but the former are rare even in the NT: ἀνεξεραύνητα occurs nowhere else, ἀνεξιχνίαστοι only here and Eph 3:8. Of the rest of the theologically significant language in the hymn, only πλοῦτος occurs elsewhere in the Pauline corpus with the meaning attached to it in 11:33. At Rom 2:4 πλοῦτος is defined as God's kindness and forebearance and patience; at 9:23 it is God's glory (cf. also Phil 4:19); and the κύριος πάντων of 10:12 is the one who bestows the wealth of salvation on all who call upon him. In 11:12 πλοῦτος is used twice, parallel to the

---

[184]Norden (*Agnostos Theos*, 240, n.1) credits T. Gataker with the observation. The translation is from Bornkamm, "The Praise of God," 108.

[185]1 Cor 8:6; Eph 4:6; Col 1:16-17; Heb 2:10.

[186]Käsemann, *Romans*, 319.

σωτηρία of v 11. Clearly the wealth of God praised in 11:33 can be understood as the same discussed previously in Romans.[187]

The knowledge, judgments, and ways of God, though, however implied by the preceding argument, are not explicitly mentioned elsewhere in Romans. Of course the knowledge of God in 11:33 is, in the OT sense of *daᶜat*, "the gracious will of God directing history according to his plan,"[188] that is, election. Israel is, after all, τὸν λαὸν αὐτοῦ ὃν προέγνω (11:2). But Paul nowhere else speaks of γνῶσις as anything but a human possession.[189] The understanding of γνῶσις θεοῦ is appropriate to the context of Romans 9-11, but Paul's customary words are κλῆσις (e.g., Rom 11:29) and ἐκλογή (9:11; 11:5, 7; 1 Thess 1:14; cf. καλέω [4:17; 8:30; 9:7, 12, 24-26], ἐκλεκτός [8:33], κλῆτος [1:1, 6-7; 8:28]). So also, Rom 11:33 is the only place Paul uses κρίμα in the plural, except when he refers to human civil actions in 1 Cor 6:7; and the only other references to God's ὁδοί are from scripture quotations (Rom 3:16-17). His other uses of ὁδός are of his own ways in Christ (1 Cor 4:17), and the more excellent way of love (1 Cor 12:31).

This abundance of unusual vocabulary and vocabulary used in uncharacteristic ways provides the final piece of evidence that Rom 11:33-36 has traditional origins. The intricacy of the hymn's structure and content fuel the suspicion that it had a life of its own prior to Romans. This is by no means to assert that Paul is incapable of rhetorical elegance: the preceding paragraph (vv 28-32) attests his skill.[190] But the abundance of non-Pauline words and concepts, coupled with the self-contained character of the hymn tip the scales in favor of a pre-Pauline origin. Furthermore, 2 Bar 75:1-5 and the two Qumran Hodayot appear to be very similar compositions, written for apparently the same purposes, and can therefore be said to demonstrate roughly contemporary parallels. Finally, in both 1 Enoch and 2 Baruch a revelation of future salvation is immediately followed by praise of God's wisdom, the latter in hymnic form. It is reasonable, therefore, to assert that Paul found this particular hymn in use in the synagogue and deemed it useful for concluding his argument in Romans because it follows a revelation of God's wisdom. Not only is its content appropriate to the context in Romans 11, but the fact that the initial line

---

[187]See above, p. 129.

[188]Bultmann, "γινώσκω, κ.τ.λ.," 707.

[189]Cf. Rom 2:20; 15:14; 1 Cor 1:5; 8:1ff; 12:8; etc.

[190]See above, p. 146.

contains the word πλοῦτος, a concept so important to the argument of Romans 9-11, may very well have been what suggested it.

3. The function of the hymn. In other searches for traditional material in Paul's letters, one of the most important questions concerns how the Apostle may have altered his source to suit his own purposes. In Phil 2:6-11, for example, Paul's addition of θανάτου δὲ σταυροῦ in v 8 disrupts the poetry but puts a distinctive Pauline stamp on the christological hymn.[191] Rom 11:33-36, however, bears few traces of such modification. Only the substitution of διά for ἐν in the τὰ πάντα formula of v 36, a move which he also makes in 1 Cor 8:6 and which the authors of Eph 4:6 and Col 1:16-17 do not think necessary, may betray Paul's editorial activity. Otherwise, the hymn stands by itself as a typical Jewish praise of God's wise ordering of the world. Paul's invocation of the hymn in response to the revelation of a saving mystery is itself traditional, as the parallels in 2 Baruch and the Qumran Hodayot indicate.

Just as 11:28-32 provide the 'logical' conclusion to the argument, so 11:33-36 offer the 'liturgical' counterpart. The hymn combines with the introductory oath of 9:1-5 to create an *inclusio* for the argument of chapters 9-11, beginning and ending with ascriptions of praise to the omnipotent God (cf. ἐπὶ πάντων, 9:5; τὰ πάντα, 11:36). The doxology ascribes glory to the One blessed in 9:5. Paul praises God for the marvelous and indeed mysterious wisdom that provides salvation for all—both Jew and Gentile. God's mercy is as unfathomable as God's justice is sure. Surely no one "has known the mind of the Lord," (11:34) but the mystery of God's saving plan (11:25-27) has been made known, and in that Paul rejoices. Käsemann points out that the doxology functions at the end of Romans 9-11 much as Dan 2:20-23 does in its context,[192] to praise God who "reveals deep and mysterious things" (Dan 2:22). But it should also be recalled that throughout the early Jewish literature examined in Chapter Two, God's wisdom is frequently identified specifically with the apocalyptic mysteries of future salvation. That Paul should praise God's wisdom for the revelation of his μυστήριον concerning Israel is very much in keeping with contemporary Jewish thought.

---

[191] See G. Bornkamm, "On Understanding the Christ-hymn (Philippians 2.6-11)" in *Early Christian Experience*, 112-122, and T. Nagata, "Philippians 2:5-11: A Case Study in the Contextual Shaping of Early Christology" (Ph.D. Dissertation, Princeton Theological Seminary, 1981) and the literature cited there.

[192] *Romans*, 319.

Just as 11:28-32 conclude not only chapters 9-11 but the whole of Romans 1:16-11:27, so the hymn in 11:33-36 expresses Paul's awe and wonder at the miracle of God's redemption of the world. "It is not only God's way of dealing with Israel which is miraculous, which surpasses [human] understanding," observes Dahl. "That no [one] holds God in his debt, so that what he receives from God is never merited, is a fundamental idea which underlies all of Romans."[193] The κρίματα and ὁδοί of God acclaimed in 11:33 are not only God's ways with Israel, but the judgment of God on pagan idolatry (1:18ff) and Jewish boasting (2:17ff), the grace of God that justifies sinners by faith (3:21ff), and the new life in Christ God granted believers (5:1ff).[194] God's dealings with the world by means of the gospel are utterly consistent with God's dealings with the world by means of Israel. It is that consistency, that trustworthiness, that simultaneous impartiality and faithfulness of God which drives the argument of Romans to its conclusion in 11:28-32. And because it is God's wisdom—in the law and in the gospel which is the τέλος of that law—which remains consistent, Paul's doxological response in 11:33-36 cannot help but laud God's wisdom.

IV. Conclusions

In this chapter we have arrived at three related conclusions. First of all, Romans 9-11 are not an appendix to the first eight chapters, a recapitulation of the theme of those eight chapters, nor a delayed conclusion to 3:1-9, but a critical component of the argument of the entire letter. The question about the relation of the church to Israel in the plan of salvation, although discussed most thoroughly in chapters 9-11, underlies the whole argument of Romans from the statement of its theme in 1:16. The gospel is "the power of God for salvation to everyone who believes"—that is, God judges and redeems impartially, without regard for ethnic or religious background. But the gospel is also "to the Jew first and also to the Greek," which means that God's faithfulness to Israel as his elect people is not negated by the inclusion of Gentiles, but is rather affirmed by it. The God who justifies the ungodly, both Jew and Gentile, is the God who may be trusted to keep his promises to Israel.

---

[193]"Israel," 157.

[194]Cf. Käsemann: "Only the judged who have been set in their proper place are saved. Only the needy who can make no boast of themselves nor insist on privileges or merits are saved. The way to salvation simply cannot be isolated from that for anyone" (*Romans*, 320).

Our second conclusion concerns the argument of Romans 9-11. The three chapters, rather than making three separate and mutually exclusive attempts to solve the problem of Israel's unbelief, are rather a single sustained argument that explains both Jewish unbelief and Gentile faith. The question that elicits Paul's argument is not only, Has God's faithfulness to Israel been nullified by Jewish unbelief? but also, Has God ceased to be impartial by calling only Gentiles to faith? Divine impartiality and faithfulness remain in dynamic tension for Paul at all three stages of the argument. First (9:6-29), he demonstrates how God elects both Israel and the Gentiles on the same basis—mercifully without regard for human behavior or worthiness. Secondly (9:30-10:21), he shows that the gospel of God's righteousness for everyone who believes has produced both Gentile faith and Jewish unbelief. The impartial world-wide proclamation of the gospel functions to harden Israel so that the Gentiles can be reached. And finally (11:1-32), he says this hardening of part of Israel is itself temporary, destined to be removed by the fulness of Gentile faith. The mystery revealed at 11:25-27 makes explicit what has implicitly driven the argument since 9:6—the interrelatedness of Jew and Gentile in salvation history and God's back-and-forth dealings with Israel and the nations are the concrete manifestations of Paul's dual claim that God is both faithful and impartial. God's saving intention for the world can be ultimately thwarted by neither Jewish unbelief nor Gentile presumption because "God has consigned all to disobedience in order that he might have mercy on all" (11:32).

Thirdly, we determined the function of apocalyptic and wisdom traditions in this argument of Romans 9-11. The line of thought is profoundly structured by the apocalyptic categories of eschatological salvation, God's wrath and wealth of mercy, and the destiny of the people of God. But Paul's argument also uses sapiential traditions to describe God's freedom to elect impartially (9:20-23), to show how the gospel is the near word of God's wisdom (10:6-8), and to reveal a heavenly mystery about God's saving intentions (11:25-27). Because this mystery and the discussion which it brings to a close provide a glimpse into God's wise ordering of history and redemption, Paul concludes his argument—and the argument of the letter to this point—with a hymn in praise of God's wisdom (11:33-36). The Apostle's ascription of praise for the marvel of salvation is a traditional Jewish hymn to God's wisdom because, inscrutable as they are from a human perspective, God's judgments and ways have indeed been proclaimed in the gospel of Jesus Christ. In sum, the intersections of apocalyptic and wisdom traditions in Romans 9-11 afford Paul the means of maintaining a theological tension between God's faithfulness and God's impartiality, a tension he never resolves because it is constitutive of the character of God.

Excursus

Paul and Anti-Semitism: The Exegesis of Lloyd Gaston

Among the most provocative contributions to the recent scholarly debate about Romans 9-11, none is so distinctive—or potentially controversial—as that of Lloyd Gaston. Particularly in response to the accusation of Rosemary Ruether that Paul is substantially responsible for laying the theological foundation for Christian anti-semitism,[1] Gaston has risen with a call for a massive reassessment of Paul's thought on Jews and Judaism. In a series of recent articles,[2] he has offered a program of reinterpretation that not only rescues Paul from the charge of anti-semitism, but portrays him as the lone NT representative of a constructive relationship between the church and Judaism.

---

[1] *Faith and Fratricide: The Theological Roots of Anti-Semitism* (New York: Seabury, 1974).

[2] "Paul and the Torah" in *Anti-Semitism and the Foundations of Christianity*, ed. A. T. Davies (New York: Paulist, 1979) 48-71; "Abraham and the Righteousness of God," *Horizons in Biblical Theology* 2 (1980) 39-68; "Israel's Enemies in Pauline Theology," *NTS* 28 (1982) 400-423; "Angels and Gentiles in Early Judaism and in Paul," *Studies in Religion* 11 (1982) 65-75; and "Works of Law as Subjective Genitive," *Studies in Religion* 13 (1984) 39-46. Gaston also cites his "Paul and the Law in Galatians Two and Three" in *Anti-Judaism in Early Christianity*, ed. P. Richardson (Waterloo, Ontario: Wilfrid Laurier University, forthcoming); and J. G. Gager (*The Origins of Anti-Semitism: Attitudes Toward Judaism in Pagan and Christian Antiquity* [New York: Oxford University, 1983] 198) makes reference to several unpublished papers of Gaston, none of which were available to the present study.

All of the positive things Paul had to sayabout the righteousness of God effecting salvation for gentiles in Christ need not imply something negative about Israel and the Torah. Indeed, it may be that Paul, and Paul alone among the New Testament writers, had no left hand.[3] ...I believe that it is *possible* to interpret Paul in this manner. That it is *necessary* to do so is the implication of the agonized concern of many in the post-Auschwitz situation.[4]

Gaston's most enthusiastic advocate and publicist in this "reinvention of Paul"[5] has been John Gager. Gager's book *The Origins of Anti-Semitism* has given Gaston's proposals their widest circulation and strongest support, labelling his program a veritable "paradigm shift" in Pauline studies.[6]

---

[3]The phrase is Ruether's: "the christological midrash and its anti-Judaic left hand" (*Faith and Fratricide*, 95).

[4]Gaston, "Paul and the Torah," 67; emphasis added. Cf. also Gager's assessment: "For Gaston and others there is a profound theological urgency behind the exegetical task. No longer is it a case of the illegitimacy of Judaism. Unless they succeed in finding within the New Testament some area which is substantially free of anti-Judaism, the issue becomes the illegitimacy of Christianity" (*The Origins of Anti-Semitism*, 202). Gager also traces the modern debate about the historical and theological sources of Christian anti-Judaism, and reviews the discussion occasioned by Ruether's book (*ibid.*, 11-37).

[5]The title of Gager's chapter on Paul is "On Reinventing Paul" (*The Origins of Anti-Semitism*, 197-212).

[6]"Of course [Gager concedes] it would be premature to speak of a paradigm shift as an accomplished fact. At the moment one can speak only of the potential for revolution. But certainly the potential is present in Gaston's work" (*ibid.*, 198).

J. T. Koenig's more popular treatment of the issue of Paul and Judaism (*Jews and Christians in Dialogue: New Testament Foundations* [Philadelphia: Westminster, 1979] 37-59) arrives at a remarkably similar thesis independently (the book is the product of lectures delivered in 1975 and thus pre-dates Gaston's published work), but his argument is of necessity presented in less exegetical detail, and avoids the sweeping conclusions Gaston draws. Koenig too says Paul allows for "two valid ways [i.e., Christ and Torah]" (44), but unlike Gaston he is convinced that ultimately "God's Messiah must be first of all Israel's Messiah" (55). The question Koenig unfortunately leaves unanswered is the precise nature of Judaism's "validity" for Paul: is it a temporary concession until the parousia or a permanent alternative? The tone of Koenig's chapter suggests the

Whether and to what extent other scholars will be able to join Gaston's revolution depends on the historical and exegetical sturdiness of that program, which has yet to be tested.

The assumptions which dictate the course of Gaston's project are not difficult to discern. First, Gaston is convinced that the Christian scriptures are the primary theological tool in what is for him a most urgently needed Jewish-Christian dialogue. This theological commitment is given free reign in both his historical and exegetical investigations.

> A Christian Church with an anti-semitic New Testament is abominable, but a Christian Church without a New Testament is inconceivable.... Whatever the general effect of the gospels, it is Paul who has provided the theoretical structure for Christian anti-Judaism.... This [reconstruction of Paul] is not being done in the spirit of a theological reparation, if that were possible, but as a search for a new and better understanding of Paul on the part of those whose eyes have been shocked open [by the history of Christian anti-semitism]. Thereby we may find a foundation within the New Testament itself for attacking the Christian anti-Judaic myth Ruether so eloquently delineates.[7]

The second presupposition apparent in Gaston's essays originates from a desire to defend Paul himself. The centerpiece of Gaston's proposal is his confessed "fundamental hermeneutical principle. Every interpretation of Paul that is based on a misrepresentation of Judaism is to be rigourously excluded."[8] He is deeply concerned to explain away what Hans Joachim

---

former, and thus distances his proposal from Gaston's in significant ways, but he never says explicitly one way or another. In his subsequent "The Jewishness of the Gospel," 57-68, especially 61-68), Koenig buttresses his case for the abiding "validity" for Paul of non-Christian Jews' Torah faithfulness by appeal to Rom 4:16 and 15:1-13.

P. Lapide argues a similar case, although without the exegetical evidence evinced by Gaston and Koenig: "Jesus became the Savior of the Gentiles *without* being the Messiah of Israel.... Certainly Pauline Christology *is* one of the ways to God. Israel's way is another" (P. Lapide and P. Stuhlmacher, *Paul: Rabbi and Apostle*, tr. L. W. Denef [Minneapolis: Augsburg, 1984] 51; emphasis his).

[7]"Paul and the Torah," 54.

[8]"Abraham," 59.

Schoeps calls "Paul's fundamental misapprehension,"[9] the Apostle's alleged misunderstanding of Judaism's view of the law and his consequent apposition of Christ to it.[10] Gaston asserts repeatedly that Paul neither misunderstands nor misrepresents the law's role in salvation *for Jews*.[11] As Apostle to the Gentiles, Paul writes to *Gentiles only*, about Gentile problems only, and therefore speaks of the law only in its relation to Gentiles.[12] When Paul says εἰμι ἐγὼ ἐθνῶν ἀπόστολος (Rom 11:13; cf. Rom 1:5, Gal 1:15-16), Gaston takes him at his word and places particular confidence in the terms of the Jerusalem agreement mentioned in Gal 2:7-9 ("that we should go to the Gentiles and they to the circumcised").

> I believe that Paul kept this agreement throughout his career, confining his preaching strictly to gentile God-fearers.... Although it is not emphasized [in Galatians 2], we note that Paul was *not* commissioned to preach among Jews, whether about Jesus Christ or the Torah or anything else.[13]

The final result of such a reading, as will become clear from the following analysis, is that for Gaston Paul ultimately advocates "two

---

[9]*Paul*, 213-216. Gaston's dispute with Schoeps underlies all his essays, but he cites the latter's phrase specifically in "Paul and the Torah," 51-52; "Abraham," 40; "Israel's Enemies," 401; and "Angels and Gentiles," 75.

[10]"It is Paul's abrogation of the law which most disturbs Jewish interpreters and those who know something of the concept of Torah in Jewish thought. Paul's invective disturbs them less than his ignorance" ("Paul and the Torah," 51).

[11]Cf. one of the "basic methodological considerations" with which he opens one essay: "If we want to avoid a Marcionite reading of Paul, it might be best to assume that he stands in continuity with the traditions of Judaism rather than in opposition to them, if this is at all possible" ("Israel's Enemies," 401).

[12]"Paul and the Torah," 55-56; "Abraham," 53; "Israel's Enemies," 402; "Angels and Gentiles," 68.

[13]"Paul and the Torah," 55; emphasis his. Nowhere does Gaston comment on 1 Cor 9:20 ("I became to the Jews as a Jew, in order that I might gain Jews"), but he creatively discerns four groups who are described in 9:21: "[1] Jews, [2] those under the law = gentiles (which Paul said he is not), [3] the lawless = the Corinthian antinomians (which Paul said he is not), and [4] the weak = those under discussion in chapters 8-10" (ibid., 63). Does Gaston really think Paul engaged in antinomian immorality as an evangelistic strategem?

180   *Function of Apocalyptic and Wisdom Traditions*

religions, two chosen people":[14] Jews are saved by their covenant relationship to God through the law, and Gentiles are saved by faith in Christ. Gaston's argument boils down to an alternative between two interpretations of Paul's relationship to Judaism:

> A There is no way to be saved except to be a Jew;
> B Paul says Gentiles are saved without becoming Jews;
> C Therefore Paul says being a Jew does not save *anyone*.
>   OR
> A There is no way to be saved except to be a Jew;
> B Paul says Gentiles are saved without becoming Jews;
> C Therefore Paul says Jews and Gentiles are saved *differently*.

The former is the traditional interpretation, the one Gaston blames for perpetuating modern anti-semitism. The latter is Gaston's own, and obviously a great deal of it depends on his understanding of Romans 9-11.

There are three difficulties involved in responding directly to Gaston's exegesis of Romans 9-11. His reading of Paul's letters rests on a prior reconstruction of first-century Jewish attitudes toward Gentiles, so that it is necessary first to understand the historical considerations that prompt his interpretation. Secondly, his reading of the three chapters in Romans is organically related to what he reads throughout the Pauline corpus, so that Romans 9-11 are just a part—albeit a most central part—of his system. And finally, Gaston has not (yet) written a commentary on Romans, so his understanding of chapters 9-11 must be gleaned from references scattered throughout his essays.

I. Historical Considerations

Underlying all of Gaston's exegesis is a complex reconstruction of Jewish attitudes toward the law and Gentiles. First-century Judaism, he maintains, operates with two parallel but distinct views of the purpose of God's law. Both derive from the equation of Torah with Wisdom, effective at least by the time of Sirach (second century, B.C.E.), and the understanding of Torah as ultimate revelation, "God in his knowability, in his presence, in his electing will, in his covenant."[15]

---

[14]*Ibid.*, 67. The phrase is the title of the epilogue to J. Parkes's *The Foundations of Judaism and Christianity* (Chicago: Quadrangle Books, 1960).
[15]*Ibid.*, 59.

On the one hand, Gaston says, Jews of the period believe that God initially offered the Torah to the whole world, but only Israel accepted the gift (Mekilta, Bahodesh 5; Lam. R. 3:1). Only Israel, therefore, lives in covenant relationship with God, and only Israel experiences the Torah as God's gracious self-revelation. On the other hand, since Torah is identical with Wisdom, and Wisdom is universally accessible (Sirach), Gentiles too are bound by its prescripts. But since from the Jewish perspective no means exist outside the covenant for repentance or atonement, God-fearers who stop short of full conversion can know God's Torah only as a crushing burden, because disobedience of the law brings death. Jews, then, know the Torah as covenant; Gentiles can know it only as commandments.[16] "For gentiles, who do not have the Torah as covenant, Torah as law functions in an exclusively negative way, to condemn."[17]

In Gaston's view, Paul maintains this two-fold understanding of the law both before and after his conversion, and his Christian preaching is therefore addressed only to those God-fearers who previously experienced the law in such an oppressive way. The reason for Paul's initial opposition to Christianity, then, becomes precisely the cornerstone of his apostolic proclamation: in Christ, God has opened up the way to a *covenant* relationship with Gentiles that is totally independent of Torah. Gaston acknowledges that Judaism has always provided for and welcomed proselytes. But the discussion had previously revolved around Gentiles' relationship to all or part of the Torah. Paul's Christian preaching takes a quantum leap by eliminating Torah altogether from the Gentiles' (*not* the Jews') covenant relationship with God. Thus for Gaston, Paul's gospel offers freedom from the law-as-curse to Gentiles without even addressing itself to the Jews' law-as-covenant. God has already acted to save Israel; now, in Christ, God acts to save Gentiles.

Gaston documents this "Torah vs. law" theory—and Paul's espousal of it—by refering to a broad collection of texts from a variety of time periods. To begin with, he says, nearly all Jews of the period consider membership in the covenant to be salvation.[18] Nevertheless, the literature seems

---

[16]*Ibid.*, 61; "Abraham," 55; "Israel's Enemies," 401-402; "Works of Law," 44-45.

[17]"Paul and the Torah," 61.

[18]*Ibid.*, 57. The only significant exception is 4 Ezra. Here (as elsewhere) Gaston relies on E. P. Sanders's conclusions in *Paul*, 422-428 and in his essay, "The Covenant as a Soteriological Category and the Nature of Salvation in Palestinian and Hellenistic Judaism" in *Jews, Greeks, and Christians: Religious Cultures in Late Antiquity: Essays in Honor of*

occasionally to speak of "righteous Gentiles," although their status as righteous and the possibility of their salvation are by no means unanimously affirmed. One verse from the Testament of Naphtali promises that in the end God will "assemble the righteous from among the nations [whom Gaston takes to be Gentiles]" (8:3), but "it is not said how the righteous are to be defined,"[19] that is, whether or not those righteous Gentiles must convert to Judaism. Similarly, Gaston invokes two texts from Josephus to document this phenomenon. In the first, Ananias considers King Izates righteous without circumcision (*Ant* 20.38-42),[20] and in the second, the reportedly wide-spread observance of Jewish practices by

---

William David Davies, ed. R. Hamerton-Kelly and R. Scroggs (Leiden: Brill, 1976) 11-44.

[19]"Paul and the Torah," 57. TNaph. 8:3 does not specifically identify the righteous, but the flow of the narrative indicates that they are members of *Israel* who have been dispersed by the Lord "over the face of the whole earth until the mercy of the Lord comes" (4:5). Elsewhere TNaph. is unambiguously hostile toward Gentiles (3:3-4; 4:2). Moreover, the definition of righteousness in TNaph. is clearly in terms of covenant obedience (8:6, 9).

[20]*Ibid.*, 58. Gaston's invocation of Josephus here is particularly puzzling, since the full narrative is intended to prove that faithful adherence to the *whole* law is what ultimately earns Izates God's protection and blessing ("God thus demonstrated that those who fix their eyes on Him and trust in Him alone do not lose the reward of their piety" (*Ant* 20.48). Ananias's willingness to allow Izates to postpone or even forego circumcision is hardly a point of theological persuasion—as though he considers the rite optional for righteous Gentiles—but a rather pragmatic recognition of the fact that obedience to the commandment would endanger the lives of the king and Ananias himself. Eleazar's more rigorist position is clearly Josephus's own, as similar stories of conversion in *Ant* 20.139 and 145 attest: the only way for a Gentile to become righteous is to convert fully and thus enter the covenant. See the discussion of L. H. Feldman in *Josephus* (LCL, vol IX [Cambridge: Harvard University, 1969] 410-411). Generally on Josephus's attitude toward piety's reward, see H. W. Attridge, *The Interpretation of Biblical History in the Antiquitates Judaicae of Flavius Josephus* HDR 7 (Missoula: Scholars, 1976).

Gentiles in Greco-Roman cities (*Ap* 2.39) "seems to sound a positive note" about God-fearers.[21] From these isolated references, as well as the existence of catechetical literature produced for God-fearers, Gaston concludes that

> their [i.e., God-fearers'] status as being "righteous," while probable, is not really certain. It is because of this unclarity that legalism—the doing of certain works in order to win God's favor and be counted righteous—arose as a gentile and not a Jewish problem at all. Salvation and God's grace were for all under the covenant who had not cast off the yoke of the Torah, but God-fearers *not* under the covenant had to establish their righteousness by the performance of certain works, compounded by uncertainty as to what those works should be.[22]

According to Gaston, this unclarity and uncertainty about the possibility of righteousness for God-fearers led to Gentile Judaizing—the imposition by some Gentiles of certain Jewish practices on themselves and other Gentiles "as a means of self-justification."[23] It is these Judaizing God-fearers who are the sole targets of Paul's preaching and make up the membership of his churches.[24] They—and certainly not the Jews—are guilty of the self-righteous legalism Paul counters in Romans and Galatians, and they alone are freed from the law by Paul's gospel, since they alone have been 'enslaved' by the law. When Paul says that perfect obedience is required of all who submit to Torah (Gal 3:10, 21; Rom 2:25), he speaks to God-fearers alone, since no Jew ever considered perfection either possible or desireable.[25] The only complaint Paul has against Jews, according to Gaston, is their refusal to support his mission to Gentiles.

> Paul never accused the Jews of lacking zeal for Torah, and certainly not of legalism, but rather of disobedience to the new revelation he (Paul) had received. Hence the reproaches in Romans 2:17-24 have

---

[21]"Paul and the Torah," 58. For some peculiar reason, Gaston attributes *Apion* to Philo. The context indicates that Josephus means to defend the reasonableness and attractiveness of Jewish practices (i.e., if these are such silly laws, then why do some non-Jews also abide by them?), rather than to say anything one way or another about the potential salvation of the Gentiles who engage in those practices.

[22]*Ibid.*; emphasis his.

[23]*Ibid.*

[24]*Ibid.*, 55.

[25]*Ibid.*, 51.

to do with Israel's relative failure to become "a light to the gentiles." Israel is said to have "stumbled" (Rom 9:32; 11:11) because most other Jews did not join Paul in proclaiming his gospel of the righteousness of God to the gentiles.[26]

The clearest evidence Gaston can muster that Jews actually considered God-fearers "under the curse of the law" comes not from first-century Judaism, but from rabbinic sources. The most important is the conviction of R. Tanhuma (fifth-generation Amora) that "the word of the Lord went forth in two aspects, slaying the heathen who would not accept it, but giving life to Israel who accepted the Torah" (Ex. Rab. 5.9).[27] Indeed this fifth-century statement is essentially the linch pin of Gaston's reconstruction of first-century Jewish attitudes, and leads him to see reflections of it in the earlier texts he cites. The most serious question raised by this and the other texts he examines is one of interpretation. In every single case, the affirmation is made that those who reject or disobey the Torah are condemned by it. With the exception of 4 Ezra, it is clear that Jews are the only people considered to have accepted and obeyed.[28] There is, moreover, no mention anywhere—even in the much touted statements of R. Tanhuma—of Gentiles who obey only *part* of the law (i.e., God-fearers) and thus place themselves in Gaston's postulated limbo between covenantal righteousness and legal condemnation. All that can legitimately be gleaned from these widely separated discussions of the law is that *anyone* who refuses the yoke of Torah is condemned. In essence, these texts function as explanations for the lostness of Gentiles: Gentiles refuse and disobey the law; therefore they are condemned.

Gaston's repeated reliance on rabbinic sources to illuminate pre-70 Judaism[29] is fraught with the serious problems to which all such studies are prone. Only once does he acknowledge (somewhat obliquely) that

---

[26]*Ibid.*, 66.

[27]"Paul and the Torah," 59; "Angels and Gentiles," 70; "Israel's Enemies," 405.

[28]Not even for 4 Ezra does there appear to be much hope that Gentiles will ultimately be counted among the righteous. 4 Ezra denies that (ethnic) membership in Israel is *alone* salvific; it does not claim that it is possible to be saved *outside* Israel (cf. 3:5-10, 28-36; 7:19-22, [37-38]; 9:7-8, 31-37) since obedience of Israel's law is what determines salvation (*contra* Sanders, *Paul*, 415).

[29]A thirteenth-century rabbinic interpretation of Gen 15:6, for example, supports his reading of Paul's interpretation of that text ("Abraham," 42-43).

methodological danger may lurk behind the practice: "We can use the rabbinic writings...not in themselves but only as the reflection in transmuted terms of earlier ideas..."[30] But for the most part, Gaston's work operates with the rhetorical question with which he concludes his study of Paul's interpretation of Gen 15:6: "Why should we not use the understanding of Scripture of later Judaism to cast light on Paul's interpretation rather than as the negative foil which Paul *ex hypothesi* must be opposed to?"[31] Unfortunately, the answer to that question is that, without controls on decisions such as these, without some means of determining which traditions actually predate the texts in which they are found, and without some demonstration that Paul really stands within the same stream of Judaism represented by these traditions, Gaston's appeals to rabbinic texts are utterly irrelevant. Moreover, the assumption that the rabbinic Judaism of the Talmuds accurately reflects the whole of pre-70 Judaism simply cannot be sustained. So also, the assumption of anything like unanimity among first-century Jews flies in the face of substantial evidence of wide diversity.

Gaston's historical reconstruction is seriously flawed on several further scores. First, in the absence of any literary evidence that God-fearers actually experienced such *Angst* about their status before God, one can only conclude that the unclarity about their possible righteousness remains a modern scholarly rather than a first-century Gentile one. We simply do not know that God-fearers actually existed as a distinct religious group, what they perceived the certainty of their salvation to be, or how they may have responded to any lack of certainty. Gaston finds ambiguous the texts refering to requirements for Gentiles; that does not mean Gentiles considered their status ambiguous. Second, Gaston can point only to the existence of *Christian* Judaizers,[32] with no evidence that their concern for legal righteousness antedates their Christianity. Third, although he refers to such verses as 1 Thess 1:9, 1 Cor 12:2, Gal 4:8,[33] and Eph 2:11-17[34] (cf. also

---

[30]"Angels and Gentiles," 71.

[31]"Abraham," 59.

[32]Outside Paul's letters, only in Rev 2:9 and 3:9, and Ign Mag 10:3 and Ign Phil 6:1 ("Paul and the Torah," 58).

[33]*Ibid.*, 55; "Israel's Enemies," 416.

[34]"Israel's Enemies," 409. Here we encounter yet another methodological blunder. Gaston considers both Ephesians and Colossians deutero-Pauline ("Paul and the Torah," 55-56), but proceeds to use them freely to interpret the *Hauptbriefe*. For example, Eph 2:3 explains Rom 2:14: Gentiles, 'by nature children of wrath' (Eph 2:3), 'are for themselves the law' and 'do by nature that which belongs to the law (= sin)' ([Rom]

Rom 1:23, 1 Cor 6:9-11) as evidence of the purely Gentile composition of Paul's congregations, he does not seem to think it odd that Paul should refer to God-fearers—presumably Jews in every respect except circumcision—as former idolaters. In the very texts Gaston invokes to prove that Paul's parishioners were *God-fearers* Paul rather reminds them that they used to behave as *pagans*. In fact, Gaston operates with a functional equation of the words "Gentile" and "God-fearer," appearing to assume that whenever a Jewish text mentions non-Jews in connection with the law, the reference must be to God-fearers.[35]

Finally—and most seriously—Rom 3:9 (which Gaston nowhere addresses) states that Jew and Gentile alike stand ὑφ' ἁμαρτίαν. Regardless of how one locates the intended audience(s) of the preceding arguments,[36] and even if Jews are called on the carpet only for being poor witnesses to the Gentiles, it is clear from 3:9 that Paul considers the sinful human situation a universal one. There is no distinction (3:22) between Jews whose covenant relationship accounts for and deals with disobedience, and Gentiles whose non-covenant status damns them if they do and if they do not obey.Even if such a two-sided view of the law exists in first-century Judaism, Paul does not appear to subscribe to it.

II. Exegetical Considerations

Although Gaston's reading of Paul's letters rests in large measure on the historical reconstruction which we have seen cannot survive methodological scrutiny, he has a number of eggs in other baskets as well. The next question, then, is whether or not Gaston's position can be defended exegetically, whether or not it is possible to claim that Paul's letters speak

---

2:14), for they have 'the work of the law (= wrath) written on their hearts' (2:15)" ("Paul and the Torah," 64). Cf. also "Works of Law," 43, where the use by "the Pauline school" of the first person plural possessive with ἔργα (Eph 2:8; 2 Tim 1:19; Tit 3:5) confirms Gaston's judgment that ἔργα νόμου refer to acts of human (Gentile) legalism: "If Paul had also written that way... [there would be no] necessity of dealing with a troublesome genitive."

[35]As a matter of fact, after his first essay, "Paul and the Torah," Gaston makes only passing mention of God-fearers, and concentrates solely on Gentiles. The unspoken premise, however, throughout the rest of the essays, is that this portrait of God-fearers somehow fits all Gentiles.

[36]Gaston sees Gentiles addressed in 3:1-8 ("Israel's Enemies," 414).

to and about Gentiles only, that what appears in them to be directed against Jews is for the most part against Judaizing Gentiles, and that for Paul, Jesus was neither a new Moses nor the messiah, nor the climax of the history of Israel, but the fulfillment of God's promises to the gentiles."[37]

Gaston makes one significant exegetical decision that precedes his attention to any specific text. Since he notes that Paul speaks both positively about νόμος ("that it is good and has been fulfilled in Christ"[38]) and negatively ("that it is bad and has been abolished in Christ"[39]), he determines to translate the word in two different ways. When he deems νόμος to refer to the Jews' covenant relationship with God, the word means "Torah" (or sometimes "scripture"); when it speaks of the Gentiles' doomed situation, the translation is "law."[40]

Particularly the phrases "under the law" (1 Cor 9:20; Gal 3:23, 4:4, 4:5, 4:21, 5:18) and "works of the law" (Rom 3:20, 3:28; Gal 2:16, 3:2, 3:10) can apply to Gentiles only,[41] since they are never used in Jewish literature to express Jews' relationship to the Torah.[42] To be ὑπὸ νόμον,

---

[37]"Paul and the Torah," 66. It would be helpful if Gaston were to discuss how 2 Cor 1:20 (ὅσαι γὰρ ἐπαγγελίαι θεοῦ ἐν αὐτῷ ['Ιησοῦς Χριστός, v 19] τὸ ναί) distinguishes between God's promises to Israel and those to the Gentiles, but he does not.

[38]*Ibid.*, 62.

[39]*Ibid.*

[40]Paul's limited vocabulary, Gaston says, is due to the fact that he "used the only word available to him in the vocabulary of the times" (*ibid.*). Cf. also: "It would have been much simpler for all concerned if Paul had used a different word than νόμος when he wanted to speak of the law outside the context of the covenant, but of course he could not, no more than could ben Sira and 4 Ezra. Because God is one, his law is one, but this law has quite a different effect when it is administered directly by God himself for his people Israel and when it is administered by the angels of the nations" ("Angels and Gentiles," 73-74).

[41]"Paul and the Torah," 62; cf. also "Works of Law," which argues that ἔργα νόμου is a simple subjective genitive describing the law's work of wrath (cf. Rom 4:15) toward Gentiles who are outside the covenant of grace. The ἔργα τῆς σαρκός of Gal 5:19 also are "the direct parallel to ἔργα νόμου" (*ibid.*, 44), although no warrant is offered for that claim.

[42]Gaston finds support also in M. Barth's studies of ἔργα νόμου ("Die Stellung des Paulus zu Gesetz und Ordnung," *EvT* 33 [1973] 496-526, and *Ephesians 1-3* AB 34 [Garden City: Doubleday, 1974] 244-248).

Gaston says, is to be outside the covenant of grace (i.e., to be a Gentile), but to impose on oneself the responsibility of obeying the commandments (i.e., to be a God-fearing Gentile). His evidence for this contention, not surprisingly, is the argument in Galatians 3-4 (especially 4:21-31), which is addressed to non-Jews who attempt to live as Jews.[43]

In this passage, according to Gaston, Paul identifies himself so closely with his readers that he includes himself among them ("that in Christ Jesus the blessing of Abraham might come upon the *gentiles*, that *we* might receive the promise of the Spirit through faith" [Gal 3:14]).[44] The στοιχεῖα (Gal 4:3, 9; Col 2:8, 20) under whose sway "we Gentiles" all formerly lived include the law, its confinement, and its curse (cf. Gal 3:10, 22, 24; 4:2).

> Not...the Torah [Gaston hastens to add], for it is the Torah as scripture which "has declared the whole world to be prisoners confined *under* sin (3:22) and has said that those who rely on "works of the law" are "*under* a curse" (3:10). For those under "the law of deeds," [Gal 3:10, var.] the Mosaic covenant is of no avail (3:19-20).... Those who interpret the passage as an attack on Torah are wrong, for it is not the past of Jews which is described but the past of gentiles.[45]

This is a provocative interpretation of an admittedly abstruse Pauline argument. It explains a number of difficulties, and rescues Paul from appearing to make a scurrilous attack on the eternal validity of Torah— which attack would be the most offensive to Jews. Gaston fails to note, however, two other verses from Galatians that raise damaging questions about his own interpretation. First of all, if Paul so identifies with the Galatians in 3:14, 23-26, and 4:3 that he counts himself a Gentile, why does he make so stark a contrast earlier in 2:15 between himself—a Jew by nature—and sinners from among the Gentiles? Even if Gaston extends the direct address beyond 2:14, as though 2:15ff are part of Paul's response to Cephas and not a commentary to the Galatians on his response, the alleged claim of solidarity in 3:14 still arrives rather suddenly, and is in some tension with what has come before. The second verse—"God sent forth his Son...born under the law" (4:4)—Gaston even cites, although without comment.[46] How can God's Son (whom Gaston must surely take for Jesus,

[43]"Israel's Enemies," 402-411; cf. "Angels and Gentiles," 73-75.
[44]"Paul and the Torah," 62-63; emphasis his.
[45]*Ibid.*, 63; emphasis his.
[46]*Ibid.*

a Jew) be γενόμενον ὑπὸ νόμον if only Gentiles outside the covenant have that status?

Furthermore, the remaining verses of the pericope describing the Antioch confrontation (especially 2:15-17) refute Gaston's claim that only Gentiles are saved from the law.

> We ourselves, Jews by nature and not sinners from among the Gentiles, knowing that a person is not justified by works of the law but through faith in Jesus Christ, even we believed inChrist Jesus, in order that we might be justified by faith in Christ and not by works of the law, because absolutely no one (οὐ...πᾶσα σάρξ) will be justified by works of the law (2:15-17).

The first person plural pronoun of v 15—repeated in v 16b—clearly refers to Paul and his "natural" Jewish brothers and sisters, and is the subject of the verbs ἐπιστεύσαμεν and δικαιωθῶμεν, and the antecedent of εἰδότες. Gaston could conceivably read "Gentiles" for ἄνθρωπος in v 16a and πᾶσα σάρξ in v 16b, since the governing conviction for him appears to be 3:8: "that God would justify the *Gentiles* by faith." But that still would not explain why the "we (Jews)" should be justified through faith in Christ at all. Why, if only Gentiles are justified apart from works of the law, do the rest of the Jews at Antioch (who do *not* share Paul's call to preach to the Gentiles) believe in Christ ἵνα δικαιωθῶμεν ἐκ πίστεως χριστοῦ καὶ οὐκ ἐξ ἔργων νόμου? If they are Jews within the covenant, what danger was there—on Gaston's reckoning—that they might have attempted to justify themselves or that they might have labored under the curse of the law?

Gaston knows that there were other Jewish Christians besides Paul, but he never says much about why they might have become Christians except to say that "for Jewish Christians, and presumably for Paul himself, Christ was seen as the fulfillment of the Sinai covenant."[47] But for Gentile Christians, he says, Christ is the fulfillment not of Sinai, but of the promise to Abraham concerning the Gentiles. "The gentile counterpart to living in the covenant community of Torah is being 'in Christ.'"[48] What Gaston never says is exactly why some Jews might consider Christ the fulfillment of Torah[49] and others might not. The only reason for Jewish

---

[47]*Ibid.*, 65.

[48]*Ibid.*

[49]Paul himself never says any such thing. In fact, Paul says only that love fulfills the law (Rom 13:8, 10; Gal 5:14; cf. Rom 8:4, Gal 6:2), never that Christ does.

opposition to Christianity, he says, is that Paul offers Gentiles "a covenant
and commandment relationship to God which was different from but parallel
to that of Sinai."[50]

If for Paul the Sinai covenant remains salvific for Jews, as Gaston
maintains, then there seems little cause to think Paul considers the gospel
"the power of God for salvation to everyone who believes, to the Jew *first*
and also to the Greek" (Rom 1:16, cf. 2:9). Indeed, Gaston's curious
translation of that phrase indicates he does not think so:

> The content of that gospel is described as the righteousness of God,
> i.e. "the power of God for salvation, for the Jew *of course* but also
> for the Greek" (Rom 1:16), or concretely, "that God would justify
> the Gentiles from faithfulness" (Gal 3:8).[51]

The ἐκ πίστεως of Gal 3:8 (and elsewhere[52]) Gaston takes to be not
human faith, but God's faithfulness. The original meaning of Gen 15:6
("And he believed in the Lord; and he reckoned it to him as righteousness"),
for example, is "And he (Abraham) put his trust in YHWH; and he
(Abraham) counted to him (YHWH) righteousness."[53]

> Seen in itself, Gen 15:1-6 is clearly about God and his promise and
> not about Abraham and his faith.... [In Gen 15:6] the righteousness
> is still God's and...the sentence is a promise that God will exercise
> his righteousness in the future for Abraham's benefit.... The sense
> would then be not that God says, "Good for you, Abraham; I call

---

[50]"Paul and the Torah," 65.
[51]"Abraham," 54; emphasis added.
[52]In Rom 3:20, 28 ("Works of Law," 43), Rom 3:30 ("Angels and
Gentiles," 74), Gal 2:16; 3:2, 5, 10, 11 ("Works of Law," 43), and Gal 3:7-
9 ("Abraham," 54). In Rom 3:26, πίστις Ἰησοῦ is the "faithfulness of Jesus"
("Israel's Enemies," 416), and πίστις χριστοῦ (Rom 3:22, 26; Gal 2:16, 20;
3:22, 26; Phil 3:9; Eph 3:12) is everywhere the "faithfulness of Christ"
("Abraham," 54). Gaston is fond of subjective genitives. "If a text speaks of
works," he muses, "they may not be our works; if it speaks of faith, it may
not be our faith; if it speaks of righteousness, it may not be our
righteousness" ("Works of Law," 41-42).
[53]"Abraham," 41. The translation and interpretation rest substantially
on those of Ramban (Nachmanides, 1194-1270) found in the Mikraoth
Gedoloth, and on Gaston's tradition-historical interpretation of Isa 51:4-6
and Sirach 44 (*ibid.*, 42-49).

that righteousness," but rather: "Good for you, Abraham; you have some righteousness coming to you, which I shall exercise on a later occasion."[54]

Even though Paul uses the verb "count" in the passive voice, this is still the meaning for him: Abraham believed God and, as a result, God promised to make Abraham a blessing to the Gentiles. God's righteousness was 'reckoned to Abraham's account' to be drawn on at a future time. That righteousness is God's promise to save the Gentiles, a promise stored up ever since Abraham was faithful and now (in Christ) delivered to its intended recipients, the Gentiles. Those who are justified by faith are not Jews faithful to the Torah, but the Gentiles on whose behalf God's righteousness=faithfulness was granted to Abraham after the fashion of "the merits of the fathers."[55]

Although Gaston deals with Romans 4 in a number of contexts,[56] he nowhere expressly addresses the notion in 4:12 that Abraham is the father of those who follow in the footsteps of his uncircumcised faith. In fact, Gaston seems to deny just that:

Attempts to understand Abraham as a hero of faith to be imitated by Christian believers [in Romans 4] cause insuperable difficulties, which the commentators gloss over. Thus, one cannot really say that the promise to Abraham came *through* the righteousness of his faith (v 13), or that the inheritance *depends* on faith (vs 16). *Pistis* is parallel to "promise" in vs 14 and to "grace" in vs 16 and must refer to God's faithfulness to his promise, as does the phrase "(God's) righteousness, i.e. faithfulness" in vs 13. Abraham's *pistis* appears in a formula "the one *ek pisteos* of Abraham," which reminds us of "the one *ek pisteos* of Jesus" in 3:26 and "those *ek pisteos* in Gal 3:7 and 9. The chapter is not about faith but about grace, expressed in the constantly recurring phrase that God "counts righteousness" to Abraham's heirs (vss 5, 6, 9, 11, 23, 24), and that "according to grace" (vs 4).[57]

---

[54]*Ibid.*, 44, 50, 51.

[55]*Ibid.*, 59. Cf. also: "Paul's major theological concern I understand to be not the justification of individuals by their faith but the justifiction of the legitimacy of his apostleship to and gospel for the Gentiles" (*ibid.*, 53).

[56]"Israel's Enemies," 407; "Abraham," 56-59; "Works of Law," 43-45; "Paul and the Torah," 64.

[57]"Abraham," 57; emphasis his.

192   *Function of Apocalyptic and Wisdom Traditions*

When in Gal 3:28 Paul affirms that "in Christ there is neither Jew nor Greek, slave nor free, male nor female," Gaston understands him still to be arguing for 'separate but equal' covenants. The verse means not that religious distinctions have been obliterated, but

> that in Christ there is *both* Jew *and* Greek, *both* male *and* female. Just as women do not need to become men nor men women to attain their full humanity, so Jews do not have to become gentiles nor gentiles to become Jews. Paul is, of course, concerned to argue for the equal rights of gentiles as members of the people of God.... But that battle has long since been won, and Pauline interpreters, in the light of subsequent history, need to emphasize the other side—the right of modern Israel to remain Israel, without being defined by someone else's "mystery" [Rom 11:25], as equal but elder recipients of the grace of God.[58]

Herein lies perhaps the most insidious of Gaston's (unexpressed) operating assumptions. He correctly reads Gal 3:27 to say that Gentiles do not have to become Jews to become Christians, nor Jews Gentiles. But instead of ἐν χριστῷ he apparently reads something equivalent to διὰ χριστόν: *because* of what Christ has done for Gentiles, there is no difference in *the people of God* (which is not coextensive with the *church*) between Gentiles and Jews. The ἐν Χριστῷ formula really has to be removed from its liturgical context (ἐβαπτίσθητε, v 27) for the verse to mean what Gaston claims, which he may just recognize when he comments somewhat wistfully that it would be somehow more appropriate if Paul were to use "God language" in Galatians 3 as he does in Romans 11.[59] Gaston apparently assumes that a Jew must become a Gentile to become a Christian, since he concludes that Paul's refusal to wish Jews to become Gentiles is equivalent to a refusal to wish that they become Christians.

Only in Romans 9-11 does Paul actually address the question, and it is therefore to Gaston's interpretation of that argument that we now turn.

---

[58]"Paul and the Torah," 67; emphasis added. Grammatically, the argument requires that οὐκ...οὐδέ be equivalent to καί....καί—ingenious, but scarcely compelling. On the religio-historical backgrounds to the text, see W. A. Meeks, "Image of the Androgyne: Some Uses of a Symbol in Earliest Christianity," *History of Religions* 13 (1974) 165-208.

[59]"Paul and the Torah," 67.

III. Romans 9-11

Gaston approaches Romans 9-11 by observing that 9:3-5 "affirm the continued election of Israel,"[60] and demonstrate that "the Torah was the great privilege of Israel...which belonged in the context of the promises to the Patriarchs and the Sinai covenant."[61] For one to whom Israel and its relationship to the Torah (and therefore to God) are supposedly "irrelevant to his gospel,"[62] the Apostle's λυπή...μεγάλη and ἀδιάλειπτος ὀδύνη do seem a bit overstated and melodramatic if none of that is in jeopardy. But Gaston does not speculate about why Paul might make so solemn a vow of solidarity with his kinfolk, even to the extent of willingness to relinquish his own relationship to Christ on their behalf (vv 2-3).

The affirmation in 9:6 that God's word has not collapsed is "stated...presumably to the same people who ask, 'Has God rejected his people?' (11.1) and who need to be warned not to boast with respect to the Jews (11.18, 20, 25)."[63] It is commonly assumed that what prompts the question in 11:1, and therefore the assurance about God's word in 9:6a, is the fact that large numbers of Jews have not believed the gospel. But Gaston counters:

> How is it that people can say that chapter 9 deals with the unbelief of Israel when it is never mentioned, and all human activity, whether doing or believing, whether Jewish or Gentile, is expressly excluded from consideration?... How can people say that the purpose of 9.6-13 is to declare that Israel is not defined by physical descent from the patriarchs when Paul later says that 'as regards election they (= all Israel) are beloved for the sake of the patriarchs' (11.28)?[64]

The whole chapter, he says, deals only with Jews and Gentiles, not Christians and (non-Christian) Jews. Every illustration Paul employs in chapter 9 makes the same distinction: Isaac, Jacob, and Moses stand for Israel; Ishmael, Esau, and Pharaoh stand for Gentiles.[65] Rom 9:6-29 argue simply that, since it is God's nature to be merciful (witness the merciful call of Israel apart from its deserving), God has now been equally merciful to

[60]"Paul and the Torah," 51.
[61]*Ibid.*, 64.
[62]*Ibid.*, 66.
[63]"Israel's Enemies," 412.
[64]*Ibid.*, 411.
[65]*Ibid.*, 416.

Gentiles. The unspoken question that elicits 9:6a is: Does the inclusion of Gentiles by faith in Christ into the people of God negate the foregoing (vv 4-5) list of Israel's privileges? The answer is: Of course not. "God's grace toward Israel, Abraham's seed, stands, even if election also involves those not chosen: Abraham's other children, those ἐξ Ἰσραήλ.... the non-chosen."[66]

Curiously, that peculiar translation of ἐξ Ἰσραήλ as 'outside of Israel' applies for Gaston not only to Gentiles (the physical descendents of Ishmael and Esau[67]), but also to "individual Jews who become apostate, ἐξ Ἰσραήλ."[68] Presumably, then, equivalent translations of 9:6b might be 'Not all outside Israel are Israel' or 'Not all Gentiles are Israel' or 'Not all apostates are Israel.'[69] In order to avoid having Paul make a nonsensical statement, he must essentially rearrange the syntax of vv 6b-7a so that οὐ... πάντες οἱ ἐξ Ἰσραήλ οὗτοι Ἰσραήλ becomes οὐ...πάντες Ἰσραήλ οὗτοι ἐξ Ἰσραήλ, and οὐδέ...σπέρμα Ἀβραὰμ πάντες τέκνα becomes οὐδέ...τέκνα Ἀβραὰμ πάντες σπέρμα. The two statements then remain parallel, and the sense is that the Gentiles have not replaced Israel as God's elect, since not all of Abraham's children are his physical descendents. The advantages of such a translation are (a) that it avoids attributing to Paul a (re)definition of Israel that includes less than the totality of ethnic Israel, and (b) it makes the subject of Paul's argument the *in*clusion of Gentiles into Israel rather than the possible *ex*clusion of (non- Christian) Jews from Israel. The problems with such a translation are that (a) Paul's syntax must be forced beyond its obvious sense; and (b) regardless of vv 6-7, οὐ τὰ τέκνα τῆς σαρκὸς ταῦτα τέκνα τοῦ θεοῦ (v 8) still makes the claim that genetic identity does not

---

[66]*Ibid.*, 413.

[67]On the strength largely of the rabbinic tradition that God offered the Torah to each of them only to be refused (*ibid.*, 405-406). Cf. also: "...it is clear [from 9:6-29] that the Jews of Paul's time are seen to be descendents of Abraham and Isaac and Jacob and not of Ishmael and Esau" (ibid., 413-414); and "The Gentiles...come into focus [in chapter 9] only as those not chosen (Ishmael, Esau) or as those God uses, not for their own sakes but solely as instruments of his grace toward Israel (Pharaoh)" (*ibid.*, 415).

[68]*Ibid.*, 413.

[69]Gaston actually translates the entire sentence in vv 6b-7a with Barrett (*Romans*, 180): "For not all who are from Israel are Israel, nor are all the children (of Abraham) Abraham's seed" ("Israel's Enemies," 413), but proceeds twice on the same page to refer to ἐξ Ἰσραήλ as outsiders even though the translation is obviously inclusive of both insiders and outsiders.

constitute Israel. For Gaston's argument to be consistent, he has to alter the sense of v 6b or v 7a, but not both.[70] As we have seen, Gaston is absolutely correct to read Romans 9 as a discussion of God's merciful election of Israel. What he fails to see, however, is the purpose to which that discussion is put in Paul's argument: God's election of Gentiles, not even mentioned until v 24, is shown to be not different from but identical to God's creation of Israel. The possibility of the Gentiles' replacing Israel—although it stands behind 9:6—is not raised explicitly until 9:30-31.

The vessels of wrath (vv 22-23), says Gaston, are to be understood as *instruments* rather than *objects* of God's wrath, since that translation "would make a better connection with what is said about Pharaoh in Vs.17,"[71] and since "there is absolutely no reference to God's wrath in the earlier section [vv 6-18]."[72] The image of the potter and the vessels explains what Paul has previously said about the archetypal Gentile, Pharaoh:

> The complaint with which the section begins [τί ἔτι μέμφεται; (9:19)] is still very much a Gentile complaint, as the close parallel in Wisdom 12.12 shows.... God was gracious toward the Egyptians and Canaanites in that he did not destroy them at once but overlooked their sin (11.23), in order by his longsuffering and limited punishment to allow them time to come to repentance (12.2, 10, 15, 20).... Paul differs from Wisdom in his understanding of God's longsuffering toward Gentiles, because what Gentiles need is more than repentance and what they receive is more than a second-class mercy.... What the Gentiles need is not repentance but life from the dead, not a turning back...but a 'turning to...God from idols' (1 Thes.1.9). What they receive is complete incorporation into the elect people of God.[73]

The vessels of mercy (both Jews and Gentiles, v 24) are on this reading instruments of mercy "who were prepared for the glorification of *others*, that is...the reference is to those who carry out the mission to the Gentiles."[74]

---

[70]The same problem obviously obtains with Barrett's own interpretation of his translation.

[71]*Ibid.*, 417.

[72]*Ibid.*, 416. "The concept of wrath is very important in Romans, and it makes sense to say that God needs people (or powers) through whom his wrath can be executed" (*ibid.*, 417).

[73]*Ibid.*, 415-416.

[74]*Ibid*; emphasis added.

Gentiles have been borne by God with much longsuffering[75] in order that through the vessels of mercy (the Jewish and Gentile Christian missionaries) God might demonstrate his power to save the vessels of wrath (all Gentiles).

This argument hangs together with a certain logic, and coheres with Gaston's interpretation of chapter 11, but it fails to correspond to what Paul actually says in chapter 9. On Gaston's reading, the vessels of *wrath* are ultimately the recipients of the δόξα that Paul explicitly says has been prepared ahead of time for the vessels of *mercy*. Moreover, Gaston falls prey to the common misconception that the two sorts of vessels in Romans 9 are images for Jews and Gentiles; what is innovative in his interpretation is simply the reversal of the traditional roles. As we have demonstrated, the image of the potter and the vessels is designed not to draw allegorical pictures of any groups of people but to demonstrate the dynamic of God's impartial and purposeful election. Why Gaston forces such a contorted reading of 9:21-23 is unclear since he sees very well that the Gentiles are saved by the same mercy that saves Israel: just as all human worthiness is excluded from God's call of Israel, so are the Gentiles saved *sola gratia*. The citations from scripture in vv 25-29 which conclude the argument must then be

> understood in a positive sense. 'Seed' (cf. vs. 7-8) will be left to Israel, God will never abandon his people. God's election of course never promised a rose garden, but just as Israel survived the Assyrians in Isaiah's time, so they will survive (the Romans?) in Paul's time.[76]

Only here does it finally become clear what Gaston considers the 'threat' to the integrity of Israel. That which could conceivably jeopardize God's faithfulness to Israel is not that they refuse to believe in Christ or only that the Gentiles consider themselves to have taken Israel's place, but that the power of imperial Rome might become hazardous to Israel's welfare! Although Gaston eschews allegorization of the historical figures (if not the metaphorical ones) in chapter 9,[77] he himself suggests that the person of Pharaoh in 9:17 may be a cipher for the Empire.

---

[75]The notion of God's patience with Gentiles is "something of a common-place within Hellenistic Judaism" (*ibid.*, 415).

[76]*Ibid.*, 416.

[77]*Ibid.*, 412.

Does Pharaoh have a counterpart in Paul's present? The answer depends on the degree to which we can read Romans, particularly 13.1-7, in the context of the political situation. If Pharaoh is seen as the example of the oppressor of Israel and if Paul were interested in hinting at the political situation, then Pharaoh's counterpart could be seen in the Roman Emperor. Esau, whom God 'hated', might have been a name for the Empire already in the first century. We recall that in the Mekilta the descendents of Esau said that 'the very heritage which our father left us was: "And by thy sword thou shalt live."' It is conceivable that all of this is reflected in Rom 13.4, where the 'one in authority ...bears the sword' and is 'the servant of God to execute his wrath'. This would bear investigation but has nothing whatsoever to do with Romans 9-11 except to account for the anticipatory 'instruments of wrath' in 9.22.[78]

Not only does the rulers' ἐξουσία (13:3) have nothing to do with Romans 9-11, as Gaston admits, but neither can those who are ὑπὸ θεοῦ τεταγμέναι (13:1), θεοῦ...διακονὸς...σοὶ εἰς τὸ ἀγαθόν (13:4) simultaneously be Israel's enemy whom God hates. And to claim that *Gentile* readers who are tempted to boast over Israel might be sympathetic to an equation of the Empire with Israel's enemies makes no sense whatsoever.

The fact is that, without such a contrived introduction of a hypothesized political situation into Romans 9, Gaston simply cannot account for the text. The vessels of wrath and mercy refuse to fall neatly into his assumed categories of Jew and Gentile, since v 24 unambiguously identifies the vessels of mercy as a mixed group. Consequently, Gaston is forced to postulate a totally different function for the third pair of illustrations from the one he claims for the first two (the patriarchs and Moses/Pharaoh). On Gaston's reading, Isaac and Ishmael, Jacob and Esau, Moses and Pharaoh illustrate the ways God has always elected Israel and not elected Gentiles; but the vessels of wrath and mercy illustrate how God has elected Jewish *and* Gentile missionaries to preach to the Gentiles. With Gaston's interpretation, Paul's reader must read Romans 11 first for Rom 9:19-24 to make any

---

[78]*Ibid.*, 418; ellipsis his. Cf. also his comment on 9:10-13: "While the supposition is not necessary for our exegesis, great poignancy would be added to the Malachi citation [Mal 1:2-3 in v 13] if the identification of Esau with Rome were old enough to be known by Paul and even more if it were known by his Roman readers" (*ibid.*, 413).

sense. There is no reason in the text to think Christian missionaries—of any ethnic background—are under discussion in chapter 9 at all.

Gaston's exegesis of Rom 9:30-10:21 and 11:1-36 is a good deal less detailed than that of chapter 9, but he nevertheless finds his conclusions affirmed here as well. Just as chapter 9 describes God's election of Israel by grace and not works, so chapter 10 details his similarly gracious election of the Gentiles.

> The chapters then are not to be seen dialectically but successively. Rom 9.30; 10.3b-18, 19b-20 deal with the theme of the inclusion of the Gentiles. Interpreters have been misled by the fact that formally Paul presents his gospel of Gentile inclusion as the content of what Israel did not understand (9.31-10.3a, 19a).[79]

Rom 9:31-32 may just be the most damaging verses in the Pauline corpus to Gaston's argument, since Paul says clearly two things Gaston claims are impossible: (a) although Israel pursues the νόμον δικαιοσύνης, it does not attain it; and (b) the reason (ὅτι) for the failure is that Israel pursues the law ἐξ ἔργων. Gaston claims Paul's only complaint against Israel is that it resists his preaching of Gentile inclusion, but just how pursuing the law ἐξ ἔργων means resistance to Gentiles Gaston fails to explain.

The λίθος προσκόμματος/πέτρα σκανδάλου of 9:32-33 Gaston identifies as the "gospel of the righteousness of God to the gentiles,"[80] and scripture says the one who believes ἐπ'αὐτῷ will not be put to shame. This reading is tantalizingly close to our own, with the critical exception of Gaston's phrase "to the gentiles." By ignoring Rom 10:1-4 altogether, Gaston conveniently avoids coming to grips with the full implications of his otherwise perceptive identification of the stone of stumbling as the gospel. The gospel's function—to trip up Israel and save Gentiles—derives from its being the realization of God's intention for the law: righteousness for all who believe. Gaston understands the subject of ο πιστευων in 9:33 to be a *Gentile* believer. Paul cites precisely the same phrase from Isa 28:16 again in Rom 10:11, though, as a proof-text for his summary of the gospel—"if you confess with your mouth that Jesus is Lord and believe in your heart that God raised him from the dead, you will be saved" (10:9)— and the second time adds πᾶς to the citation. Now all this could still apply

---

[79]"Israel's Enemies," 418.
[80]"Paul and the Torah," 66.

only to Gentiles, as Gaston maintains, were it not for vv 12-13. The reassertion of divine impartiality (cf. Rom 3:22, 29) explains why the same one is κύριος πάντων, that is, of both Jew and Greek, and why *all* who call upon his name will be saved.

One of the subtlest features of Gaston's exegesis of chapter 10 is his claim that vv 18 and 19 speak of different groups: v 18a asks, "(the Gentiles) have surely heard, have they not?" and v 19a asks, "Israel did not understand, did it?" What Israel did not understand is "that the time had come to do this [i.e., include the Gentiles]."[81] The very inclusiveness of 10:12-13, however, forbids such a reading. If everyone—both Jew and Greek—who calls on the Lord's name is saved, then the subject of each of the third person plural verbs in 10:14 must be the same mixed company included in the πᾶς of v 13. Accordingly, the same must be the subject of the third person plural verbs in 10:16 and 18. The naming of Israel in v 19, then, cannot be the fortuitous change of subject Gaston thinks it is.

As for chapter 11, Gaston's comments are very brief. He takes primary note of the second-person address to Gentiles in 11:13ff and asserts that 11:1 ("Has God rejected his people?") is a question asked by Gentiles.[82] Paul's fervent denial, μὴ γένοιτο, is supported by reference to himself and a list of his ethnic qualifications. On Gaston's reading, the fact that Paul uses the word λεῖμμα in v 5 has nothing to do with Jewish Christians, any more than did the reference from Isaiah 10 to ὑπόλειμμα in 9:27.[83] In chapter 9, the reference was allegedly to a "saved remnant"[84] of Israel (presumably saved from Rome); in chapter 11, the word refers to "a saving remnant, for the only example given of that remnant is the Apostle to the Gentiles himself."[85] Gaston does not say just how the presence of a "saving remnant," a single Jew who preaches to Gentiles, demonstrates that God has not rejected Israel. Interestingly, the same Paul who in Romans 11 ostensibly rattles his ancestral chain to demonstrate Israel's continuing covenant relationship makes very similar claims in Phil 3:3-11[86] to prove that his covenant righteousness is σκύβαλα (3:8)—a fact Gaston fails to notice.

---

[81]"Paul and the Torah," 66.
[82]"Israel's Enemies," 412.
[83]*Ibid.*, 416.
[84]*Ibid.*, 417.
[85]*Ibid.*
[86]᾽Ισραηλίτης, ἐκ γένους᾽Ισραήλ; φυλῆς Βενιαμίν.

The parable of the olive tree occupies most of Gaston's attention to chapter 11. Since he has decided that Israel's stumbling (11:11) is its resistance to the Gentile mission,[87] the natural and wild olive branches must refer also to missionaries. It is clear that his understanding of this image has informed his reading of 9:19-24 and the potter's vessels, and *vice versa*.

> God would have preferred to use as his instruments of mercy the good olive branches, but since they would not he had to make do with wild olive branches, Gentiles, as his missionaries. Israel is an unwitting instrument of mercy in 11.11-12, and in 11.30-31 Jews and Gentiles are instruments of mercy each to the other.[88]

The "holy root" (v 16), although Gaston does not say so explicitly, must be the promise of God concerning the Gentiles. What the natural branches relinquished was not their status as righteous, but their role as "light to the nations." The wild branches grafted in κατὰ φύσιν (vv 21, 24) are Gentile Christians who preach to other Gentiles in the absence of Jews whose responsibility it ought to be. God is able, however, to reinstate Jews in the Gentile mission whenever they share Paul's understanding of the gospel (v 23). Jewish ἀπιστία, then, as in Rom 3:3, is not refusal to believe the gospel, but refusal to help *Gentiles* believe.

This vision might be convincing were it not for Paul's use of the word σωθήσεται in 11:26. Why, if Paul considers covenant faithfulness alone salvific for Jews, might their refusal to preach to Gentiles endanger their salvation? Can it be that for Paul the definition of covenant faithfulness has been reduced to the single act of evangelizing the nations? Gaston of course denies that Paul—or any Jew—believes salvation rests on any human work. But how can he account for the undeniable fact that Paul's μυστήριον concerns Israel's salvation? Gaston acknowledges that Jews and Gentiles are mutually agents of mercy in 11:28-32, although each has been disobedient.

> Just before his final great doxology, Paul sums up what he has said in these chapters in 11.28-32. 'In the spreading of the Gospel' (NEB) Jews are enemies..., but 'as regards election they are beloved for the sake of the patriarchs' (9.1-18). 'For irrevocable are the χαρίσματα (the "privileges" of 9.4-5) and the κλῆσις (the καλεῖν of 9.7, 12) of God.' Everything is 'not a matter of human willing

---

[87]"Paul and the Torah," 66.
[88]"Israel's Enemies," 417.

or running but of God being merciful' (9.16), and ultimately all 'instruments' turn out to be instruments of mercy, even though all disobeyed.[89]

In order to account for the obvious allusion to God's impartiality in v 32, Gaston must see here also the continuing 'separate but equal' status of Jews and Gentiles. Each has disobeyed in a different fashion: Gentiles disobeyed God's law, and Jews disobeyed the "new revelation...Paul had received."[90] God's mercy, too, comes in separate ways: God's mercy to Israel is by means of the covenant, and to the Gentiles by means of Christ.

A Gentile might well wonder at that sort of impartiality, however. On Gaston's reading Gentiles, although eventually saved, still retain their second-class citizenship in this life beside their Jewish brothers and sisters who decline to join the church. While Gaston supposes Paul encourages *Christian* Jews to abrogate at least selected parts of the law (such as requirements that Gentiles be denied table fellowship and all but the most limited social relationships [Rom 14:1-15:13]), he also thinks Paul expects nothing of the kind from *non-Christian* Jews. There is no consideration in Gaston's program of what *behavioral* implications the gospel might have for this group—only *attitudinal* implications. Paul's plan is apparently for nothing empirical to change between Jews and Gentiles except that Jews are to consider Christian Gentiles saved. What this does mean in practical terms is that Paul expects Israel to give up its proselytizing of Gentiles altogether:

> Had all Israel followed Paul's example, we could have had an Israel loyal to the righteousness of God expressed in the Torah alongside a gentile church loyal to the righteousness of God expressed in Jesus Christ and his fulfillment of the promises to Abraham.[91]

After the first "bridge generation" of Jewish Christians, then, the call to be a light to the nations passes totally from Israel to the church, which carries sole responsibility for converting a lost world. Since God does not want Gentiles converting to Judaism because that inevitably brings boasting and Gentile legalism,[92] and God has instead opened a separate means of salvation to Gentiles, then Israel's role as herald of God is terminated. The new spokespeople for God in the pagan world are now Christians. This is a peculiar expression of impartiality indeed. God deals equally graciously with

---

[89]*Ibid.*, 418.
[90]"Paul and the Torah," 66.
[91]*Ibid.*
[92]See especially "Israel's Enemies," 406-407.

Jew and Gentile, but the net effect is that the torch passes from Israel to the church. Christians take over the work of proclaiming the one God, and Israel retires to an existence of self-maintenance. It appears that Gaston, having rescued Paul from one charge of anti-semitism—maligning the law and Jews' covenant righteousness—, effectively accuses Paul of another— denying Israel any relevant role in salvation history at all after the coming of Christ.

The hardest exegetical question of chapter 11 Gaston fails even to address. The parallelism of 11:28 sets up three pairs of opposites:

κατὰ μὲν τὸ εὐαγγέλιον	κατὰ δὲ τὴν ἐκλογὴν
ἐχθροὶ	ἀγαπητοὶ
δι' ὑμᾶς	διὰ τοὺς πατέρας

Although Gaston resorts to the NEB translation of κατὰ...τὸ εὐαγγέλιον ("in the *spreading* of the Gospel"[93]) to protect his interpretation, "gospel" and "election" are nevertheless opposed, as are "enemies" and "beloved," and "for your sake" and "for the fathers' sake." Israel's election, while not forfeited, is not by itself salvific—Israel remains both "beloved" and "enemies"—since "God has consigned all to disobedience in order that he might have mercy on all" (11:32). Gaston himself concedes that that gospel is "the power of God for salvation" (Rom 1:16),[94] but persists in maintaining that it is somehow salvific for Gentiles alone. Despite his inventive exegesis of it, Romans 9-11 simply does not support him.

IV. Conclusions

We noted at the beginning of this excursus that Gaston's program is essentially theologically motivated. He assumes—as do others who are similarly engaged[95]—that Christians must repent of anti-semitism and be involved in creative and reconciling conversation with Jews, and that they must carry on that conversation in biblical terms. He therefore sets out to demonstrate that the Apostle Paul, alone of the NT writers, can and must be rescued from charges of anti-semitism so that Jewish-Christian dialogue can be both reconciling (i.e., not anti-semitic) and authentically biblical.

---

[93]*Ibid.*, 418; emphasis added.
[94]"Abraham," 54.
[95]Cf. the similar attempts to salvage Paul offered by Gager, Koenig, and Lapide mentioned in n. 6, pp. 177-178 above.

We have seen, however, that the historical and exegetical program by which Gaston seeks to accomplish this goal collapses on a number of scores. To begin with, there are simply insufficient data to demonstrate that Paul shares the perception of the law's dual function Gaston postulates, i.e., that God gave Torah as covenant to Israel but as law to Gentiles. Second, without this dualistic function of the law, there is no reason to assume Paul perceives the human predicament *coram deo* to be different for Jews and for Gentiles. Third, and most importantly, Paul's letters themselves—particularly Romans and Galatians, on which Gaston relies so heavily to support his case—are suffused with a conviction of God's impartial treatment of Jews and Gentiles, in both judgment and redemption. This final observation and the exegetical ramifications of it speak conclusively against Gaston's claim that God justifies Israel through the law and the Gentiles through faith in Christ. Our own study of Romans 9-11 has shown that Paul's unwillingness to dispense with either God's impartiality or God's faithfulness to Israel means Jews and Gentiles indeed retain their distinct identities. But it also means the Torah acheives its divinely intended goal in the preaching of the gospel, God's righteousness for everyone who believes. Paul is absolutely convinced that God will save πᾶς Ἰσραήλ; Gaston rightly discerns that conviction. It is impossible, though, to argue as Gaston does that Paul conceives of Israel's salvation apart from the gospel.

To what extent is it possible to share this desire to engage in Jewish-Christian dialogue in a manner that is both constructive and biblical without relinquishing historical and exegetical thoroughness? Can Paul's perception of the relationship between Judaism and Christianity function as scripture for Christians and still contribute positively to the church's contemporary conversation with Jews?

It seems that, for all Gaston's very proper attempts to distance Paul from the other NT authors on this subject, he fails to question Ruether's basic claim that Jewish-Christian relations hinge on the question of christology.[96] It is clear that christology is central to many of the NT attitudes toward Judaism. There is no question, for example, that for the Fourth Gospel the issue of Jesus' identity as the Christ is at the heart of the church's relationship to the synagogue.[97] So also, Hebrews[98] appears

---

[96]See above, nn. 1 and 3, pp. 176-177 above.

[97]Cf. Jn 5:39-40; 8:39-47; etc. See the seminal works of J. L. Martyn (*History and Theology in the Fourth Gospel* [Nashville: Abingdon, 1979[rev]; original, 1968]) and R. E. Brown (*The Gospel According to John I-XII* AB 29 [Garden City: Doubleday, 1966] lxx-lxxv; *The Community of the Beloved Disciple: The Life, Loves, and Hates of an Individual*

204 offers the most fruitful assistance. For Paul the question of Judaism's

similarly to espouse a replacement theory to explain why the majority of Jews have not joined the church: rejection of Jesus means rejection by God. Matthew speaks in most bitter terms of God's rejection of unbelieving Israel,[99] although D. R. A. Hare has argued persuasively that the evangelist's polemic is directed less at Israel than at Israel's leaders.[100] The central issue in Jewish-Christian relations for Matthew, then, is more a matter of ecclesiology than christology, although the two are of course intimately related in Matthew's thought.[101] The same is not the case with Paul, however, and this is the point at which our own study of Romans 9-11 offers the most fruitful assistance. For Paul the question of Judaism's relation to Christianity is not asked from the perspective of christology but of theology. Paul's primary concern as he addresses the problem is not the identity of Jesus but the nature of God who elects both Israel and the Gentiles.[102]

The theocentric—rather than christocentric—argument of Romans 9-11 and Paul's refusal to allow the gospel to abrogate Israel's covenant relationship with God make the most significant contribution to Jewish-Christian dialogue in the words of Rom 10:4: the aim of Torah is to lead all, without regard for ethnic or religious heritage, to trust God's impartial righteousness. This is undeniably a Christian rather than a Jewish interpretation of Torah, since for Paul trusting in God's righteousness means confessing that Jesus is Lord and believing God raised him from the dead (10:9-10). But for Christians to talk with Jews this way on Paul's terms is nevertheless to speak first of the meaning of Torah and the God

---

Church in New Testament Times [New York: Paulist, 1979] particularly 25-91).

[98]Most telling is Heb 8:13, but see G. B. Caird, "The Exegetical Method of the Epistle to the Hebrews," *Canadian Journal of Theology* 5 (1958) 44-51 for a very succinct description of how the author of Hebrews argues that biblical promises to Israel are fulfilled only in the church.

[99]Cf. Mt 21:33-43; 22:1-10; 23:1-39.

[100]The Theme of Jewish Persecution of Christians in the *Gospel According to St. Matthew* SNTS Monograph Series 6 (Cambridge: University, 1967).

[101]Correctly emphasized by J. P. Meier in *The Vision of Matthew: Christ, Church and Morality in the First Gospel* (New York: Paulist, 1979).

[102]Cf. also Beker's repeated insistence on the theocentricity of Paul's gospel (*Paul, passim*) and his specific recognition of the *theo*logical nature of the argument of Romans 9-11 (*ibid.*, 331).

who is revealed in Torah, and thus to share a common premise. Christology cannot be eliminated from the agenda, but in Pauline terms the person and work of Christ can be understood only in terms of the God who elected Israel, who gave the law, and who is faithful.

> If the three pillars on which Judaism stands are God, Torah, and Israel [Gaston asserts], then a fundamental attack on any of the three would be anti-Jewish, i.e., a denial of the right of Jews to exist in terms of their own self-understanding. Is Paul guilty?[103]

The Apostle's answer to that question is surely μὴ γένοιτο, but not for the reasons Gaston claims. It is the latter's final phrase, "in terms of their own self-understanding," that Paul would challenge, precisely because he affirms what precedes it. Paul's Christian preaching rests on the same three pillars of Judaism, but he interprets the middle pillar differently from his non-Christian kinfolk. From Paul's perspective, Judaism's dispute with the church is fundamentally an exegetical one: "their own self-understanding" (cf. Rom 10:2-3) for Paul is rooted in their misapprehension of Torah, but that misapprehension is itself a function of God's abiding faithfulness to Israel (9:33; 10:19-21; 11:7, 25-26). Christians can engage with Jews in meaningful conversation about Torah interpretation as Paul pursues it in Romans 9-11 without perpetuating anti-semitism or relinquishing their Christian confession.

---

[103]"Paul and the Torah," 50. With Ruether, Gaston considers the "theological anti-Judaism" of the NT (the phrase is Hare's alternative to "NT anti-semitism" [*The Theme of Jewish Persecution*]) to be "the fundamental root of later cultural and political anti-semitism" ("Paul and the Torah," 50).

4

Conclusions

This study was prompted by two related questions: (1) What is the nature of Paul's relationship to Jewish apocalyptic thought? Why is his theology both like and unlike that of some of his contemporaries who write apocalypses? (2) Why does the argument of Romans 9-11, which seems to have so much in common with apocalyptic thought, also contain wisdom traditions and conclude with a sapiential hymn? How is it that traditions from two so different kinds of literature—apocalyptic and wisdom—can coexist in the same text? In the course of our investigation, we have come to see that the answer to the first question is determined in part by the answer to the second.

In Chapter One we traced the study of Paul's relationship to Jewish apocalyptic and wisdom traditions and determined that, with very rare exceptions, interpreters have focused solely on one or the other. The scholarly descendents of Albert Schweitzer, on the one hand, and Hans Windisch, on the other, have seldom taken seriously each other's perspectives on Paul's theological heritage and outlook. As a result, evidence of wisdom or apocalyptic material in the letters has been either exaggerated or ignored, depending on a scholar's conviction about which tradition is constitutive of Paul's thought. The recent exceptions to this tendency in the history of research have recognized the essentially apocalyptic shape of Paul's theology, but have detected in parts of his letters evidence of wisdom thought as well. The results of these few studies suggested that further inquiry into the confluence of apocalyptic and wisdom traditions in the Pauline corpus would prove fruitful.

In Chapter Two we saw that some students of early Jewish literature have been similarly curious about the relationship between the apocalyptic and wisdom traditions, and have for twenty-five years looked for ways to explain why two so different types of literature often share similar language and thought. Although the conversation has frequently bogged down in history of religions debates about the ancestry of one tradition or the other, the persistence of the search indicates these scholars have identified a phenomenon worthy of further investigation. We therefore adopted an exegetical and theological approach, rather than a purely historical one, to examine the function of confluent apocalyptic and wisdom traditions in specific texts: the Wisdom of Solomon, 1 Enoch, 4 Ezra, the Qumran library, and 2 Baruch.

Using descriptive criteria drawn from the classical wisdom corpus and the apocalypses of the period, we discovered that although each of these documents is fundamentally either apocalyptic or sapiential in character, each makes use of material from both traditions. A theological continuum exists among these Jewish writers of the second century B.C.E. through the first century C.E. that is relatively independent of their historical contexts. Among these writers who use both apocalyptic and wisdom traditions to express themselves, it appears that the more prominent are the traditional wisdom themes, the less traditional are the apocalyptic ones, and *vice versa*. To discern the shape of that contiuum, we asked five questions of the documents under consideration:

Where is wisdom located?

Who has access to wisdom?

What is the means of access?

What is the content of wisdom?

What is the potential for meaningful human life before the eschaton?

From the answers to these questions emerged a pattern of usage that suggests the more an apocalyptic writer employs traditional wisdom language and motifs, the more he sees potential for meaningful human life before the eschaton. Similarly, the more transcendent is God's wisdom, and the more it is hidden in heavenly mysteries, the more the author locates hope for meaningful life in the disjunctive future.

In Chapter Three we moved from examination of Jewish literature to Paul's letter to the Romans. We established first the significance of chapters 9-11 to the argument of the letter. Paul's conviction that God judges and redeems Jew and Gentile impartially remains in dynamic tension with his conviction that God remains faithful to Israel, and both sides of that argument continue in the discussion of Israel's role in the plan of salvation. Paul's presentation of the gospel which is "the power of God for salvation to everyone who believes, to the Jew first and also to the Greek" (1:16) reaches its conclusion in the summary statements of 11:29, 32: "for the gifts and the call of God are irrevocable," and "for God has consigned all to disobedience in order that he might have mercy on all."

Secondly, we showed that a single sustained argument in Romans 9-11, rather than three distinct ones, moves Paul to that conclusion in 11:28-32. God's election of Israel and the Gentiles by the same impartial mercy (9:6-29) raises the question why only Gentiles have responded. That question is answered (9:30-10:21) by pointing to the gospel as the stumbling stone God has put in Israel's path to make possible Gentile faith. Israel's stumbling is not final, however (11:1-27), since already some Jews believe and the eschatological fulness of Gentile faith will provoke the rest of Israel to faith, "and in this manner, all Israel will be saved" (11:26).

Finally in Chapter Three we established that Paul's argument in Romans 9-11 is substantially influenced not only by apocalyptic thought but by sapiential traditions as well. The confluence of those traditions enables Paul to maintain a balanced tension between God's impartial treatment of all and God's faithfulness to Israel. In chapter 9, the wisdom theme of a potter and two sorts of vessels demonstrates how God elects purposefully to demonstrate his wrath, power, and glory. In chapter 10, the sapiential tradition that God's wisdom is accessible in Torah helps show how the gospel, the goal of Torah, is universally available. In chapter 11, the revealed μυστήριον of Israel's salvation, itself a mystery of God's wisdom, evokes from Paul a hymn in praise of God's wisdom. Since Romans 9-11, like the Jewish documents we studied in Chapter Two, contains a confluence of apocalyptic and wisdom traditions, it is now time to ask of Paul's argument the questions we asked of those Jewish texts.

(1) Where is wisdom located? By his exegesis of Deut 30:12-14 in Rom 10:6-8 which is influenced by Bar 3:29-30, Paul indicates first of all that he considers the gospel, "the word of faith which we preach" (v 8), to be God's wisdom, the word that is near. He has previously said the gospel is the goal of the law (Rom 10:4), so his identification of wisdom with the gospel is functionally similar to the equation of wisdom with Torah in Sirach, 4 Ezra, 2 Baruch, and throughout early Judaism. Secondly, by calling God's plan to save both Israel and the Gentiles a μυστήριον (11:25-27) and immediately quoting a sapiential

hymn (11:33-36), Paul locates God's wisdom in heavenly secrets, much as 1 Enoch, 4 Ezra, and the Qumran covenanters do. The relationship of the specific wisdom of Paul's mystery to the wisdom of the gospel is not immediately clear. Given the explicit uses of σοφία in 1 Corinthians 1-2 to identify both the gospel (Χριστός [1:24] = λόγος τοῦ σταυροῦ [1:18]) and mystery (θεοῦ σοφίαν ἐν μυστηρίῳ [2:7]), it is reasonable to say that in Romans 9-11 also the two are distinct. That Paul describes God's wisdom as both the gospel and specific mysteries is functionally parallel to the descriptions in 1 Enoch, 4 Ezra, and Qumran of wisdom as both Torah and heavenly secrets.

(2) Who has access to wisdom? The central argument of Romans 10 is that *all* have access to the gospel. Its nearness to both Jew and Gentile is a function of God's impartiality (vv 12-13) and the world-wide preaching of the gospel (v 18). But in much the way Ezra's Torah-righteous wise are alone entitled to receive the secret wisdom of his revelations (4 Ez 14:21, 45-47), so Paul's Christian readers who possess the wisdom of the gospel are granted the μυστήριον of God's wise plan to save Israel and the Gentiles.

(3) What is the means of access? Although the preaching and hearing of the gospel are available to all (Rom 10:14-17), and the mission has reached the ends of the earth (v 18), it may be that only those who are members of the church at Rome have access to Paul's mystery. Although Scroggs[1] maintains on the basis of 1 Cor 2:6 that Paul reserves his wisdom teaching for the τέλειοι of his churches, the fact that he makes tantalizing reference to the content of divine mysteries in 1 Cor 2:9 and reveals one of those mysteries in the same letter (15:51) suggests that the distinction between general and specific wisdom is not a rigid one, and that the designation τέλειοι is something less than technical.[2] The wisdom of God as the gospel and wisdom as heavenly mysteries are related as components of Christian preaching.

---

[1]"Paul: ΣΟΦΟΣ and ΠΝΕΥΜΑΤΙΚΟΣ," 37.

[2]As Scroggs rightly observes, by distinguishing between the immature Corinthians and the τέλειοι who are capable of grasping deeper levels of wisdom, "Paul cannot be charged with setting up a new division in the church at the same time as he is trying to destroy the ones that exist.... Paul nowhere denies that valid *distinctions* in maturity, spiritual gifts, intellectual levels, or productivity exist. What he attacks is rather *divisions* based upon a prideful evaluation of such distinctions" (*ibid.*, 38, n.4; emphasis his).

This means that one has access to God's wisdom as Paul understands it in the context of Christian proclamation.

(4) What is the content of wisdom? Although God's wisdom is located both in proclamation of the gospel and in the specific mystery of Israel's salvation, the line between these two cannot be sharply drawn. The gospel as Paul preaches it includes Christ crucified and raised, but embraces as well the whole horizon of God's past creative sovereignty and faithfulness, and his coming triumph and glory. The content of wisdom was defined by 1 Enoch, 4 Ezra, 2 Baruch, Qumran, and the Wisdom of Solomon as God's plan for the cosmic future, Torah, the good life, and immortality. There is a sense in which Paul's definition includes all of these. Clearly wisdom contains God's plan for the cosmic future, but it also contains the gospel of Christ crucified and raised, the (Pauline interpretation of) Torah as God's impartial righteousness to all who believe, the good life as Christians experience it in the present, and eternal life.

(5) What is the potential for meaningful human life before the eschaton? Here Paul stands closest to Qumran and 2 Baruch. It is only in the church, the elect community called from both Jews and Gentiles, that God's wisdom in the gospel and apocalyptic mysteries may be known, and only in the church where human life has authentic meaning. But far more than Qumran or 2 Baruch, Paul has great hope for order beyond the church as well. The dawning day of salvation promises to restore not only Jews and Gentiles in the church, but the entire suffering creation (Rom 8:18-25). The mystery of God's dealings with Israel and the Gentiles demands that Paul's evangelistic ministry be carried out with great urgency (11:13; cf. 1 Cor 9:16). Because in God's wisdom the Gentile mission serves both Israel and the Gentiles, the present is a time of enormous potential. Indeed Paul views the διακονία for Jerusalem whose delivery is imminent (Rom 15:30-32) as at least partial fulfillment of that potential.[3] But a more immediate restoration of order accomplished by Paul's mystery is anticipated by the hortatory section of the argument (11:17-24), where he corrects Gentile boasting and outlines the mutuality and interdependence of Gentiles and Jews in salvation history. Because the transcendent wisdom of God has come near in the gospel of Christ and the mystery of Israel's salvation, that wisdom is ordering the church even as it will ultimately restore order in the whole creation.

---

[3]Munck, *Paul*, 305-308.

Just as we saw in the Jewish literature of Paul's time, so in Romans the use of traditional wisdom material places the author at some distance from the "ideal" apocalyptic perspective inasmuch as the present and the eschatological future are not drastically disjunctive. Although for Paul it is only at Christ's parousia that God will ultimately redeem the creation, already that redemption is breaking into human history as the righteousness of God justifies sinners and brings together Jew and Gentile in the church.

Scholars who urge the importance of Jewish apocalyptic language and ideas in Paul are inevitably faced with the differences as well as the similarities between the Apostle and his contemporaries. As much as Paul sounds like 1 Enoch or 4 Ezra or 2 Baruch or Qumran in some respects, he also speaks in distinctive ways that set him very much apart from them. Even Beker, for whom apocalyptic categories are most central to Paul's thought, concedes:

> The modification of apocalyptic is evident in the fact that Paul (1) does not employ the traditional terminology of "this age" in conjunction with that of "the age to come"; (2) significantly modifies the traditional apocalyptic view of the escalation of the forces of evil in the end time; and (3) rarely uses the terminology "the kingdom of God" (or "the day of the Lord"), and when he does, it is mainly in traditional contexts.... Paul does not engage in apocalyptic timetables, descriptions of the architecture of heaven, or accounts of demons and angels. He does not relish the rewards of the blessed or delight in the torture of the wicked....[4]

The results of our study indicate that this Pauline "modification" of apocalyptic thought is itself somewhat traditional. Even among some of the Jewish documents that define what it means to be apocalyptic, wisdom traditions in varying measures contribute to "modifications" of the ideal apocalyptic perspective. The use of sapiential traditions is obviously not the only variable in the diversity of Jewish and Christian apocalyptic literature—an author's social situation and religious experience substantially affect the ways he appropriates apocalyptic categories. But it is clear that wisdom language and motifs are one of the means available for expressing one's particular sense of apocalyptic reality.

---

[4]*Paul*, 145.

The distinctiveness of Paul's apocalyptic world view is, as Beker rightly observes, his experience of the Christ event.[5] In the death and resurrection of Jesus, Paul understands God's redemption to have broken into the world, and the Spirit's presence in the community of faith to be a foretaste of the glory to come. But untold eschatological riches still await the world for which Christ died, and the tension between the already and not yet of God's saving activity is a salient quality of the Pauline gospel. As greatly as that gospel is indebted for its perspective to apocalyptic thought, its contours are also shaped by sapiential traditions.

---

[5]*Ibid.*, cf. 192.

Bibliography

Texts and Translations

Charles, R. H., ed. *Apocrypha and Pseudepigrapha of the Old Testament.* 2 Vols. Oxford: Clarendon, 1913.
_____., ed. *The Book of Enoch.* Oxford: Clarendon, 1912[2].
Charlesworth, J. H., ed. *The Old Testament Pseudepigrapha.* 2 Vols. Garden City: Doubleday, 1983-1985.
Gaster, T. H. *The Dead Sea Scriptures With Introduction and Notes.* Garden City: Anchor-Doubleday, 1976[3].
Hennecke, E. *New Testament Apocrypha.* Ed. W. Schneemelcher. Tr. R. McL. Wilson. 2 Vols. Philadelphia: Westminster, 1965.
Josephus. *Works.* Tr. L. H. Feldman. LCL. 9 Vols. Cambridge: Harvard University, 1969.
Knibb, M. A., ed. *The Ethiopic Book of Enoch: A New Edition in the Light of the Aramaic Dead Sea Fragments.* 2 Vols. Oxford: Clarendon, 1978.
Lohse, E., ed. *Die Texte aus Qumran: Hebräisch und Deutsch mit masoretischen Punktation.* Munich: Kösel, 1971 2 .
Milik, J. T., ed. *The Books of Enoch: Aramaic Fragments of Qumran Cave 4.* Oxford: University, 1976.
Vermes, G. *The Dead Sea Scrolls in English.* Hammondsworth, England: Penguin, 1968[3].

Books and Articles

Aageson, J. W. "Scripture and Structure in the Development of the Argument in Romans 9-11." *CBQ* 48 (1986) 265-289.
Achtemeier, P. J. "An Apocalyptic Shift in Early Christian Tradition: Reflections on Some Canonical Evidence." *CBQ* 45 (1983) 231-248.

Allison, D. C. "The Background of Romans 11:11-15 in Apocalyptic and Rabbinic Literature." *Studia Biblica et Theologica* 10 (1980) 229-234.

Alt, A. "Die Weisheit Salomos," *TLZ* 76 (1951) 139-143.

Althaus, P. *Der Brief an die Römer*. NTD 6.11. Göttingen: Vandenhoeck and Ruprecht, 1970.

Andersen, F. I. "Introduction" to 2 Enoch in *The Old Testament Pseudepigrapha*, Vol. 1, 91-100. Ed. J. H. Charlesworth. Garden City: Doubleday, 1983.

Attridge, H. W. *The Interpretation of Biblical History in the Antiquitates Judaicae of Flavius Josephus*. HDR 7. Missoula: Scholars, 1976.

Aune, D. *Prophecy in Early Christianity and the Ancient Mediterranean World*. Grand Rapids: Eerdmans, 1983.

Aus, R. D. "Paul's Travel Plans to Spain and the 'Full Number of the Gentiles' of Rom. XI.25." *NovT* 21 (1979) 232-262.

Badenas, R. "The Meaning of *Telos* in Romans 10:4." Ph.D. Dissertation, Andrews University, 1983.

Bandstra, A. J. *The Law and Elements of the World: An Exegetical Study in Aspects of Paul's Teaching*. Kampen: J. H. Kok, 1964.

Barrett, C. K. *The Epistle to the Romans*. New York: Harper and Row, 1957.

_____. "Romans 9.30-10.21: Fall and Responsibility of Israel" in *Die Israelfrage nach Römer 9-11*, 99-121. Ed. L. de Lorenzi. Rome: Abtei von St. Paulus vor den Mauern, 1977.

Barth, K. *Church Dogmatics*. 4 Vols. Ed. G. W. Bromiley and T. F. Torrence. Edinburgh: T & T Clark, 1957.

_____. *The Epistle to the Romans*. Tr. E. C. Hoskyns. London: Oxford, 1933[6].

Bassler, J. M. *Divine Impartiality: Paul and a Theological Axiom*. SBLDS 59. Chico: Scholars, 1982.

Batey, R. "So All Israel Will Be Saved: Rom. 11:25-32." *Int* 20 (1966) 218-231.

Batsch, H. W. "The Historical Situation of Romans." *Encounter* 33 (1972) 329-339.

Baur, F. C. *Paul the Apostle of Jesus Christ: His Life and Works, His Epistles and Teachings*. Tr. A. Menzies. Edinburgh: Williams and Norgate, 1873[2].

Beare, F. W. *St. Paul and His Letters*. Nashville: Abingdon, 1962.

Beasley-Murray, G. R. "The Righteousness of God in the History of Israel and the Nations: Romans 9-11." *Review and Expositor* 73 (1976) 437-445.

Beker, J. C. *Paul the Apostle: The Triumph of God in Life and Thought.* Philadelphia: Fortress, 1980.

_____. *Paul's Apocalyptic Gospel: The Coming Triumph of God.* Philadelphia: Fortress, 1982.

Benoit, P. "Conclusion par mode de synthese" in *Die Israelfrage nach Römer 9-11,* 217-236. Ed. L. de Lorenzi. Rome: Abtei von St. Paulus vor den Mauern, 1977.

Betz, H. D. "On the Problem of the Religio-Historical Understanding of Apocalypticism." *Journal for Theology and the Church* 6 (1969) 134-156.

_____. "The Concept of Apocalyptic in the Theology of the Pannenberg Group." *Journal for Theology and the Church* 6 (1969) 192-207.

_____. Review of *Paul the Apostle: The Triumph of God in Life and Thought,* by J. C. Beker. *JR* 61 (1981) 457-459.

Betz, O. "Die heilsgeschichtliche Rolle Israels bei Paulus." *Theologische Beiträge* 9 (1978) 1-21.

Black, M. *Romans.* Grand Rapids: Eerdmans, 1981².

Bläser, P. *Das Gesetz bei Paulus.* NTA 19.1-2. Münster: Aschendorfer, 1941.

Bloch, J. *On the Apocalyptic in Judaism.* JQRMS 2. Philadelphia: Dropsie College, 1952.

Boers, H. "The Problem of Jews and Gentiles in the Macro-Structure of Romans." *Neotestamentica* 15 (1981) 1-11.

Bornkamm, G. *Das Ende des Gesetzes: Paulusstudien: Gesammelte Aüfsatze I.* Munich: Chr. Kaiser, 1963.

_____. "μυστήριον" in *TDNT* (1967). Vol. 4, 802-828.

_____. "On Understanding the Christ-hymn (Philippians 2:6-11" in *Early Christian Experience,* 112-122. Tr. P. L. Hammer. New York: Harper and Row, 1969.

_____. *Paul.* Tr. D. M. G. Stalker. New York: Harper and Row, 1971.

_____. "The Praise of God" in *Early Christian Experience,* 105-111. Tr. P. L. Hammer. New York: Harper and Row, 1969.

Bourke, M. M. "The Eucharist and Wisdom in First Corinthians." *AnBib* 17 (1963) 367-381.

Bousset, W. "Eine jüdische Gebetssammlung in siebensten Buch der Apostolischen Konstitutionen" in *Nachrichten von der Königlichen Gesellschaft der Wissenschaften zu Göttingen,* 438-485. Berlin: Weidmann, 1916.

_____. *Die Religion des Judentums im späthellenistischen Zeitalter.* Tübingen: J. C. B. Mohr, 1926.

Brandenburger, E. "Paulinische Schriftauslegung in der Kontroverse um das Verheissungswort Gottes (Röm 9)." *ZTK* 82 (1985) 1-47.

Breech, E. "These Fragments Have I Shored Against My Ruins: The Form and Function of 4 Ezra." *JBL* 92 (1973) 267-274.

Bring, R. "Paul and the Old Testament: A Study of the Ideas of Election, Faith and the Law in Paul With Special Reference to Rom. 9:30-10:30 [sic]." *ST* 25 (1971) 20-60.

Brown, R. E. *The Community of the Beloved Disciple: The Life, Loves, and Hates of an Individual Church in New Testament Times.* New York: Paulist, 1979.

_____. *The Gospel According to John I-XII.* AB 29. Garden City: Doubleday, 1966.

_____. *The Semitic Background of the Term "Mystery" in the New Testament.* FBBS21. Philadelphia: Fortress, 1968.

_____. and Meier, J. P. *Antioch and Rome: New Testament Cradles of Catholic Christianity.* New York: Paulist, 1983.

Bruce, F. F. "Paul and the Law of Moses." *BJRL* 57 (1975) 259-279.

_____. *Romans.* Tyndale New Testament Commentaries. Grand Rapids: Eerdmans, 1985 2.

_____. "The Romans Debate—Continued." *BJRL* 64 (1982) 334-359.

Bultmann, R. "Die Bedeutung der neuerschlossenen mandäischen und manichäischen Quellen für das Verständnis des Johannesevangeliums." *ZNW* 24 (1925) 100-146.

_____. "Christ the End of the Law" in *Essays Philosophical and Theological*, 36-66. Tr. J. C. G. Grieg. London: SCM, 1955 (original, 1940).

_____. "γινώσκω" in *TDNT* (1964). Vol. 1, 689-719.

_____. *The Gospel of John: A Commentary.* Tr. G. R. Beasley-Murray, *et al.* Philadelphia: Westminster, 1971 (original, 1941).

_____. "History and Eschatology in the New Testament." *NTS* 1 (1954) 5-16.

_____. "The Interpretation of Mythological Eschatology" in *Jesus Christ and Mythology*, 22-34. New York: Charles Scribners' Sons, 1958.

_____. "Neueste Paulusforschung." *ThRu* 8 n.f. (1936) 1-22.

_____. "The New Testament and Mythology" in *Kerygma and Myth*, 1-44. Ed. H. W. Bartsch. New York: Harper and Brothers, 1961 (original, 1948).

_____. "Der religionsgeschichtliche Hintergrund des Prologs zum Johannesevangeliums" in Ἐυχαριστήριον: *Studien zur*

Religion und Literature des Alten und Neuen Testaments, 3-26.
FRL 36. Ed. H. Schmidt. Göttingen: Vandenhoeck and Ruprecht,
1923.

_____. *Theology of the New Testament*. 2 Vols. Tr. K. Grobel.
New York: Charles Scribners' Sons, 1951-1955.

Burrows, M., ed. *The Dead Sea Scrolls of St. Mark's Monastery*. 2
vols. New Haven: ASOR, 1950-1951.

Caird, G. B. "The Exegetical Method of the Epistle to the Hebrews."
Canadian Journal of Theology 5 (1958) 44-51.

_____. "Expository Problems: Predestination; Romans 9-11."
Expository Times 68 (1957) 324-327.

Campbell, W. S. "The Freedom and Faithfulness of God in Relation
to Israel." *JSNT* 13 (1981) 27-45.

_____. "The Place of Romans ix-xi Within the Structure and
Thought of the Letter." *TU* 71 (1982) 121-131.

_____. "Some Recent Literature on Paul's Letter to the
Romans: A Critical Survey." *Biblical Theology* 25 (1975) 25-34.

Carroll, J. T. "Eschatology and Situation in Luke-Acts." Ph. D.
Dissertation, Princeton Theological Seminary, 1986.

Cerfaux, L. "Le titre Kyrios et la dignité royale de Jésus" in *Recueil
Lucien Cerfaux*, 3-63. Gembloux: J. Duculot, 1954.

_____. *Christ in the Theology of St. Paul*. Tr. G. Webb and A.
Walker. New York: Herder and Herder, 1959².

_____. "Paul's Eschatological Message to the Nations" in *The
Spiritual Journey of St. Paul*, 40-61. New York: Sheed and Ward,
Inc., 1968. Reprinted in *A Companion to Paul: Readings in
Pauline Theology*, 101-118. Ed. M. J. Taylor. New York: Alba,
1975.

Charles, R. H. *A Critical History of the Doctrine of a Future Life in
Israel, in Judaism, and in Christianity*. London: A and C Black,
1913.

Charlesworth, J. H. "Jewish Hymns, Odes, and Prayers, ca. 167
B.C.E.-135 C.E." *JJS* 33 (1982) 411-436.

_____. *The Old Testament Pseudepigrapha and the New
Testament: Prolegomena for the Study of Christian Origins*.
SNTS Monograph Series 54. Cambridge: University, 1985.

_____. "A Prolegomenon to a New Study of the Jewish
Background of the Hymns and Prayers in the New Testament" in
Early Judaism and its Modern Interpreters, 265-285. Ed. R. A.
Kraft and G. W. E. Nickelsburg. Atlanta: Scholars, 1986.

_____. *The Pseudepigrapha and Modern Research With A Supplement.* Septuagint and Cognate Studies 7s. Chico: Scholars, 1981.

_____. "The Triumphant Majority as Seen by a Dwindled Minority: The Outsider According to the Insider of the Jewish Apocalypses, 70-130" in *To See Ourselves As Others See Us: Christians, Jews, "Others" in Late Antiquity,* 285-313. Ed. J. Neusner and E. S. Frerichs. Chico: Scholars, 1985.

Charue, A. *L'Incrédulité des Juifs dans le Nouveau Testament: Etude historique, exégétique et théologique.* Gembloux: Duculot, 1929.

Clements, R. E. "A Remnant Chosen By Grace (Romans 11:5)" in *Pauline Studies: Essays Presented to F. F. Bruce,* 106-121. Ed. D. A. Hagner and M. J. Harris. Exeter and Grand Rapids: Paternoster and Eerdmans, 1980.

Collins, A. Y. "The Early Christian Apocalypses." *Semeia* 14 (1979) 61-121.

Collins, J. J. *The Apocalyptic Vision of the Book of Daniel.* Harvard Monograph Series 16. Missoula: Scholars, 1977.

_____. "Cosmos and Salvation: Jewish Wisdom and Apocalyptic in the Hellenistic Age." *History of Religions* 17 (1977) 121-142.

_____. "The Court Tales in Daniel and the Development of Apocalyptic." *JBL* 94 (1975) 218-234.

_____. *Daniel, First Maccabees, Second Maccabees: With An Excursus on the Apocalyptic Genre.* Wilmington, DE: Michael Glazier, 1981.

_____. "Introduction: Towards the Morphology of a Genre." *Semeia* 14 (1979) 1-20.

_____. "The Jewish Apocalypses." *Semeia* 14 (1979) 21-59.

Conzelmann, H. "Current Problems in Pauline Research." *Int* 22 (1968) 171-186.

_____. "The Mother of Wisdom" in *The Future of Our Religious Past: Essays in Honor of Rudolf Bultmann,* 230-243. Ed. J. M. Robinson. Tr. C. E. Carlston and R. P. Scharlemann. New York: Harper and Row, 1964.

_____. "Paulus und die Weisheit." *NTS* 12 (1965) 231-244.

_____. "Wisdom in the New Testament" in *IDBS* (1976) 956-960.

Cooper, C. "Romans 11:25-26." *Restoration Quarterly* 21 (1978) 84-94.

Corley, B. "The Jews, the Future, and God (Rom. 9-11)." *Southwestern Journal of Theology* 19 (1976) 42-56.

Coughenour, R. A. "Enoch and Wisdom: A Study of the Wisdom Elements in the Book of Enoch." Ph. D. Dissertation, Case Western Reserve University, 1972.

Craddock, F. B. *The Pre-Existence of Christ in the New Testament.* Nashville: Abingdon,1968.

Cranfield, C. E. B. *The Epistle to the Romans.* ICC. 2 Vols. Edinburgh: T & T Clark, 1979
_____. "St. Paul and the Law." *SJT* 17 (1964) 43-68.

Crenshaw, J. L. "Method in Determining Wisdom Influence Upon 'Historical' Literature." *JBL* 88 (1969) 129-142.
_____. "Prolegomenon" in *Studies in Ancient Israelite Wisdom*, 1-45. Ed. J. L. Crenshaw. New York: KTAV, 1976.

Cross, F. M. "New Directions in the Study of Apocalyptic." *Journal for Theology and the Church* 6 (1969) 157-165.

Cullmann, O. "Le caractère eschatologique du devoir missionaire et de la conscience apostolique de S. Paul: Etude sur le κατέχον(ων) de II Thess.2.6-7." *RHPR* 16 (1936) 210-245.

Dahl, N. A. "Contradictions in Scripture" in *Studies in Paul: Theology for the Early Christian Mission*, 159-177. Minneapolis: Augsburg, 1977.
_____. "The Future of Israel" in *Studies in Paul: Theology for the Early Christian Mission*, 137-158. Minneapolis: Augsburg, 1977.
_____. "The Neglected Factor in New Testament Theology." *Reflection* 73 (1975) 5-8.
_____. "The One God of Jews and Gentiles" in *Studies in Paul: Theology for the Early Christian Mission*, 178-191. Minneapolis: Augsburg, 1977.

Davids, P. H. *The Epistle of James: A Commentary on the Greek Text.* Grand Rapids: Eerdmans, 1982.

Davies, J. A. *Wisdom and Spirit: An Investigation of I Corinthians 1.18-3.20 Against the Background of Jewish Sapiential Traditions in the Greco-Roman Period.* Lanham, NY and London: University Press of America, 1984.

Davies, P. R. "Qumran Beginnings" in *1986 SBL Seminar Papers*, 361-368. Ed. K. H. Richards. Atlanta: Scholars, 1986.

Davies, W. D. *The Gospel and the Land.* Berkeley: University of California, 1974.
_____. "The Jewish Background of the Teaching of Jesus: Apocalyptic and Pharisaism" in *Christian Origins and Judaism*, 19-30. Philadelphia: Westminster, 1962.

_____. *Paul and Rabbinic Judaism: Some Rabbinic Elements in Pauline Theology.* New York: Harper and Row, 1955[2].

_____. "Paul and the People of Israel." *NTS* 24 (1977) 4-39.

Deichgräber, R. *Gotteshymnus und Christushymnus in der fruhen Christenheit.* Göttingen: Vandenhoeck and Ruprecht, 1967.

Deissmann, A. *Paul.* Tr. W. E. Wilson. London: Hodder and Stoughton, 1926[2].

DeVries, S. J. "Observations on Qualitative and Quantitative Time in Wisdom and Apocalyptic" in *Israelite Wisdom: Theological and Literary Essays in Honor of Samuel Terrien,* 263-276. Ed. J. G. Gammie, W. A. Brueggemann, W. L. Humphreys, J. M. Ward. New York: Union Theological Seminary, 1978.

Dibelius, M. "Vier Worte des Römerbriefs: 5,5. 5,12. 8,10. und 11,30f." *Symbolae Biblicae Upsalienses,* 3-17. SEA Supp. 3. Uppsala: Wretmans, 1944.

Dinkler, E. "The Historical and Eschatological Israel in Rom. 9-11: A Contribution to the Problem of Predestination and Individual Responsibility." *JR* 36 (1956) 109-127.

_____. "Prädestination bei Paulus" in *Festschrift für Günther Dehn,* 81-102. Ed. W. Schneemelcher. Neukirchen: Kreis Moers, 1957.

Dinter, P. E. "The Remnant of Israel and the Stone of Stumbling According to Paul (Romans 9-11)." Ph. D. Dissertation, Union Theological Seminary, 1979.

Dodd, C. H. *According to the Scriptures.* London: Nisbet and Co., 1952.

_____. *The Epistle of Paul to the Romans.* New York: Harper and Row, 1932.

Donfried, K. P. "False Presuppositions in the Study of Romans" in *The Romans Debate,* 120-148. Ed. K. P. Donfried. Minneapolis: Augsburg, 1977.

_____. "Paul and Judaism: I Thessalonians 2:13 As A Test Case." *Int* 38 (1984) 242-253.

Drane, J. W. *Paul: Libertine or Legalist?* London: SPCK, 1975.

Ebeling, G. "The Ground of Christian Theology." *Journal for Theology and the Church* 6 (1969) 47-68.

Eichholz, G. *Die Theologie des Paulus im Umriss.* Neukirchen-Vluyn: Neukirchener, 1972.

Ellis, E. E. "Midrash *Pesher* in Pauline Hermeneutics" in *Prophecy and Hermeneutic in Early Christianity: New Testament Essays,* 173-181. WUNT 18. Grand Rapids: Eerdmans, 1978.

_____. *Paul and His Recent Interpreters.* Grand Rapids: Eerdmans, 1961.

_____. *Paul's Use of the Old Testament.* Edinburgh and London: Oliver and Boyd, 1957.

_____. "'Wisdom' and 'Knowledge' in I Corinthians" in *Prophecy and Hermeneutic in Early Christianity: New Testament Essays,* 45-62. WUNT 18. Grand Rapids: Eerdmans, 1978.

Ellison, H. L. *The Mystery of Israel.* Grand Rapids: Eerdmans, 1966.

Evans, C. A. "Paul and the Hermeneutics of 'True Prophecy': A Study of Romans 9-11." *Bib* 65 (1984) 560-570.

Farrell, H. "The Eschatological Perspective of Luke-Acts." Ph. D. Dissertation, Boston University, 1972.

Feiler, P. F. "Jesus the Prophet: The Lukan Portrayal of Jesus and the Prophet Like Moses." Ph. D. Dissertation, Princeton Theological Seminary, 1986.

Feuillet, A. *Le Christ Sagesse de Dieu d'après les Epîtres pauliniennnes.* Paris: J. Gabalda, 1966.

_____. "L'énigme de I Cor.II.9: Contribution à l'étude des sources de la christologie paulinienne." *RB* 70 (1963) 52-74.

Fichtner, J. *Die altorientalische Weisheit in ihrer israelitischjüdischen Ausprägung.* Giessen: A. Töpelmann, 1933.

_____. "Die Stellung der Sapientia Salomonis in der Literature- und Geistesgeschichte ihrer Zeit." *ZNW* 36 (1937) 113-132.

Finkel, A. "The *Pesher* of Dreams and Scriptures." *RQ* 4 (1963-1964) 357-370.

Fitzmyer, J. A. *The Gospel According to Luke X-XXIV.* AB 28.2. Garden City: Doubleday, 1983.

_____. "St. Paul and the Law." *The Jurist* 27 (1967) 18-36. Reprinted as "Paul and the Law" in *A Companion to Paul: Readings in Pauline Theology,* 73-88. Ed. M. J. Taylor. New York: Alba, 1975.

_____. *Pauline Theology: A Brief Sketch.* Englewood Cliffs: Prentice-Hall, 1967.

_____. "The Use of Explicit Old Testament Quotations in Qumran Literature and in the New Testament." *NTS* 7 (1960-1961) 297-333.

Flückiger, F. "Christus, des Gesetzes Telos." *TZ* 11 (1955) 153-157.

Foerster, W. "κύριος, κ.τ.λ." in *TDNT* (1965). Vol. 3, 1039-1098.

_____. "σώζω, κ.τ.λ." in *TDNT* (1971). Vol. 7, 965-1024.

Francis, F. O. and Meeks, W. A., eds. *Conflict at Colossae.* Missoula: Scholars, 1975.

Freedman, D. N. "The Flowering of Apocalyptic." *Journal for Theology and the Church* 6 (1969) 166-174.

Fuchs, E. "On the Task of a Christian Theology." *Journal for Theology and the Church* 6 (1969) 69-98.

Funk, R. W. "Apocalyptic as an Historical and Theological Problem in Current New Testament Scholarship." *Journal for Theology and the Church* 6 (1969) 175-191.

Gager, J. G. *The Origins of Anti-Semitism: Attitudes Toward Judaism in Pagan and Christian Antiquity.* New York: Oxford University, 1983.

_____. "Functional Diversity in Paul's Use of End-Time Language." *JBL* 89 (1970) 325-337.

Gamble, H. Y. *The Textual History of the Letter to the Romans: A Study in Textual and Literary Criticism.* SD 42. Grand Rapids: Eerdmans, 1977.

Gammie, J. G. "Spatial and Ethical Dualism in Jewish Wisdom and Apocalyptic Literature." *JBL* 93 (1974) 356-385.

Gaston, L. "Abraham and the Righteousness of God." *Horizons in Biblical Theology* 2 (1980) 39-68.

_____. "Angels and Gentiles in Early Judaism and in Paul." *Studies in Religion* 11 (1982) 65-75.

_____. "Israel's Enemies in Pauline Theology." *NTS* 28 (1982) 400-423.

_____. "Paul and the Torah" in *Anti-Semitism and the Foundations of Christianity*, 48-71. Ed. A. T. Davies. New York: Paulist, 1979.

_____. "Works of Law as Subjective Genitive." *Studies in Religion* 13 (1984) 39-46.

Gaugler, E. *Der Brief an die Römer.* 2 Vols. Zürich: Zwingli, 1945-1952.

Geiger, R. *Die Lukanische Endzeitreden.* Bern: Herbert Lang, 1973.

Georgi, D. *Die Geschichte der Kollekte des Paulus für Jerusalem.* Hamburg: Herbert Reich, 1965.

_____. "The Records of Jesus in the Light of Ancient Accounts of Revered Men" in *SBL Proceedings 1972*, vol. 2, 527-542. Ed. L. C. McGaughy. SBL, 1973.

_____. "Der vorpaulinische Hymnus Phil 2,6-11" in *Zeit und Geschichte: Dankesgabe an Rudolf Bultmann zum 80. Geburtstag*, 263-293. Ed. E. Dinkler. Tübingen: J. C. B. Mohr (Paul Siebeck), 1964.

Gese, H. "Der Johannesprolog" in *Zur biblischen Theologie*, 152-201. Munich: Chr. Kaiser, 1977.

_____. "Natus ex Virgine" in *Vom Sinai zum Zion*, 130-146. Munich: Chr. Kaiser, 1974.

_____. "Die Weisheit, der Menschensohn und die Ursprüunge der Christologie als konsequente Entfaltung der biblischen Theologie." *SEA* 44 (1979) 77-114.

Getty, M. A. "An Apocalyptic Perspective on Rom. 10:4." *Horizons in Biblical Theology* 4-5 (1982-1983) 79-131.

_____. "The Apostle of Romans: Paul's Message for Today's Church." *TBT* 91 (1977) 1281-1288.

Gilbert, M. "Wisdom Literature" in *Jewish Writings of the Second Temple Period: Apocrypha, Pseudepigrapha, Qumran Sectarian Writings, Philo, Josephus*, 283-324. Compendia Rerum Iudaicarum ad Novum Testamentum II. Ed. M. E. Stone. Assen and Philadelphia: Van Gorcum and Fortress, 1984.

Ginsburg, L. "Some Observations on the Attitude of the Synagogue Towards the Apocalyptic-Eschatological Writings." *JBL* 41 (1922) 115-136.

Gloer, W. H. "Homologies and Hymns in the New Testament: Form, Content, and Criteria for Identification." *Perspectives in Religious Studies* 11 (1984) 115-132.

Godet, F. *Commentary on St. Paul's Epistle to the Romans*. 2 Vols. Tr. A. Cusin. Edinburgh: T & T Clark, 1890[2].

Goppelt, L. "Apokalyptik und Typologie bei Paulus." *TLZ* 89 (1964) 321-344.

_____. *Jesus, Paul, and Judaism*. Tr. E. Schroeder. New York: Thomas Nelson and Sons, 1964.

_____. "Paul and Heilsgeschichte." *Int* 21 (1967) 315-326.

Gorday, P. *Principles of Patristic Exegesis: Romans 9-11 in Origin, John Chrysostom, and Augustine*. New York and Toronto: Edwin Mellon, 1983.

Grafe, E. "Das Verhältnis der paulinischen Schriften zur Sapientia Salomonis" in *Theologische Abhandlungen: Carl von Weizsäcker zu seinem siebzigsten Geburstag 11 December 1892*, 253-286. Ed. A. Harnack, *et al*. Freiburg: J. C. B. Mohr (Paul Siebeck), 1892.

Güttgemanns, E. *Heilsgeschichte bei Paulus oder Dynamik des Evangeliums? Zur strukturellen Relevanz von Römer 9-11 für die Theologie des Römerbriefs*. BEvT 60, 1971.

Gunkel, H. *Schöpfung und Chaos in Urzeit und Endzeit: Eine religionsgeschichtliche Untersuchung über Gen.1 und Ap.Joh.12*. Göttingen: Vandenhoeck and Ruprecht, 1895.

224   *Function of Apocalyptic and Wisdom Traditions*

Haacker, K. "Das Evangelium Gottes und die Erwählung Israels: Zum Beitrag des Römerbriefs zur Erneuerung des Verhältnis zwischen Christen und Juden." *Theologische Beitrag* 13 (1982) 59-72.

Hahn, F. "Das Geseztverständnis in Römer- und Galaterbrief." *ZNW* 67 (1976) 49-51.

Hamerton-Kelly, R. G. *Pre-Existence, Wisdom, and the Son of Man: A Study in the Idea of Pre-Existence in the New Testament.* Cambridge: University, 1973.

Hanson, A. T. *The New Testament Interpretation of Scripture.* London: S.P.C.K., 1980.

_____. *Studies in Paul's Technique and Theology.* Grand Rapids: Eerdmans, 1974.

_____. "Vessels of Wrath or Instruments of Wrath? Romans IX.22-3." *JTS* 32 (1981) 433-443.

Hanson, P. D. "Apocalypticism" in *IDBS* (1976) 28-34.

_____. *The Dawn of Apocalyptic.* Philadelphia: Fortress, 1979[2].

_____. "Prolegomena to the Study of Jewish Apocalyptic" in *Magnalia Dei: The Mighty Acts of God*, 389-413. Ed. F. M. Cross, W. E. Lemke, P. D. Miller. Garden City: Doubleday, 1976.

Harder, G. *Paulus und das Gebet.* Gütersloh: C. Bertelsmann, 1936.

Hare, D. R. A. *The Theme of Jewish Persecution of Christians in the Gospel According to St. Matthew.* SNTS Monograph Series 6. Cambridge: University, 1967.

Harnisch, W. *Verhängnis und Verheissung der Geschichte: Untersuchungen zum Zeit und Geschichtsverständnis im 4. Buch Esra und in der syr. Baruchapokalypse.* FRLANT 97. Göttingen: Vandenhoeck and Ruprecht, 1969.

Harrisville, R. A. *Romans.* Augsburg Commentary on the New Testament. Minneapolis: Augsburg, 1980.

Hartman, L. *Prophecy Interpreted: The Formation of Some Jewish Apocalyptic Texts and of the Eschatological Discourse Mark 13 Par.* Tr. N. Tomkinson. Lund: Gleerup, 1966.

_____. "The Functions of Some So-Called Apocalyptic Timetables." *NTS* 22 (1976) 1-14.

Hauck, F. and Kasch, W. "πλοῦτος, κ.τ.λ." in *TDNT* (1968). Vol. 6, 318-332.

Hawkins, R. M. "The Rejection of Israel: An Analysis of Romans 9-11." *ATR* 23 (1941) 329-335.

Heitmüller, W. *Taufe und Abendmahl bei Paulus: Darstellung und religionsgeschichtliche Beleuchtung.* Göttingen: Vandenhoeck and Ruprecht, 1903.

Helfgott, B. W. *The Doctrine of Election in Tannaitic Literature*. New York: King's Crown, 1954.

Hengel, M. *Judaism and Hellenism: Studies in Their Encounter in Palestine During the Early Hellenistic Period*. 2 Vols. Tr. J. Bowden. Philadelphia: Fortress, 1974.

_____. *The Son of God: The Origin of Christology and the History of Jewish-Hellenistic Religion*. Tr. J. Bowder. Philadelphia: Fortress, 1976.

Hermisson, H. J. "Observations on the Creation Theology in Wisdom" in *Israelite Wisdom: Theological and Literary Essays in Honor of Samuel Terrien*, 43-57. Ed. J. G. Gammie, W. A. Brueggemann, W. L. Humphreys, J. M. Ward. New York: Union Theological Seminary, 1978.

Hill, M. *A Sociology of Religion*. London: Heinemann Educational, 1973.

Hölscher, G. "Die Entstehung des Buches Daniels." *Theologische Studien und Kritiken* 92 (1919) 113-138.

Howard, G. E. "Christ the End of the Law: The Meaning of Romans 10:4ff." *JBL* 88 (1969) 331-337.

Hübner, H. *Gottes Ich und Israel: Zum Schriftgebrauch des Paulus in Römer 9-11*. FRLANT 136. Göttingen: Vandenhoeck and Ruprecht, 1984.

Hyldahl, N. "Jesus og jøderne ifolge I Tess 2,14-16." *SEA* 27-28 (1972-1973) 238-254.

Isaac, E. "Introduction" to I Enoch in *The Old Testament Pseudepigrapha*. Vol. 1, 5-12. Ed. J. H. Charlesworth. Garden City: Doubleday, 1983.

Jeremias, J. "Einige vorwiegend Beobachtungen zu Röm. 11,25-36" in *Die Israelfrage nach Römer 9-11*, 193-205. Ed. L. de Lorenzi. Rome: Abtei von St. Paulus vor den Mauern, 1977.

_____. *The Eucharistic Words of Jesus*. Tr. N. Perrin. New York: Charles Scribners' Sons, 1966[2] (original, 1935).

Jervell, J. "The Letter to Jerusalem" in *The Romans Debate*, 61-74. Ed. K. P. Donfried. Minneapolis: Augsburg, 1977.

Jewett, R. "The Law and the Coexistence of Jews and Gentiles in Rome." *Int* 39 (1985) 341-356.

_____. "Romans as an Ambassadorial Letter." *Int* 36 (1982) 5-20.

Jocz, J. *A Theology of Election: Israel and the Church*. New York: Macmillan, 1958.

226   *Function of Apocalyptic and Wisdom Traditions*

Kabisch, R. *Die Eschatologie des Paulus in ihren Zusammenhängen mit dem Gesamtbegriff Paulinismus.* Göttingen: Vandenhoeck and Ruprecht, 1893.

Käsemann, E. *Commentary on Romans.* Tr. G. W. Bromiley. Grand Rapids: Eerdmans, 1980.

_____. *Essays on New Testament Themes.* Tr. W. J. Montague. London: SCM, 1964.

_____. *New Testament Questions of Today.* Tr. W. J. Montague. London: SCM, 1969.

_____. *Perspectives on Paul.* Tr. M. Kohl. London: SCM, 1971.

Kasch, W. "ῥύομαι" in *TDNT* (1968). Vol. 6, 998-1003.

Keck, L. E. "Paul and Apocalyptic Theology." *Int* 38 (1984) 229-241.

Kennedy, G. *New Testament Interpretation Through Rhetorical Criticism.* Chapel Hill, NC: University of North Carolina, 1984.

Kinoshita, J. "Romans—Two Writings Combined: A New Interpretation of the Body of Romans." *NovT* 7 (1965) 258-277.

Kittel, B. P. *The Hymns of Qumran.* SBLDS 50. Chico, Scholars, 1981.

Kittel, G. "δοκέω, κ.τ.λ." in *TDNT* (1964). Vol. 2, 232-255.

Knibb, M. A. "Apocalyptic and Wisdom in 4 Ezra." *JSJ* 13 (1981) 56-74.

_____. "The Dating of the Parables of Enoch: A Critical Review." *NTS* 25 (1979) 345-359.

_____. "Prophecy and the Emergence of the Jewish Apocalypses" in *Israel's Prophetic Heritage: Essays in Honour of Peter J. Ackroyd,* 155-180. Ed. R. J. Coggins, A. Phillips, M. A. Knibb. Cambridge: University, 1982.

Knight, G. A. F. "Israel—A Theological Problem." *Reformed Theological Review* 17 (1958) 33-43.

Knox, W. L. *St. Paul and the Church of the Gentiles.* Cambridge: University, 1939.

Koch, K. *The Rediscovery of Apocalyptic.* Tr. M. Kohl. London: SCM, 1972.

Koenig, J. T. "The Jewishness of the Gospel: Reflections of a Lutheran." *Journal of Ecumenical Studies* 19 (1982) 57-68.

_____. *Jews and Christians in Dialogue: New Testament Foundations.* Philadelphia: Westminster, 1979.

Koester, H. "Paul and Hellenism" in *The Bible in Modern Scholarship,* 187-195. Ed. J. P. Hyatt. Nashville: Abingdon, 1965.

_____. Review of *Weisheit und Torheit*, by U. Wilckens. *Gnomon* 33 (1961) 590-595.

Küchler, M. *Frühjüdische Weisheitstraditionen: Zum Fortgang weisheitlichen Denkens im Bereich des Frühjüdischen Jahwehglaubens.* OBO 26. Göttingen: Vandenhoeck and Ruprech, 1979.

Kümmel, W. G. "'Das Gesetz und die Propheten gehen bis Johannes'—Lukas 16,16 in Zusammenhang der heilsgeschichtlichen Theologie der Lukasschriften" in *Verborum Veritas: Festschrift für Gustav Stählin zum 70. Geburtstag*, 89-102. Ed. O. Böcher and K. Haacker. Wuppertal: R. Brockhaus, 1970.

_____. *The New Testament: The History of the Investigation of its Problems.* Tr. S. M. Gilmour and H. C. Kee. Nashville: Abingdon, 1972.

_____. "Die Probleme von Römer 9-11 in der gegenwärtigen Forschungslage" in *Die Israelfrage nach Römer 9-11*, 13-33. Ed. L. de Lorenzi. Rome: Abtei von St. Paulus vor den Mauern, 1977.

_____. *The Theology of the New Testament According to its Major Witnesses: Jesus, Paul, John.* Tr. J. E. Steely. Nashville: Abingdon, 1973.

Kuss, O. *Der Römerbrief.* 3 Vols. Regensburg: Pustet, 1978.

Lagrange, M. -J. *Saint Paul Epître aux Romains.* Paris: Victor Lecoffre, 1916.

Langevin, P. -E. "Sur la Christologie de Romains 10,1-13." *Laval Théologique et Philosophique* 35 (1979) 35-54.

Lapide, P. and Stuhlmacher, P. *Paul: Rabbi and Apostle.* Tr. L. W. Denef. Minneapolis: Augsburg, 1984.

Larcher, C. *Le Livre de la Sagesse ou La Sagesse de Salomon. EBib* n.s. 1. Paris: J. Gabalda, 1983.

Lebram, J. C. "Die Theologie der späten Chokma und häretisches Judentum." *ZAW* 77 (1965) 202-211.

Leenhardt, F. J. *The Epistle to the Romans.* Tr. H. Knight. London: Lutterworth, 1961.

R. Lehmann. "Ben Sira and the Qumran Literature." *RevQ* 3 (1961) 103-116.

Lenski, R. C. H. *The Interpretation of St. Paul's Epistle to the Romans.* Columbus, OH: Book Concern, 1936.

Lietzmann, H. *An die Römer.* HNT 3.1. Tübingen: J. C. B. Mohr (Paul Siebeck), 1928.

Limbeck, M. *Die Ordnung des Heils: Untersuchungen zum Gesetzverständnis des Frühjudentums.* Düsseldorf: Patmos, 1971.

Lindemann, A. "Die Gerechtigkeit aus dem Gesetz: Erwägungen zur Auslegung und zur Textgeschichte von Römer 10:5." *ZNW* 73 (1982) 231-250.

Lipscomb, W. L. and Sanders, J. A. "Wisdom at Qumran" in *Israelite Wisdom: Theological and Literary Essays in Honor of Samuel Terrien,* 263-276. Ed. J. G. Gammie, W. A. Brueggemann, W. L. Humphreys, J. M. Ward. New York: Union Theological Seminary, 1978.

Lohse, E. *Colossians and Philemon.* Tr. W. R. Poehlmann and R. J. Karris. Philadelphia: Fortress, 1971.

Longenecker, R. N. *Biblical Exegesis in the Apostolic Period.* Grand Rapids: Eerdmans, 1973.

Lütgert, W. *Freiheitspredigt und Schwarmgeister in Korinth.* Gütersloh: Gütersloher, 1908.

Luz, U. *Das Geschichtsverständnis des Paulus.* BEvT 49. Munich: Chr. Kaiser, 1968.

Mack, B. L. *Logos und Sophia: Untersuchungen zur Weisheitstheologie im hellenistischen Judentum.* Göttingen: Vandenhoeck and Ruprecht, 1973.

_____. "Wisdom Myth and Myth-ology." *Int* 24 (1970) 46-60.

Macrae, G. W. "The Jewish Background of the Gnostic Sophia Myth." *NovT* 12 (1970) 86-101.

Maillot, A. "Essai sur les citations vétérotestamentaires contenues dans Romains 9 à 11, ou comment se servir de la Torah pour montrer que le 'Christ est la fin de la Torah'." *Etudes Théologiques et Religieuses* 57 (1982) 55-73.

Maly, E. H. *Romans.* Wilmington, DE: Michael Glazier, 1979.

Marcus, J. "Mark 4:10-12 and Marcan Epistemology." *JBL* 103 (1984) 557-574.

Marquardt, F. -W. *Die Juden in Römerbrief.* Theologische Studien 10. Zürich: Theologischer, 1971.

Martin, R. P. *Worship in the Early Church.* Grand Rapids: Eerdmans, 1974.

_____. "Aspects of Worship in the New Testament Church." *Vox Evangelica* 2 (1963) 2-9.

Marxsen, W. *Introduction to the New Testament.* Tr. G. Buswell. Philadelphia: Fortress, 1968.

Meeks, W. A. "Image of the Androgyne: Some Uses of a Symbol in Earliest Christianity." *History of Religions* 13 (1974) 165-208.

_____, ed. *The Writings of St. Paul*. New York: W. W. Norton, 1972.

Meier, J. P. *The Vision of Matthew: Christ, Church and Morality in the First Gospel*. New York: Paulist, 1979.

Metzger, B. M. "Introduction" to 4 Ezra in *The Old Testament Pseudepigrapha*, Vol. 1, 517-523. Ed. J. H. Charlesworth. Garden City: Doubleday, 1983.

_____. *A Textual Commentary on the Greek New Testament*. London and New York: United Bible Societies, 1975 2 .

Meyer, P. W. "Romans 10:4 and the 'End' of the Law" in *The Divine Helmsman*, 59-78. Ed. J. R. Crenshaw and S. Sandmel. New York: KTAV, 1980.

Michel, O. *Paulus und seine Bibel*. MeyerK 4. Gütersloh: Gütersloher, 1929.

Milik, J. T. "4Q Visions de 'Amram et une citation d'Origène." *RB* 79 (1972) 77-97.

_____. "Prière de Nabonide et autres écrits araméens de Qumrân 4." *RB* 63 (1956) 407-415.

Millar, W. R. *Isaiah 24-27 and the Origin of Apocalyptic*. Missoula: Scholars, 1976.

Minear, P. S. *The Obedience of Faith*. London: SCM, 1971.

Montgomery, J. A. *The Book of Daniel*. ICC. New York: Charles Scribner's Sons, 1927.

Moule, H. C. G. *The Epistle of Paul the Apostle to the Romans*. Cambridge: University, 1952.

Müller, C. *Gottes Gerechtigkeit und Gottes Volk: Eine Untersuchung zu Römer 9-11*. Göttingen: Vandenhoeck and Ruprecht, 1964.

Müller, H.-P. "Mantische Weisheit und Apokalyptik" in *Congress Volume Uppsala. VT* Supp. 22, 268-293. Leiden: Brill, 1972.

Munck, J. *Christ and Israel: An Interpretation of Romans 9-11*. Tr. I. Nixon. Philadelphia: Fortress, 1956.

_____. "Israel and the Gentiles in the New Testament." *JST* 2 (1951) 3-16.

_____. *Paul and the Salvation of Mankind*. Tr. F. Clarke. Richmond: John Knox, 1959.

_____. "Pauline Research Since Schweitzer" in *The Bible in Modern Scholarship*, 166-177. Ed. J. P. Hyatt. Nashville: Abingdon, 1965.

Murdock, W. R. "History and Revelation in Jewish Apocalypticism." *Int* 21 (1967) 167-187.

Murphy, R. E. "Assumptions and Problems in Old Testament Wisdom Research." *CBQ* 29 (1967) 407-418.

_____. "Hebrew Wisdom." *JAOS* 101 (1981) 21-34.

_____. *Wisdom Literature: Job, Proverbs, Ruth, Canticles, Ecclesiastes, and Esther.* Grand Rapids: Eerdmans, 1981.

Mussner, F. "'Christus (ist) des Gesetzes Ende zur Gerechtigkeit für jeden, der glaubt' (Röm 10,4)" in *Paulus: Apostat oder Apostel? Jüdische und christliche Antworten,* 31-44. Regensburg: Pustet, 1977.

_____. "'Ganz Israel wird gerettet werden' (Röm 11,26): Versuchener Auslegung." *Kairos* 18 (1976) 241-255.

_____. "Heil für Alle: Der Grundgedanke des Römerbriefs." *Kairos* 23 (1981) 207-214.

Nagata, T. "Philippians 2:5-11: A Case Study in the Contextual Shaping of Early Christology." Ph. D. Dissertation, Princeton Theological Seminary, 1981.

Neill, S. *The Interpretation of the New Testament: 1861-1961.* London: Oxford University, 1964.

Nickelsburg, G. W. E. "Future Life in Intertestamental Literature" in *IDBS* (1976) 348-351.

_____. *Jewish Literature Between the Bible and the Mishnah: A Historical and Literary Introduction.* Philadelphia: Fortress, 1981.

_____. *Resurrection, Immortality, and Eternal Life in Intertestamental Judaism.* Cambridge: University, 1972.

_____. "Revealed Wisdom as a Criterion for Inclusion and Exclusion: From Jewish Sectarianism to Early Christianity" in *"To See Ourselves As Others See Us": Christians, Jews, "Others" in Late Antiquity,* 73-91. Ed. J. Neusner and E. S. Frerichs. Chico: Scholars, 1985.

Nock, A. D. "Gnosticism." *HTR* 57 (1964) 255-279.

Noack, B. "Celui qui court: Rom. IX,16." *ST* 24 (1970) 113-116.

_____. "Current and Backwater in the Epistle to the Romans." *ST* 19 (1965) 155-166.

Norden, E. *Agnostos Theos: Untersuchungen zur Formengeschichte religioser Rede.* Leipzig: Teubner, 1913.

Nygren, A. *Commentary on Romans.* Tr. C. Rasmussen. Fortress: Philadelphia, 1949.

Oepke, A. "ἀνίστημι, κ.τ.λ." in *TDNT* (1964). Vol. 1, 368-372.

Oesterreicher, J. M. "Israel's Misstep and Her Rise—The Dialectic of God's Saving Design in Romans 9-11." *TBT* 1 (1964) 768-774.

O'Neil, J. C. *Paul's Letter to the Romans.* Baltimore: Penguin, 1975.

von der Osten-Sacken, P. *Die Apokalyptik in ihrem Verhältnis zu Prophetie und Weisheit.* TEH 157. Munich: Kaiser, 1969.

Parkes, J. *The Foundations of Judaism and Christianity.* Chicago: Quadrangle, 1960.

Pearson, B. "Hellenistic-Jewish Wisdom Speculation and Paul" in *Aspects of Wisdom in Judaism and Early Christianity*, 43-66. Ed. R. L. Wilken. Notre Dame, IN: University of Notre Dame, 1975.

_____. *The Pneumatikos-Psychikos Terminology in I Corinthians: A Study in the Theology of the Corinthian Opponents of Paul and its Relation to Gnosticism.* SBLDS 12. Missoula: Scholars, 1973.

Peterson, E. "ἀνεξιχνίαστος" In *TDNT* (1964). Vol. 1, 358.

Perrin, N. "Wisdom and Apocalyptic in the Message of Jesus" in *SBL Proceedings 1972*, vol. 2, 543-572. Ed. L. C. McGaughy. SBL, 1972.

van der Ploeg, J. *The Church and Israel.* Washington, DC: Catholic Distributors, 1956.

Plöger, O. *Theokratie und Eschatologie.* WMANT 2. Neukirchen-Vluyn: Neukirchener, 1962².

Porter, F. C. "The Pre-Existence of the Soul in the Book of Wisdom and in the Rabbinical Writings." *American Journal of Theology* 12 (1908) 53-118.

Porteus, N. W. *Daniel: A Commentary.* London: SCM, 1965.

von Rad, G. *Old Testament Theology.* 2 Vols. Tr. D. M. G. Stalker. New York: Harper and Row, 1965.

_____. *Wisdom in Israel.* Tr. J. D. Martin. London: SCM, 1972.

Reese, J. M. *The Book of Wisdom, Song of Songs.* Old Testament Message 20. Wilmington, DE: Michael Glazier, 1983.

_____. *Hellenistic Influence on the Book of Wisdom and its Consequences.* AnBib 41. Rome: Biblical Institute, 1970.

_____. "Paul Proclaims the Wisdom of the Cross: Scandal and Foolishness." *Biblical Theology Bulletin* 9 (1979) 147-153.

_____. "Plan and Structure in the Book of Wisdom." *CBQ* 27 (1965) 391-399.

Rengstorf, K. H. "Das Ölbaum-Gleichnis in Röm.11,11ff.: Versuch einer weiterführenden Deutung" in *Donum Gentilicium: New Testament Studies in Honour of David Daube*, 126-164. Ed. E. Bammel, C. K. Barrett, W. D. Davies. Oxford: Clarendon, 1978.

Rese, M. "Die Vorzüge Israels in Röm.9,4f. und Eph.2,12: Exegetische Anmerkungen zum Thema Kirche und Israel." *TZ* 31 (1975) 211-222.

Rhyne, C. T. *Faith Establishes the Law.* SBLDS 55. Chico: Scholars, 1981.

Richardson, P. *Israel in the Apostolic Church*. Cambridge: University, 1969.
Ridderbos, H. *Aan de Romeinen*. Kampen: J. H. Kok, 1959.
_____. *Paul: An Outline of His Theology*. Tr. J. R. deWitt. Grand Rapids: Eerdmans, 1975.
Ringgren, H. *The Faith of Qumran*. Philadelphia: Fortress, 1963.
Robinson, J. A. T. *Wrestling With Romans*. Philadelphia: Westminster, 1979.
Roetzel, C. "*Diatheke* in Romans 9,4." *Bib* 51 (1970) 377-390.
Romaniuk, C. "Le Thème de la Sagesse dans les Documents de Qumrân." *RevQ* 9 (1977-1978) 429-435.
van Roon, A. "The Relation Between Christ and the Wisdom of God According to Paul." *NovT* 16 (1974) 207-239.
Rowland, C. *The Open Heaven*. New York: Crossroad, 1982.
Rowley, H. H. *The Biblical Doctrine of Election*. London: Lutterworth, 1950.
_____. *The Revelance of Apocalyptic*. New York: Association, 1964[3].
Ruether, R. R. *Faith and Fratricide: The Theological Roots of Anti-Semitism*. New York: Seabury, 1974.
Russell, D. S. *The Method and Message of Jewish Apocalyptic*. Philadelphia: Westminster, 1964.
Sanday, W. and Headlam, A. C. *A Critical and Exegetical Commentary on the Epistle to the Romans*. Edinburgh: T & T Clark, 1902.
Sanders, J. A. "Two Non-Canonical Psalms in 11QPs[a]." *ZAW* 76 (1964) 57-75.
Sanders, E. P. "The Covenant as a Soteriological Category and the Nature of Salvation in Palestinian and Hellenistic Judaism" in *Jews, Greeks, and Christians: Religious Cultures in Late Antiquity: Essays in Honor of William David Davies*, 11-44. Ed. R. Hamerton-Kelly and R. Scroggs. Leiden: Brill, 1976.
_____. *Paul and Palestinian Judaism: A Comparison of Patterns of Religion*. Philadelphia: Fortress, 1977.
_____. "Paul's Attitude Toward the Jewish People." *USQR* 33 (1978) 175-187.
_____. *Paul, the Law, and the Jewish People*. Philadelphia: Fortress, 1983.
Sayler, G. B. *Have the Promises Failed? A Literary Analysis of 2 Baruch*. SBLDS 72. Chico: Scholars, 1984.
Schelkle, K. H. *The Epistle to the Romans: Theological Meditations*. New York: Herder and Herder, 1964.

_____. *Paulus: Lehrer der Väter: Die altkirchliche Auslegung von Römer 1-11.* Düsseldorf: Patmos, 1956.

Schlier, H. *Der Römerbrief.* HTKNT 6. Freiburg: Herder, 1977.

Schmidt, J. M. *Die jüdische Apokalyptik: Die Geschichte ihrer Erforschung von den Anfägen bis zu den Textfunden von Qumran.* Neukirchen-Vluyn: Neukirchener, 1976².

Schmithals, W. *Gnosticism in Corinth.* Tr. J. E. Steely. Nashville: Abingdon, 1971.

_____. *Der Römerbrief als historisches Problem.* StNT 9. Gütersloh: Gütersloher (G. Mohn), 1975.

Schoeps, H. J. *Paul: The Theology of the Apostle in the Light of Jewish Religious History.* Tr. H. Knight. Philadelphia: Westminster, 1961.

Schweitzer, A. *The Mysticism of the Apostle Paul.* Tr. W. Montgomery and F. C. Burkitt. New York: H. Holt, 1931.

_____. *Paul and His Interpreters.* Tr. W. Montgomery. London: SCM, 1912.

_____. *The Quest of the Historical Jesus.* Tr. W. Montgomery. London: SCM, 1910.

Schweizer, E. "ὑιός, κ.τ.λ." in *TDNT* (1972). Vol. 8, 363-392.

_____. "Zum religionsgeschichtliche Hintergrund des 'Sendungsformel' Gal 4:4f. Rm 8:3f. Joh 3:16f. I Joh 4:9." *ZNW* 57 (1966) 199-210.

Scott, R. B. Y. *The Way of Wisdom in the Old Testament.* New York: Macmillan, 1971.

Scroggs, R. "Paul as Rhetorician: Two Homilies in Romans 1-11" in *Jews, Greeks, and Christians: Religious Cultures in Late Antiquity: Essays in Honour of William David Davies,* 271-298. Ed. R. Hamerton-Kelly and R. Scroggs. Leiden: Brill, 1976.

_____. "Paul: ΣΟΦΟΣ and ΠΝΕΥΜΑΤΙΚΟΣ." *NTS* 14(1967) 33-55.

Seifrid, M. A. "Paul's Approach to the Old Testament in Rom 10:6-8." *Trinity Journal* 6 n.s. (1985) 3-37.

Sharvit, B. "The Virtue of the Image of the Righteous Man in 1QS." [in Hebrew] *Beth Mikra* 19 (1974) 526-530.

Siegert, F. *Argumentation bei Paulus gezeigt an Röm 9-11.* Tübingen: J. C. B. Mohr (Paul Siebeck), 1985.

Smith, J. Z. "Wisdom and Apocalyptic" in *Religious Syncretism in Antiquity: Essays in Conversation With Geo Widengren,* 131-156. Ed. B. A. Pearson. Missoula: Scholars, 1975.

Stählin, G. "ὀργή, κ.τ.λ." in *TDNT* (1967). Vol. 5, 419-447.

Stauffer, E. *New Testament Theology.* Tr. J. Marsh. London: SCM, 1948.

Stendahl, K. *Paul Among Jews and Gentiles.* Philadelphia: Fortress, 1976.

Stone, M. E. "Apocalyptic Literature" in *Jewish Writings of the Second Temple Period: Apocrypha, Pseudepigrapha, Qumran Sectarian Writings, Philo, Josephus,* 383-441. Compendia Rerum Iudaicarum ad Novum Testamentum II. Ed. M. E. Stone. Assen and Philadelphia: Van Gorcum and Fortress, 1984.

_____. "The Book of Enoch and Judaism in the Third Century B.C.E." *CBQ* 40 (1978) 479-492.

_____. "Lists of Revealed Things in the Apocalyptic Literature" in *Magnalia Dei: The Mighty Acts of God,* 415-452. Ed. F. M. Cross, W. E. Lemke, P. D. Miller. Garden City: Doubleday, 1976.

Stowers, S. K. *The Diatribe and Paul's Letter to the Romans.* SBLDS 57. Chico: Scholars, 1981.

_____. "Paul's Dialogue With a Fellow Jew in Romans 3:1-9." *CBQ* 46 (1984) 707-722.

Strack, H. L. *Introduction to Talmud and Midrash.* Philadelphia: Jewish Publication Society of America, 1931⁵.

Strugnell, J. "Notes en marge du Volume V des *Discoveries in the Judean Desert of Jordan.*" *RevQ* 7 (1970) 163-276.

Stuhlmacher, P. "'Das Ende des Gesetzes': Über Ursprung und Ansatz der paulinischen Theologie." *ZTK* 67 (1970) 14-39.

_____. *Gerechtigkeit Gottes bei Paulus.* Göttingen: Vandenhoeck and Ruprecht, 1965.

_____. "Zur Interpretation von Römer 11,25-32" in *Probleme biblischer Theologie: Gerhard von Rad zum 70. Geburtstag,* 555-570. Ed. H. W. Wolff. Munich: Chr. Kaiser, 1971.

Suggs, M. J. "Wisdom of Solomon 2.5-5.1: A Homily Based on the Fourth Servant Song." *JBL* 76 (1957) 26-33.

_____. "'The Word Is Near to You': Romans 10:6-10 Within the Purpose of the Letter" in *Christian History and Interpretation: Studies Presented to John Knox,* 289-312. Ed. W. R. Farmer, *et al.* Cambridge: University, 1967.

Suter, D. W. *Tradition and Composition in the Parables of Enoch.* SBLDS 47. Missoula: Scholars, 1979.

Thompson, L. L. "The Form and Function of Hymns in the New Testament: A Study in Cultic History." Ph. D. Dissertation, University of Chicago, 1968.

Towes, J. E. "The Law in Paul's Letter to the Romans: A Study of Rom. 9.30-10.13." Ph. D. Dissertation, Northwestern University, 1978.

Trocme, E. "The Jews as Seen by Paul and Luke" in *To See Ourselves As Others See Us*: *Christians, Jews, "Others" in Late Antiquity*, 145-161. Ed. J. Neusner and E. S. Frerichs. Chico: Scholars, 1985.

Via, D. O. "A Structuralist Approach to Paul's OT Hermeneutic." *Int* 28 (1974) 201-220.

Vielhauer, P. "Apocalyptic in Early Christianity" in E. Hennecke, *New Testament Apocrypha*, Vol. 2, 608-642. Ed. W. Schneemelcher. Tr. R. McL. Wilson. Philadelphia: Westminster, 1965.

_____. "Introduction" to Apocalypses and Related Subjects in E. Hennecke, *New Testament Apocrypha*, Vol. 2, 581-642. Ed. W. Schneemelcher. Tr. R. McL. Wilson. Philadelphia: Westminster, 1965.

_____. "Paulus und das Alte Testament" in *Oikodome*, 1966-228. Munich: Chr. Kaiser, 1979.

de Villiers, J. L. "The Salvation of Israel According to Romans 9-11." *Neotestamentica* 15 (1981) 199-221.

de Waard, J. *A Comparative Study of the OT Text in the Dead Sea Scrolls, and in the New Testament*. Leiden: Brill, 1965.

Weber, W. "Die Composition der Weisheit Salomo's." *Zeitschrift für wissenschaftliche Theologie* 47 (1904) 145-169.

Weisengoff, J. P. "Death and Immortality in the Book of Wisdom." *CBQ* 3 (1941) 104-133.

Weiss, J. *Jesus' Proclamation of the Kingdom of God*. Tr. R. H. Hiers and D. L. Holland. Philadelphia: Fortress, 1971 (original, 1882).

Wendland, P. *Die hellenistische-römische Kultur in ihren Beziehung zu Judentum und Christentum*. HNT I/2. Tübingen: J. C. B. Mohr, 1907.

Whybray, R. N. *The Intellectual Tradition in the Old Testament*. BZAW 135. Berlin: deGruyter, 1974.

Wiefel, W. "The Jewish Community in Rome and the Origins of Roman Christianity" in *The Romans Debate*, 100-119. Ed. K. P. Donfried. Minneapolis: Augsburg, 1977.

Wilckens, U. *Der Brief an die Römer*. 3 Vols. Zürich: Neukirchener, 1980.

_____. "σοφία" in *TDNT* (1971). Vol. 7, 465-528.

_____. "Was heisst Paulus: 'Aus Werken des Gesetzes wird kein Mensch gerecht'?" in *Evangelisch-Katholischer Kommentar zum*

Neuen Testament, 51-77. Ed. J. Blank and E. Schweizer. Neukirchen: Neukirchener, 1969.

_____. *Weisheit und Torheit: Eine exegetischreligionsgeschichtliche Untersuchung zu I Kor. 1 und 2.* BHT 26. Tübingen: J. C. B. Mohr (Paul Siebeck), 1959.

Willi-Plein, I. *Prophetie am Ende: Untersuchungen zu Sacharja 9-14.* BBB 42. Cologne: P. Hanstein, 1974.

Windisch, H. "Die göttliche Weisheit der Juden und die paulinische Christologie" in *Neutestamentliche Studien für Georg Heinrici*, 220-234. Ed. H. Windisch. Leipzig: J. C. Hinrichs, 1914.

Winston, D. *The Wisdom of Solomon: A New Translation With Introduction and Commentary.* AB 43. Garden City: Doubleday, 1979.

Winter, M. *Pneumatiker und Psychiker in Korinth.* Marburg: N. G. Elwer, 1975.

Worgul, G. S. "Romans 9-11 and Ecclesiology." *Biblical Theology Bulletin* 7 (1977) 99-109.

Worrell, J. E. "Concepts of Wisdom in the Dead Sea Scrolls." Ph. D. Dissertation, Claremont Graduate School, 1968.

Wrede, W. *Paul.* Tr. E. Lummis. London: P. Green, 1907.

Wright, A. G. "The Structure of the Book of Wisdom." *Bib* 48 (1967) 168-173.

Zeller, D. *Juden und Heiden in der Mission des Paulus: Studien zum Römerbrief.* Stuttgart: Katholisches Bibelwerk, 1973.

Zerbe, G. "Jews and Gentiles as People of the Covenant: The Background and Message of Romans 11." *Direction* 12 (1983) 20-28.

Zimmerli, W. "The Place and Limit of Wisdom in the Old Testament Theology." *SJT* 17 (1964) 146-158.

van Zutphen, V. "Studies on the Hymn in Romans 11,33-36." Ph. D. Dissertation, Würzburg, 1973.

Index of Modern Authors

Wilckens, U., 31, 32, 33, 34, 39, 44, 45, 141, 152, 164

Windisch, H., 6, 23-25, 26, 27, 28, 29, 30, 31, 34, 38, 40, 41, 42, 44, 48, 49, 133, 136, 206

Winston, D., 75, 77
Winter, M., 32
Worrell, J. E., 62, 96, 100
Wrede, W., 4
Wright, A. G., 75

Zeller, D., 151
Zimmerli, W., 80
Zutphen, V. van, 163

Index of Ancient Authors

Old Testament

Genesis

2:7	45
15:1-6	191
15:6	184, 185, 190, 191
21:12	130
41:8	59

Leviticus

18:5	135, 152, 155, 156, 157

Deuteronomy

4:5-6	81
8:15	30
9:4	156, 157
9:4-5	157
10:17	77
16:19	77
29:3	160, 161
30:11-14	22, 40
30:12-14	130, 133, 134, 135, 136, 152, 155, 156, 157, 158, 208
30:12	134
30:13	40, 41, 135, 157
30:14	135, 157
32:21	159, 161

2 Samuel

7	52

1 Kings

3:6ff	78
19:10-18	159
19:18	160

2 Chronicles

19:6-7	77

Esther

1:13	59

Job

5:9	166
9:10	166
9:12	132
19:25	128
28	52, 85, 88
28:12-13	85
28:12-28	134
28:16-18	91
28:23-28	85
34:19	77
34:24	166
36:26-27	91
38	88
41	49
41:3	48, 167, 168, 170

Apocrypha

Pseudepigrapha

Qumran Library

16:16	130		174, 190,
20:17	154		202, 208
21:24	130	1:16-8:39	111, 121
		1:16-11:27	173
John		1:17	14
1:1-18	52	1:18	127
3:16ff	47	1:18ff	34, 35,
5:39-40	203		173
6	29	1:18-3:20	115
8:39-47	203	1:18-11:36	111
		1:23	127, 186
Acts		2-5	120
3:19-20	125	2:1-5	112
4:11	154	2:4	129, 171
7:56	53	2:5	127
9	16	2:5-11	137
19:9-10	34	2:6	120
22	16	2:7	128
26	16	2:8	127
		2:9	190
Romans		2:9-10	118
1-4	112	2:11	118, 149
1-5	111	2:14	118, 186
1-8	110, 112,	2:15	120, 186
	114, 115,	2:17	118, 120
	116, 120,	2:17ff	173
	121, 143	2:17-24	183
1-11	119	2:17-3:20	112
1:1	172	2:20	171
1:3ff	53	2:23	120
1:3-4	121	2:24	118, 153
1:5	118, 179	2:25	183
1:6-7	172	2:28-29	118, 139
1:13	118, 121	3:1	118, 119
1:14	118	3:1-2	118
1:16	118, 120,	3:1-8	186
	122, 127,	3:1-9	116, 119,
	128, 136,		120, 123
	138, 146,	3:2	119
	149, 153,	3:3	119, 143,
	154, 158,		144, 200
		3:4	144

Other Early Christian Literature

NOV 2 2 1990	DATE DUE	
DEC 14 1992		
APR 0 8 1993		
DEC 0 4 199		
DEC 1 7 1996		
DEC 1 7 1996		